IN THE SHADOW OF THE ALABAMA

IN THE SHADOW OF THE ALABAMA

THE BRITISH FOREIGN OFFICE AND THE AMERICAN CIVIL WAR

RENATA ELEY LONG

NAVAL INSTITUTE PRESS
ANNAPOLIS, MARYLAND

This book has been brought to publication with the generous assistance of Marguerite and Gerry Lenfest.

Naval Institute Press
291 Wood Road
Annapolis, MD 21402

Library of Congress Cataloging-in-Publication Data
Long, Renata Eley.
In the shadow of the Alabama : the British Foreign Office and the American Civil War / Renata Eley Long.
pages cm
Includes bibliographical references and index.
ISBN 978-1-61251-836-7 (hardcover : alk. paper) — ISBN 978-1-61251-837-4 (ebook) 1. United States—Foreign relations—1861-1865. 2. Buckley, Victor, 1838-1882. 3. United States—Foreign relations—Great Britain. 4. Great Britain—Foreign relations—United States. 5. Great Britain. Foreign Office—History—19th century. 6. Alabama (Screw sloop) I. Title.
E469.L915 2015
327.73041'09034—dc23
2015010699

♾ Print editions meet the requirements of ANSI/NISO z39.48-1992 (Permanence of Paper).
Printed in the United States of America.

23 22 21 20 19 18 17 16 15 9 8 7 6 5 4 3 2 1
First printing

For my sons, Richard and Kit,
and for Freddie and Nicole

The Foreign Office requires of the clerks . . . that they should take such interest in the Office as to consider its credit and reputation their own.

—Edmund Hammond, Permanent Under-Secretary, 1855

CONTENTS

ACKNOWLEDGMENTS

I am indebted to several people in the U.S.A. who have waited patiently for many years while I promised this finished work—in particular, Dr. Norman Delaney, historian and author to whom I wrote in 1991 having read an article by him. He not only replied, but also passed my name on to a friend, Dr. Frank J. Merli, author and professor of history at Queen's College, New York. Frank's first letter to me opened with the sentence: "How may I help you?"—and thus began years of correspondence between the three of us, circulating letters with exchanges of ideas, mostly concerning Captain James D. Bulloch. In the American spirit of generosity, Norman Delaney and Frank Merli were truly the founders of the feast.

My thanks also go to Frank's widow Margaret Merli, for her kindness and generosity in offering me access to his papers after his untimely passing, although, of course, they deserved the attention of academics, of which I cannot claim to be one. Dr. David M. Fahey edited Frank's papers for publication.

Many people have assisted me in my research during the years it has taken to produce this book and I have valued their patience and helpfulness. If I have inadvertently missed anyone's name, I hope they will forgive me.

In Great Britain, I am grateful for the permission of Her Majesty Queen Elizabeth II for the use of material from the Royal Archives. My thanks also to the great grandsons of Victor Buckley—Ed Buckley for his permission to use the photograph of his ancestor, and Canon Walter King, for the copy of his thesis and the information he has provided; also the Rt. Hon. the Earl of Radnor for his observations in the early days of my work.

My thanks also to Kate Crowe and Helen Glass at the FCO for their considerable help; Joan Butcher, granddaughter of Captain Mathew Butcher for kindly sharing his memoir; Felicia Taylerson and Cynthia Chamberlain for kindly permitting me to quote from the books of their late husbands; the late Major David Batt of the Worshipful Company of Gunmakers; also Colonel W. J. Chesshyre and Honorary Archivist Derek Stimpson; Alan Ray-Jones; Brian D. Hope; Mrs. P. Hatfield, Eton College Library; Eileen Edwards at the Merseyside

Maritime Museum; Liverpool historian Jerry Williams for unreservedly sharing his knowledge of the American Civil War with me twenty years ago and loaning me his books as I got started; Jaqueline Cox, Malcolm Underwood, St. John's College, Cambridge; John Owston, Librarian, Oxford and Cambridge University Club; Valerie Hart, the Guildhall Library; Prof. P. N. Davies who kindly provided information on Frederick Bond; also James E. Cowden, for help and expertise on the African Steam Ship Company; the late Marianne Laird (granddaughter of John Laird) for her letters and information on the Laird family; Philip Somervail; Rory Laird; Ted Molyneux, National Rifle Association; Jenny Mountain, archivist at The Royal Bank of Scotland Group plc; Prof. Richard Crockatt, University of East Anglia who provided an academic reference for me to access material in the library of Cambridge University, and Prof. Thomas Otte; Jack Davis, Librarian, and staff, at the Mitchell Library, History and Glasgow Room, Glasgow City Council; Glasgow University Archive Services; Andrew Bethune, Edinburgh Central Library; The Secretary of the Reform Club; Ernie Ruffler (Cammell Laird Archives); Wiltshire County Council Archives; Wirral Museum at Birkenhead Town Hall; Graham Miller of Fawcett Christie Hydraulics Ltd. (for trusting me with his rare copy of the bicentenary book *A History of Fawcett Preston & Co. Ltd.*); Sarah Walpole, Archivist, Royal Anthropological Institute, London; Tunbridge Wells Family History Society; Norfolk Family History Society; Bob Newman of the Joshua Nunn Lodge, Essex, for the gift of a book and the photo of Joshua Nunn. I am also grateful to my two sons for their patience over the years as they grew up with this book in the making, and for the memories that my husband and I shared of the detours we took from our work so that we could visit places and archives of interest. My thanks to son Kit for his help with formatting the manuscript.

In the United States: Ethel Trenholm Seabrook Nepveux, descendant of George Alfred Trenholm who, at the outset of my research, very kindly sent me a copy of her book, *George Alfred Trenholm and the Company That Went to War*; the late Regina Rapier, author of The Saga of Felix Senac; also her family; Dr. David M. Fahey; Prof. Lonnie A. Burnett; Whitney Stewart, author, and A. George Scherer III, great, great grandson of Francis B. Carpenter; the archivists at the Library of Congress in Washington, D.C.; Alicia Clarke and staff at the Henry Sheldon Sanford Archive, Sanford Museum, Florida; staff at the Tredegar Iron Works, Richmond, VA; in Georgia—staff at Bulloch Hall, Roswell, the Georgia Historical Society, and the Andrew Low House in Savannah; Helen Matthews, Kenan Research Center at the Atlanta History Center; Sharon G. Whitney, Professor Emerita, political science; the librarians at the University of South Florida, Tampa; Philip Thrapp, for keeping an old copy of the Edinburgh phone directory, numerous airport runs, and words of encouragement.

My thanks are also due to Adam Kane, Adam Nettina, Claire Noble, Mindy Conner, and Marlena Montagna at the Naval Institute Press for their patience and assistance as my manuscript developed into a book.

In Australia: Jim Elliott, great grandson of Captain James D. Bulloch, who has kindly provided photographs of his ancestor; Pamela Statham Drew, biographer of Admiral Sir James Stirling; Tracy Willet, Museum Curator, the Stirling History Collection, City of Stirling, W.A.; Jane Whisker, Mitchell Library, State Library of New South Wales, Sidney.

In the Canary Islands: My thanks to Teresa Hamilton Moore for her help, for finding an elusive portrait, and for sending me the gift of a book, *La Casa Hamilton*.

Dr. Norman Delaney kindly agreed to read my manuscript, and his corrections and advice have been invaluable. However, any errors are entirely my own.

Introduction

In 1872 a tribunal of arbitration sitting in Geneva found against Great Britain in a claim for damages brought by the United States. That claim stemmed from the destruction of commercial shipping during the American Civil War by Confederate raiders whose origins could be traced back to Britain. The most famous of these cruisers was the CSS *Alabama*, built on Merseyside, which captured sixty-four Yankee ships and destroyed most of them by burning. So celebrated was her name and so great her share of the depredations committed that the Geneva Tribunal hearings were known as the *Alabama* Claims.

The *Alabama*'s escape from the Mersey in 1862, just hours ahead of a detention order issued by the British government, gave rise to suspicions and recriminations. At the American legation in London a tenacious secretary acquired a copy of a note allegedly written by one Victor Buckley, a Foreign Office clerk, warning the Confederates of the ship's imminent seizure, and in later years the man responsible for building the *Alabama* referred in his memoirs to a "private and most reliable source" from whom he had received that vital information.

In the postmortem of events after the Civil War, an American newspaper published for the first time the implication that Buckley's position was worthy of scrutiny. The allegation that he had written a warning note was later repeated by a son of the wartime American foreign minister, Charles Francis Adams.

For almost 150 years historians have debated the circumstances surrounding the *Alabama*'s remarkable and timely departure to wreak havoc on the high seas. Was there a Foreign Office leak, and if so, was it sanctioned by the British government? The radical MP John Bright suspected the worst and said so. The prime minister at the time, Lord Palmerston, and his foreign secretary, Lord John Russell, denied it. With the passage of time, insufficient evidence, and events clouded by an extraordinary catalogue of errors and mishaps, the accusations seemed to die a natural death.

Yet when the dust of the American Civil War finally settled, it was British taxpayers who were called upon to make reparation to the United States—payment in gold of $15.5 million. Was Victor Buckley really the mole the Confederates claimed to have on their payroll, and was the British government's support for the Confederacy such that it would stand by while his fateful message winged its way to Liverpool? Abraham Lincoln's secretary of state, William Seward, thought the situation so compromising that Britain might be prepared to part with the Bahamas or even Canada in lieu of the *Alabama* Claims, but with the passing of time, insufficient proof, and a willingness by historians to believe that Victor Buckley was nothing more than an insignificant clerk, determination to prove his guilt abated.

A relieved British government walked away from the *Alabama* Claims with its pride intact—the settlement heralding, it has been suggested, the beginning of the Anglo-American "special relationship." The writer Arthur Conan Doyle considered the issue of the claims a "burning question," and in the aftermath of the events the master of detection himself would find his life curiously entwined with one of the most enduring mysteries of the nineteenth century.

New perspectives on British attitudes toward the American Civil War and fresh evidence revealed from hitherto neglected sources now point to the interesting conclusion that the young Foreign Office clerk was anything but insignificant.

Note for Historians

In the Shadow of the Alabama is essentially a primary research–based work. Although the evidence presented here sheds new light on the role of the British government during the American Civil War, the book does not seek to be a purely academic, revisionist text challenging the prevailing narrative offered in secondary sources. The inquiry-based research centers on the key actors, their personal stories, and the ways they influenced important naval and diplomatic events in this period.

CHAPTER 1

Family and Foreign Office

Victor Buckley was not the stuff of which Foreign Office spies are traditionally made. Unlike one of his predecessors, William Gregg, who attempted to sell state secrets to the French in 1707, or Charles Marvin, who revealed the gist of the Anglo-Russian Convention to the *Globe* newspaper on the eve of the Congress of Berlin in 1878, Buckley had started his Foreign Office career with neither a passion for deviance nor cynicism. If at any time prior to the American Civil War he had spared a thought for disloyalty, he might have been reminded of William Gregg's treachery, the price he had paid, and the loathsome place he occupied in Foreign Office annals. When Gregg's dark past as a spy in Scotland was revealed at his Old Bailey trial, he was sentenced to hang at Tyburn, a fate likely to strike fear into any young clerk contemplating betrayal.[1]

While Gregg's motivation had been egotistical—he fancied himself a proven and valuable spy—Charles Marvin would take the moral high ground in his defense, justifying the sale of a copied document for forty pounds by claiming he acted in the interests of open government. Buckley was neither a hardened spy nor transparently high principled, and the Official Secrets Act, which might have provided pause for thought, would not be passed until 1889. Yet a drama would unfold culminating in an accusation of betrayal against him—one that, if proven, would have burdened this young clerk with responsibility for a massive claim for damages made against Great Britain. It would also have impugned the integrity of senior statesmen to be challenged, affected political ambitions, and incurred the wrath of Queen Victoria. The American Civil War, which would create the climate for such espionage, started in the spring of 1861, but a series of events that occurred prior to that date set the stage for Buckley's eventual implication in the betrayal.

Before those events took place, the course of Buckley's life had run smoothly. Born in the New Forest village of Minstead on April 28, 1838, he was of aristocratic parentage with an impeccable pedigree. His mother, Lady Catherine Pleydell Bouverie, was the daughter of the 3rd Earl of Radnor and a granddaughter of the 2nd Duke of Newcastle. Victor's father, Edward Pery Buckley, was a distinguished military man, the son of Colonel Edward Pery Buckley of Woolcombe Hall, Dorset, and Minstead Lodge, Hampshire, and a general by the time of Victor's birth.[2]

The senior Edward Pery Buckley had served as a major in the Dorset militia and as lieutenant colonel in the South West Hampshire militia, commanded by Viscount Palmerston. The family also had a history of service in the royal household. For thirty years Colonel Edward Pery Buckley Sr. was groom of the bedchamber to King George III while his wife, Lady Georgiana West, served as lady of the bedchamber to their Royal Highnesses, the Princesses, daughters of George III.[3]

Victor's birth into this upper echelon of English society carried with it a proud legacy from the battle of Waterloo. Having served as a young officer in the 1st Regiment of Foot Guards, Edward Pery Buckley Jr. was revered as a "Waterloo man" when he returned to England after the historic battle in 1815. A tide of patriotism was engulfing the nation then, sweeping through the ballrooms of the great country houses and spawning rows of Waterloo Terraces in towns throughout the land. Buckley, the dashing young hero with his Peninsular and Waterloo medals, was a highly eligible bachelor, yet for him and his family the triumphal mood was tempered by mourning. Buckley's young brother, George Richard Buckley, had also fought at Waterloo. An ensign in the Coldstream Guards, he died of "battle fatigue" in Paris on August 16 at the age of seventeen.[4]

The initial euphoria of victory soon subsided, leaving many redundant soldiers hungry for work, but Buckley Junior had no such problem; by 1827 he was a half-pay captain devoting his time to courting Lady Catherine Pleydell Bouverie. The couple married on May 13, 1828, and might well have expected the military tradition to continue with their offspring. Twins, William and Alfred, were born in 1829, and two sons and a daughter followed within five years. In 1837 Buckley became equerry to Queen Victoria.[5] His wife was pregnant with their fifth son, Victor, the following year when the Queen wrote in her journal of meeting Lady Catherine Buckley "with her five nice children, four boys and a girl: William and Alfred, twins 8 years old, Bat, six years old, Frances, 5 and Felix, 3."[6]

The birth of Victor completed the Buckleys' family. The choice of name for the baby echoed his father's military prowess, but it was also, by chance or otherwise, the male equivalent of the monarch's name, and Queen Victoria became his godmother. Victor was the first child to receive that honor since her accession to the throne, and she marked the event with the gift of a silver-gilt christening cup and cover.[7] Lady Catherine served Queen Victoria as a lady of the bedchamber and was one of the valued companions the Queen was determined to retain when, in 1839, incoming prime minister Robert Peel demanded that she dispense with the services of the largely aristocratic, Whig-appointed staff. This challenge to the monarch's choice of close confidantes precipitated an impasse that became known as the Bedchamber Crisis. The Queen prevailed, Peel felt obliged to decline the premiership, and her former prime minister and personal friend, Lord Melbourne, was returned to government.

In 1843 Buckley inherited from a relative the estate of New Hall at Bodenham, near Salisbury, Wiltshire, which became his countryseat. The following year, for the family's London residence, he took a lease of 12 South Audley Street, Mayfair, a fashionable stuccoed property that was part of the Grosvenor Estate.[8] Keenly interested in politics, Buckley seized the opportunity to stand for Parliament when the member for the Salisbury constituency died in 1853. In the by-election of that November he was elected as a Liberal MP and began a twelve-year parliamentary career. So safe was the Salisbury seat that in the subsequent general election of 1858 Buckley and his fellow Liberal candidate ran unopposed.[9]

In that election the prime minister, Lord Palmerston, won a substantial vote of confidence in a fierce contest that saw such progressive politicians as John Bright, Richard Cobden, Thomas Milner-Gibson, and Austen Henry Layard lose their seats. Their absence was to be temporary, however; successfully fought by-elections reversed the political mood and reinstated some of the country's most radical voices on the benches. Bright and Cobden, representing working-class areas of England and often regarded as anti-aristocracy, were vocally pro-American and admirers of the style of republicanism practiced in the slave-free Northern states. His fellows in Parliament dubbed Bright "the Honourable Member for the United States."

In the volatile politics of that time, there followed a defeat of Palmerston's Whig party after a debate skillfully engineered by Disraeli to bring the government down, but by the following spring the persistently thorny subject of electoral reform had destroyed Lord Derby's new administration. Again the country went to the polls, returning Palmerston to his premiership and General Buckley to Salisbury, although this surprise election had elicited a challenge to the seat from a hopeful Conservative candidate.

In the summer of 1850, twelve-year-old Victor was sent to Eton, where he joined the house of Mr. Balston. Victor's time there was unremarkable. He apparently did not excel at any subject, won no major prizes, and was not elected to the Eton Society; nor did he row in the annual Procession of Boats on June 4. He left five years later, seemingly ill suited for university and with no inclination to follow in the family's military footsteps, although the Buckley men combined varied achievements in intellectual and military pursuits. Victor's grandfather had been up at Oxford, as had an uncle. The eldest of his brothers, Alfred, earned a BA at Trinity College, Cambridge, in 1852 and went on to join the Admiralty, where he was appointed secretary to the Duke of Somerset. Felix Buckley, who would become a clergyman, entered Merton College, Oxford, in 1854 and later attained an MA. The Buckleys' third son, Duncombe Frederick Bat, joined the army and was sent to Crimea as a captain in the Scots Fusilier Guards.[10] In 1855, when Victor was leaving Eton, news came of Bat's death. "Heard to our great regret," Queen Victoria wrote in her journal, "that poor General Buckley's son, so severely wounded at the Alma, and about whom there had been such anxiety before Inkerman, the father being in such ecstasy when I told him his son was safe, has now been killed 2 days ago, in the trenches!"[11]

Victor had grown into a tall, upright young man, but there was something vaguely delicate about his appearance, and he made no pretense to a military stature. There was no reflection of the Waterloo man in Victor, but rather an impeccably dressed young nobleman with a silk cravat tied flamboyantly around his neck and a cane swung rakishly at his side. He had the type of confidently handsome looks that would turn a pretty head, but he craved none of the adventures that had fueled his father's youth. With no taste for the army and modest academic achievements, Victor was considered a candidate for a career in the Foreign Office.

A life spent scratching away daily at countless letters and documents might not have suited many a young man's temperament, but the Foreign Office, still regarded as the preserve of the aristocracy, defied the generally held view of a clerk's life. The writer Charles Marvin, whose betrayal still lay twenty years hence, would note pithily of his place of employment: "As a house of call to gossip and smoke and read the morning papers, the Foreign Office is a most admirable institution. It so nicely takes up the time between the one o'clock lunch hour and the seven o'clock dinner. I doubt not that many men envy the Downing Street clerks in their easy and convenient hours at the luxurious Foreign Office."[12]

For some young clerks of noble birth the Foreign Office represented simply a transitional period prior to inheriting their aristocratic responsibilities or moving on to a parliamentary career. There was already a precedent in Victor Buckley's family. An uncle, the Honorable Edward Pleydell Bouverie, who was a barrister-at-law (Trinity, Cambridge), had joined the Foreign Office as a précis writer for Palmerston in 1840. Pleydell Bouverie progressed to the Board of Trade and the Lord Advocate's department but eventually moved on to further his political aspirations, becoming MP for Kilmarnock and nursing a personal ambition to become Speaker of the House, a prize that would ultimately be denied him.

There were also in the Foreign Office "career clerks" who were dedicated to the service and whose private means enabled them to disregard the very modest salary. For those men, the frisson of omnipotent decisions being made around them and the respect their confidential positions invoked outweighed the financial rewards. There was an air of privilege, not to say arrogance, about the Foreign Office. Great men had paced its corridors and embraced its ethos vigorously. Palmerston, it was said, had read each letter and paper that passed through during his time there—as many as two thousand items every day.

In the mid-nineteenth century the Foreign Office was divided between two buildings in Downing Street and neighboring Fludyer Street, an insalubrious area of narrow streets and grim alleys that had once provided a route for pilgrims making their way to the shrine of Edward the Confessor at Westminster Abbey. The medieval hostels had long since disappeared, and the streets were now home to bawdy public taverns, livery stables, and dressmaking workshops. Cheap lodging houses for Irish and Scottish MPs stood alongside private residences and departments of state, and the air was filled with the incessant rattle of carriages and the traditional "cries of London" voiced by street hawkers.[13]

Those Foreign Office clerks killing time before assuming the responsibilities of their class found plenty to enjoy in these questionable surroundings, and their exuberance was sometimes inclined to undermine the dignity of the office. A career clerk's reliance on an unblemished record might have weighed heavily on him at times, but the spirited young men found distraction from the tedium by tossing hot pennies down to street singers, buying strawberries by artfully dangling baskets from strings of red tape, and flashing mirrors flirtatiously at the girls in the local dressmakers.[14]

Victor Buckley entered this enigmatic institution on December 17, 1856, for a probationary period as a junior clerk. Such an appointment was predicated on a system of personal nomination at the highest level, and the path to his chosen career would most certainly have been smoothed by his family. Appointment prior to 1857 was by the patronage of the secretary of state for foreign affairs, at that time Lord Clarendon, whose wife was the sister of Lady Folkestone, Buckley's aunt by marriage; the Buckley estate at Bodenham bordered that of Lord and Lady Folkestone.[15] Victor's maternal grandfather, the Earl of Radnor, also maintained a close interest in politics, so his relationship may have carried weight, as indeed would that of the Honorable Edward Pleydell Bouverie, although for a family of the Buckleys' standing, with their connections to Palmerston and Queen Victoria, there would have been no barrier to their son's acceptance. Nepotism would prevail for many years to come, but moves were already under way, instigated by Permanent Under-Secretary Edmund Hammond, to introduce a formal examination as a means of entry into the Foreign Office, and Buckley was obliged to sit for the exam the following month.[16] He already satisfied the other qualifications stipulated by Hammond for consideration, such as "whether the family of a young candidate resides in town or not, for it is not desirable that a young man under twenty years of age should be appointed to a clerkship in the Foreign Office without his family having a home in the metropolis."[17]

Hammond's other stipulations might have found less favor with a young man: "The labour required of the Foreign Office clerks is great, the attendance long, and the hours late and uncertain. . . . The Foreign Office requires of the clerks great sacrifices of time, of comfort and amusement and that they should take such an interest in the Office as to consider its credit and reputation their own."[18]

Buckley passed the qualifying exam "in a good bold hand," although his Foreign Office biographical note would later state somewhat derisorily that he had passed "a simple qualifying test." He was four months away from his nineteenth birthday when he was officially accepted as a junior clerk, third class, at a salary of about one hundred pounds per annum, and he joined three other clerks under the supervision of (Sir) Francis Beilby Alston. Closest to his own age was William Owen, son of an eminent professor. The two older men were fellow Etonian Charles Stuart Aubrey Abbott, aged twenty-two, and thirty-one-year-old Hon. Edward Scott Gifford; all were "career clerks," although Abbott was to undergo something of a metamorphosis later, from which he would emerge as an important figure in Buckley's story.

Victor Buckley could be found daily, or at least in the afternoons, at his desk in Alston's department, which dealt with matters relating to the intriguing combination of Sweden, Italy, China, Central America, and, fatefully, the United States, an arrangement that would change slightly the following year when Sweden was jettisoned to a new political department. The work was hardly strenuous. Again, it would be left to Charles Marvin in future years to reveal the ethos of the workplace: "In the morning, the office is given up to the housemaids and the messengers. Officially, the business of the place begins at twelve and closes at six . . . and John Bull having, out of his great respect for the Downing Street barnacles, conceded them the morning for their fashionable calls, what is more natural than that they should take the edge off the afternoon by staying away until one?"[19]

The first hour of the day was spent in opening dispatch boxes and answering private letters, after which the clerks, "with appetites sharpened by the social calls of the morning," went to lunch. Marvin concluded his description of a typical day for a Foreign Office clerk: "At half past five, he arouses himself into the belief that he has done a very hard day's work and after performing his toilette (the materials for which are provided at a grateful country's expense), he scowls at Big Ben booming six."[20]

At the end of his first year of service Buckley was promoted to junior clerk, second class. The Foreign Office was undoubtedly an agreeable place for its clerks. The rigors of Palmerston's control were no longer in evidence, although the specter of the great man continued to haunt it. His successor, the Earl of Clarendon, had won the approval of the clerks by lifting Palmerston's ban on smoking when he took office at the end of 1852, but the British public remained unstintingly loyal to Palmerston and felt that his rightful place was back in the Foreign Office—that the Crimean War itself might have been averted by his presence there.[21] The Foreign Office seal was briefly passed to the Earl of Malmesbury in 1858–59 and then reverted to a former prime minister, Lord John Russell (later Earl Russell), who had held the office between 1852 and 1853.

In the spring of 1861, as Buckley was slowly but surely climbing the Foreign Office career ladder, Palmerston, at the grand old age of seventy-six, was a prime minister nursing a slender majority and Lord John Russell was his foreign secretary. During the summer, Russell's inheritance of his family title, albeit at the age of sixty-eight, necessitated the appointment of an under-secretary of state for foreign affairs. That post went to the forty-four-year-old MP Austen Henry Layard, a renowned dilettante, traveler, diplomat, student of the fine arts, and archaeologist, who had unearthed wonderful treasures at the excavation of Ninevah. Layard, who came from an intellectual background (his uncle employed the young Disraeli for a short time in his London law chambers), was experienced in foreign affairs and an outspoken radical who had publicly aligned himself with "men of the people" such as Richard Cobden and John Bright. He spoke tellingly of "our good, easy, aristocratic families, who look upon ministries as their perquisites" and since the previous year had been the MP for the largely poor industrial area of Southwark, home to the Marshalsea Debtors Prison that Charles Dickens immortalized in *Little Dorrit*. Despite his sometimes contrary temperament and an unfortunate knack for alienating the aristocracy (a trait Queen Victoria found hard to forgive, vehemently opposing his appointment and, having uncharacteristically bent to Palmerston's insistence, subsequently denying Layard a peerage), he was generally acceptable to politicians on all sides, and so the Foreign Office over which Earl Russell presided was at peace with itself.[22]

Buckley was now twenty-three years old, and nothing had so far occurred in his Civil Service career to call into question his loyalty. The Foreign Office, however, was about to embark upon a fresh chapter of history—one that would test its patience and integrity to the full and in which the young Victor Buckley would become a pawn in a very dangerous game. The Crimean War had barely ended when a new international crisis loomed.

The conflict in America had been brewing for some years and broke into war on April 12, 1861, when Confederate forces opened fire on the Union-held Fort Sumter in the harbor of Charleston, South Carolina. With those shots America launched itself into a war that would have serious repercussions in Europe. Yet long before that conflagration, the seeds of support for each side had been sown across the Atlantic; sympathies had been won, personal and commercial friendships forged. Britain's textile industry maintained an insatiable appetite for slave-grown cotton from America's South, and more than a million workers relied directly or indirectly on its importation. The publication of Harriet Beecher Stowe's *Uncle Tom's Cabin* in 1851 had jarred consciences in Britain and raised awareness of the "peculiar institution" and its continued existence in the Southern states, yet while abhorrence of slavery seemed a natural instinct for the British people, the nation's social system was too complex for public opinion to be so easily swayed.

The "Young England" movement of Disraeli's youth, when a generation of aristocrats reverted to the romantic ideals of feudalism and chivalry, had found empathy in the plantation-owning gentry of America's South. That same generation had now come into its inheritance and when it searched its conscience discovered a rather different instinct. It saw in the contentious issue of electoral reform and in the eloquence of radical politics an ominous reflection of America's problems. The power of the ruling classes stood in danger of being undermined if the economic ideals of the Union states prevailed. When they thought of "American cousins," the vision that presented itself was not one of bankers or railroad magnates but cultured Southern gentlemen residing in stately mansions with Greek Doric columns, in leisurely control of their vast lands and slave labor. To protect that comfortable image, many of the British aristocracy were prepared to dig deep into their pockets and into their political passions.

Such sentiments might have colored Buckley's own youthful view of the war as he analyzed the newspaper reports in the Foreign Office, yet there is no reason to suppose that the beliefs of this particular young man were so deeply entrenched as to render him a risk to Foreign Office security. However, an apparently insignificant event had taken place in London on July 3, 1858, that was to precipitate a chain of irrevocable, fateful connections. For the purposes of examining the allegation later made against Buckley, that date is the beginning of the story.

CHAPTER 2

Guns, Ships, and Victorian Values

The renowned gun maker Robert Adams was famously photographed in 1857 loading one of his percussion revolvers for his illustrious client Prince Albert. His admirers might well have supposed that someone held in such high esteem on both sides of the Atlantic would ultimately die a wealthy man, but Adams became bedeviled by financial problems and in time would endure the stigma of bankruptcy before dying in relative obscurity. If any single event triggered Adams' eventual downfall, it was undoubtedly that which occurred on July 3, 1858. On that date he lost his job.

The man who ousted Adams as manager of the London Armoury Company was himself a member of an old gun-making family, but to his expert knowledge of arms the twenty-eight-year-old Frederick William Bond would add other talents. A highly intelligent and Machiavellian character, Bond possessed sharp business acumen and polished social skills. With his broad shoulders, black hair, dark eyes, and olive complexion, he appeared to be the archetypal Victorian City gentleman. He was born on March 23, 1830, into a family that, like Victor Buckley's, seemed to ensure his prosperity. The Bonds were the gentry of the City of London—the commercial counterpart of the aristocratic Buckleys—and members of the prestigious Worshipful Company of Gunmakers, the industry's body, which had been established in 1637 during the reign of Charles I.

Frederick William Bond's father was Edward James Bond, a celebrated gun maker, sword cutler, and goldsmith with premises at 45 Cornhill in the City. On August 27, 1834, the business fraternity was shocked by the news that forty-three-year-old Edward Bond had gone to a bathhouse in St. Mary Axe and shot himself. The subsequent inquest found he had "speculated large in one of the steam companies," which had not turned out well; but he had also met with other disappointments and had become despondent. He grieved at the recent loss of a sister and complained that his business had been latterly falling off. Several of his friends were called to give evidence as to his state of mind but conceded that, while "his intellects of late had been somewhat disordered," his circumstances were not embarrassed and were not calculated to induce him to commit so rash an act. The jury returned a verdict that "the deceased put a period to his existence while labouring under temporary derangement."[1]

Had it not been for his father's premature death, Frederick Bond might have grown up to apply his enterprising abilities to the family business. The direction of the family's life, however, turned dramatically after the suicide. His mother was also an experienced gun maker and was able to maintain the business with the help of her sister-in-law. Frederick's eldest brother, Edward Philip, apprenticed himself to an uncle, William Thomas Bond, before training in the business of John Edward Barnett and eventually trading in partnership with his uncle as Edward and William Bond. The Barnett family, like that of the Bonds, had a proud pedigree in the gun-making industry.[2] Both families supplied guns to the East India Company and the Hudson's Bay Company, and such was the stature of the Bonds' business that on one occasion Edward was called upon to give evidence to a parliamentary committee. Thomas Barnett is recorded as having supplied muskets for the African trade in 1824, and in 1837 William Thomas Bond was supplying single-barreled fowlers (fusils) for native chiefs in West Africa. He had also supplied fusils to the shah of Persia.[3]

By 1862 Edward Philip Bond was established at premises in Hooper Square, London. A third brother, Eyton, had pursued other business interests, forming a partnership in the City with Malcolm Inglis to trade as Inglis, Bond, and Company, merchants and ship insurance agents, dealers, and chapmen, at 54 Old Broad Street. The business collapsed in 1854, resulting in bankruptcy for the partners, and Eyton moved to the gun-making industry in Birmingham, where he subsequently joined the group who formed the Birmingham Small Arms Company.

Frederick William Bond therefore grew up in an environment that, on the one hand, combined the elite of arms manufacturing with the heady figures of City trade and finance, and, on the other, punished failed ambitions with financial disaster. The power of the City, with its political bedfellows and tributaries of trade throughout the world, would always have first hold on his heart. At the age of nineteen he was accepted by Cambridge University and went up in the autumn of 1849, taking residence at St. John's College that October.

However, Bond was soon to suffer a severe setback. The gun-making industry on which he relied for financial support was prone to vicissitudes, and after a while he found university life too expensive. His seven terms of residence were not sufficient to qualify him for a degree, but he nevertheless retained a lifelong interest in the university. In 1852 Bond embarked on a career that was to qualify him uniquely for the opportunities that lay ahead. He became secretary to a prominent figure in the world of shipping, a post that opened up for him the possibilities of international trade, particularly with newly explored regions of Africa. Through that City job he became connected with the shipbuilding industry on Merseyside and established contacts and friendships that were to figure largely in his later life.

Bond was soon to learn, though, that the shipping industry, like the gun-making business, was prone to economic fluctuations. The Crimean War adversely affected the African trade, and in 1855 his employer relinquished his managing directorship to pursue other interests. A commercial crisis over the following two years, precipitated by a recession, resulted in further changes to the business, and the young secretary, while continuing his association with the company, was clearly free to explore other possibilities. Comfortable in the presence of major bankers and businessmen and used to dealing with large sums of money, Bond had already earned the respect of City financiers and wealthy merchants. Content to remain in the shadows orchestrating shrewd maneuvers, he had become a valuable commodity for any commercially aggressive company.

Bond's failure to graduate from Cambridge with a degree was now of little importance. He had emerged as a confident man of business with natural commercial instincts and excellent connections that he was prepared to exploit to the full. In the course of time, employing his seductive mix of financial astuteness and ruthless ambition, he would reveal to agents of the Confederate States of America that he had a "near kinsman" holding a confidential position in the Foreign Office. Before a claim to such a fortuitous relationship would acquire some currency value, however, the circumstances surrounding the formation of the London Armoury Company and Bond's subsequent usurpation of Robert Adams' position would form a solid foundation for the coming events.

The London Armoury Company had been founded by Archibald Hamilton, an inscrutable City merchant and arms expert who, with a group of other businessmen, had identified a niche in the market. The company was formed in September 1856 with Hamilton as its chairman and gun maker Robert Adams as a director and salaried manager. Until that time Adams had been a partner in the firm of Deane, Adams, and Deane, a partnership that he then dissolved.

The prospectus of the London Armoury Company stated that its directors had entered into arrangements with Mr. Adams "whereby the present well-known manufactory of that firm has been secured to the Company, together with the exclusive right of manufacturing, at a small Royalty, Adams' Patent Revolving Fire Arms, which have been adopted by Her Majesty's War Department and the East India Company."[4] Under the terms of its contract with Adams, the London Armoury Company agreed to employ his services as manager, "superintending the whole manufacturing department of the Company's business," for seven years. "His well known experience and reputation," the company prospectus pointed out, "will prove a guarantee for the superior quality of the Arms."[5]

Before he entered into his agreement with the newly formed company Adams had borrowed money to invest in substantial premises (including "the old railway arches") on land formerly owned by the South Eastern Railway Company at Henry Street, Bermondsey, the "well-known manufactory" referred to in the prospectus. A lease of those premises was negotiated on terms providing for its reversion to Adams in the event of the London Armoury Company deciding to vacate. The reversion could take place in seven, fourteen, or twenty-one years, and there was an option for the company to purchase the freehold within the first fourteen years.[6]

On the face of it, Adams had assured himself of a long period of financial stability and security, with the London Armoury Company now being the sole manufacturer of his famous patent revolvers in Britain, supplying them wholesale to the trade. From the outset, however, conflicts of interest and disagreements subverted Adams' relations with his new business colleagues. Soon it seemed that even his bankers were conspiring with the directors of the London Armoury Company against him.[7]

Adams' percussion revolvers were also being manufactured under license in the United States (between 1857 and 1859) by the Massachusetts Arms Company of Chicopee Falls, which was in turn controlled by the Ames Manufacturing Company, also of Chicopee. The Ames Company, a major player in the manufacture of both arms and arms-making machinery, had as its chief James Tyler Ames, an export-minded businessman who expanded the company's sale of machinery into Britain, in particular to the government-owned Royal Small Arms factory at Enfield. Before long he had supplied the London Armoury Company with gunmaking machinery, which arrived in Bermondsey sometime after December 1857, accompanied by Corey P. McFarland, an Ames Company engineer. McFarland would remain at the London Armoury Company until 1860, when the crisis of the Civil War looming on the horizon would take him temporarily back to the United States.[8]

By July 1858 Adams' relations with the directors of the London Armoury Company had sufficiently soured for matters to reach a head. Suddenly, on July 3, his name was dropped from the company's customary advertisement in the *Field* magazine. The London Armoury Company now proclaimed as its manager Frederick William Bond. Adams, his position peremptorily terminated, hastened to insert a "late advertisement" giving notice of his removal to premises at 76 King William Street. Accordingly, it was Bond who, in the autumn of 1859, stepped forward to shake the hand of the company's latest visitor from the United States.

Caleb Huse was a nephew by marriage of James Tyler Ames, a graduate of the U.S. Military Academy at West Point, and, at the age of twenty-nine, an officer in the U.S. Army. He was also a close friend of Senator Charles Tillinghast James of Rhode Island, a noted abolitionist as well as a military strategist, engineer, and developer of the rifle cannon and the "James shell"—advantageous credentials, no doubt, when James used his influence to help Huse obtain a period of leave from his army duties in 1859. Citing business opportunities in his request for leave, Huse was soon en route to England, first for meetings at the London Armoury Company, then to Shoeburyness for a range trial of a 12-pounder rifled gun firing the James shell. From there he went to Europe, armed with prices supplied by his new London associates and intending to make sales to the Austrian government in Vienna. The armory there, he later stated, "had . . . the most magnificent building and the most inferior machinery in Europe," an observation that would certainly have raised a speculative glint in the eyes of Archibald Hamilton and his manager, Frederick Bond.[9]

The working relationship between Archibald Hamilton and Frederick Bond had been established before the founding of the London Armoury Company. Hamilton was the son of Hugh Hamilton, an affluent merchant from Greenock on the river Clyde, and Menzies Sinclair of Garvel Park, Greenock, a member of the wealthy Scott, Sinclair shipbuilding family. Menzies died in 1861, but her name lived on in the business Archibald had founded with his brother Robert Sinclair Hamilton in 1854. The firm of Sinclair, Hamilton, and Company, ship insurance and general commission agents and merchants, with premises in St. Helen's Place in the City, could turn its hand to any profitable commercial venture.[10] It was through their shipping and City connections that Hamilton and Bond had become closely acquainted.

For the moment, the rapport Caleb Huse had established with Hamilton and Bond at the London Armoury Company was obliged to remain dormant. With his six months' leave expiring, Huse returned to the United States and took up an appointment as superintendent of the University of Alabama in the heart of Dixie. Charged with introducing military-style discipline to the university,

"Yankee Huse," a Massachusetts man and friend of abolitionists, was not warmly received by his cadets and had to overcome their prejudices and a near mutiny before the final descent into war demanded that every man in America state his allegiance. Huse tendered his resignation to the U.S. Army early in 1861, and by April this Yankee of Puritan stock, with family and friends in the North, had made his choice. His sympathies, surprisingly, were with the South. The Confederate president, Jefferson Davis, a former West Point man himself, was quick to recognize Huse's abilities and experience, and ordered the secretary of war in his fledgling government to dispatch the newly promoted Major Huse immediately to Europe with a commission to purchase arms and military supplies.

Huse's initial orders were to purchase 12,000 rifles and a battery of field artillery as well as 1 or 2 guns of larger caliber as models. On his arrival in London he checked into Morley's Hotel in Trafalgar Square and proceeded the next day to the offices of the London Armoury Company, where, to his surprise, he found Ames' engineer Corey McFarland, newly returned to England on behalf of the federal government with orders, like his own, to procure arms. The irony of the situation apart, Huse was genuinely alarmed by McFarland's unexpected presence and announced assertively that he was there to buy for the Confederate government. As soon as McFarland left the office, Huse put forward a bold proposal—he wanted to purchase all the arms the London Armoury Company could manufacture. "I was now more determined than ever," he later wrote in his memoirs, "to secure the London Armoury Company as a Confederate States arms factory."[11]

Hamilton and Bond must have been delighted at Huse's ill-concealed enthusiasm, and Hamilton carefully demurred from giving a price, pointing out that the company was contracted also to the British government, that he would have to consult with his fellow directors, and in any event he would prefer to consider the matter overnight. Hamilton might have reflected that the order for the British government had not been without its problems, and he and Bond had been obliged to call a meeting of shareholders to raise further financing. Shortly before Huse arrived, Bond (describing himself as an ironmonger) had visited the factory of the government's Royal Small Arms Company in Enfield where the Ames Company's machinery was producing almost two thousand rifles each week. The scale on which this highly efficient machine shop was operating was so advanced and impressive that visitors were flocking to admire "the American system." Bond's observation of its efficient assembly-line practice and techniques was undoubtedly of benefit to the London Armoury Company in light of the opportunities that were about to present themselves.

Flattering though it was to be wooed by both sides, Hamilton and Bond recognized that the Confederacy's urgent need for arms represented the best financial bet. In January, Alabama's *Mobile Advertiser* had boasted, "During the past year 135,430 muskets have been quietly transferred from the Northern Arsenal at Springfield alone, to those in the Southern States." However, such covert stockpiles would be woefully inadequate for the task ahead. The agrarian South had no arms factories of its own, and although the North too had an urgent need for weapons in these early days of the fighting, in time, its own gun makers might fulfill that requirement.[12]

The day after their meeting, Hamilton threw Huse some crumbs of comfort. The company would endeavor to bring to a close the comparatively small orders it had outstanding for the British government and the United States agent and then, for the next three years, would be prepared to turn all its output over to Huse for the Confederate army.

The price quoted for the first order was rather higher than Huse had envisaged or indeed was authorized to pay, but this was a seller's market and the Confederacy's need was great. A few days later, a formal contract was closed and thus was sealed the relationship between Huse, Bond, and Hamilton. From that point on, Hamilton and Bond would nurture their Confederate customers, provide them with lavish meals and entertainment; take them to the theaters, dance halls, and prostitutes' dens of London; and, as long as the Confederacy was the hen that laid the golden eggs, go to considerable lengths to secure the arms and ammunitions it required. Those they could not supply themselves, they would purchase from other manufacturers. Hamilton and Bond knew every arms maker in the country (their equipment supplier, the American Ames Company, had sold machinery to the Birmingham gun industry, with which the Bond and Barnett families were also connected), and through the senior man's merchant business of Sinclair, Hamilton, and Company, they could acquire and coordinate deliveries of everything necessary to fulfill Huse's orders—all at a commission of 2.5 percent. And lest Corey McFarland be dispossessed of suppliers, Bond passed him promptly over to his family's associated gun makers John, Robert, and Edward Barnett, with an order for a large quantity of Enfield rifles. McFarland would also become well acquainted with the factory in Hooper Square where Bond's brother, Edward, was now in business on his own account.

Anxious not to lose out again, McFarland was soon requisitioning funds from the U.S. government to pay the deposit required by his new suppliers before they would make any delivery. It was a very satisfactory situation for Bond, who might already have glimpsed his future as a merchant prince in his own right. For his part, Archibald Hamilton was content with keeping a low profile, playing a quiet but, as time would prove, highly significant role in the South's operations in Britain while enjoying the lucrative challenge of fulfilling the Confederacy's insatiable appetite for arms for the duration of the war. In fact, were it not for the men's unwavering shrewdness, the fortunes of the London Armoury Company might have declined along with those of the Confederate government.

Hot on Huse's heels with more purchasing orders for the South was Capt. James Dunwody Bulloch, who arrived in Liverpool on June 4 and soon joined Huse in London.[13] Bulloch, at thirty-eight, was a former U.S. Navy officer whom the Confederate navy secretary, Stephen R. Mallory, had sent to Europe with one of the most formidable commissions of the Civil War—to create a navy for the South. Against overwhelming odds, this sophisticated and determined Southerner, with his distinctive bushy side-whiskers and commanding air of confidence, was intent on getting cruisers to sea to harass and destroy American mercantile shipping and to distract the U.S. fleet from its blockade of the Southern ports. In short, he was to provide, almost singlehandedly, a unique answer to the might of the U.S. Navy.

Bulloch employed his own brand of shrewdness. It was not well-honed business skills but rather something inherent in his personality that made him cautious yet audacious. Of Georgia gentry with a noble Scottish ancestry, he might have been an archetypal Southern gentleman, but a reversal in family fortunes had left him self-reliant and he had forsaken the navy for a captaincy in commercial shipping, taking his cultured intellect and maritime skills to New York. His half-sister, Mittie, escaped the Bullochs' reduced circumstances by marrying into the wealthy Roosevelt family of New York, a union that was to produce a future president, Theodore Roosevelt.

Bulloch's background and his schooling in the world of New York shipping alone would have qualified him for the task ahead, but he had also gained experience in a potentially explosive diplomatic wrangle in 1854, when the authorities in Cuba had seized the ship of which he was captain. The *Black Warrior* affair, as it became known, sparked a diplomatic crisis and brought the United States close to war with Spain over Cuba. In that incident he had come to appreciate the nuances of diplomatic posturing and had learned the value of sound legal advice and how best to apply it. When the shortage of shipbuilding facilities in the Confederacy prompted Navy Secretary Mallory to turn his eyes toward Europe, he looked particularly to Britain because historic bonds already existed between the country's prime ports (particularly Liverpool) and the South. It would be Bulloch's task, within the confines of British law, to find among those ports and shipyards the materiel for a Confederate navy.

Bulloch had a great love of linguistics. As a young naval officer during the war with Mexico he had encountered the mellifluence of the Spanish language and he developed a liking for poetic expression. The names of the two famous warships he would have built in Britain would bear testimony to this, and in his later memoirs he would tantalize his readers with cues and clues, particularly in the chapters dealing with the most sensitive areas of his covert operations in Britain—the high-level support and the betrayal of confidences that enabled him to achieve many of his objectives. But when Bulloch joined Huse in London in 1861, neither man could have suspected that the Civil War, expected to last just a few months, would keep America locked in battle with itself for four long years, providing both of them with ample material for memoirs.

Bulloch and Huse were quick to establish a harmonious working relationship, and soon they were alternating between Hatchetts Hotel in Piccadilly and rooms at 58 Jermyn Street, where they jokingly referred to the glass-roofed sitting room as "the casemate." Bulloch's base, however, was in Liverpool. The finance house of Fraser, Trenholm, and Company provided an office within its impressive premises at 10 Rumford Place, a building that was to become regarded as "the Confederate embassy" in Liverpool and which, conveniently, had a back door through which Bulloch could leave discreetly when avoiding the attention of the private detectives engaged by the U.S. consul to monitor his movements.

Fraser, Trenholm was an offshoot of a Charleston firm founded by John Fraser, a Scotsman who had immigrated to South Carolina. At the time it was poised to advantage in the American Civil War, the business was being run by the handsome and exceedingly wealthy Charles Alfred Trenholm, who would later be appointed the Confederate treasury secretary and who would one day be considered the inspiration for Margaret Mitchell's character Rhett Butler in *Gone with the Wind.* Also from South Carolina was the man sent to England in 1854 to manage the firm's office, Charles Kuhn Prioleau, who married "the belle of Liverpool," Miss Mary Wright. Prioleau lavished much of his wealth on their properties—Allerton Hall (her family's home), Balkail Hall, Carlisle, and a luxurious town house in Abercromby Square that, with its elaborate decorations reflecting aspects of the South, was something of a shrine to Prioleau's Dixie roots.

Even before funds reached England from the new and still disorganized Confederate government, Fraser, Trenholm (aptly described a century later by a descendant as *The Company That Went to War*) was extending a line of considerable credit to enable Huse and, later, Bulloch, to start making purchases.[14] That was not the high-risk venture it might at first appear, for Prioleau lived at the cutting edge of transatlantic economics and knew how heavily the scales seemed to weigh in favor of the Confederacy, at least in these early stages of the war. He would have known too of the powerful sympathies the upper classes in Britain were expressing for his beloved South. Emotive pamphlets and essays in support of the Confederacy were already hitting the presses, and the custodians of some of the country's most venerable titles and grandest estates were pledging support. Indeed, the partisanship of Robert Cecil, the future Lord Salisbury, was so passionate that it provoked the pro-abolition MP William E. Forster to accuse him of supporting the Confederacy because the aristocratic, land-owning Southerners were "the natural allies of the noble Lord and of the order to which he belonged."[15]

While political battle lines were being drawn and the British press was speculating on the government's response to events in America, shrewd businessmen were assessing the opportunities that were rapidly emerging. Abraham Lincoln's announcement of a blockade of Southern ports sparked a rush to identify vessels capable of keeping open the trade between Britain and the Southern states, in particular the flow of cotton that fed the mills of England's industrial north. Some members of Parliament had interests in shipping, among them William Gregory and William Shaw Lindsay, who would become vocal supporters of the Confederacy. A former MP, Ross Donnelly Mangles, who represented Guildford, Surrey, from 1841 to 1858, appears to have been one of those quick to scent profit in the prevailing climate.

Mangles had a long association with the East India Company and had become its chairman in 1858. He was also a director of the London and North Western Railway Company (L&NWR) and the Chester and Holyhead Railway Company. In 1847, in the belief that it would win a valuable contract to carry the mail to Holyhead and thence by sea to Kingstown, Ireland, the Chester and Holyhead Railway Company had, through a subsidiary, made a major investment in four new paddle steamers. To the directors' dismay, the sea-crossing element of the mail contract was awarded to the City of Dublin Steam Packet Company. When a House of Commons select committee sanctioned the Dublin company's purchase of faster steamers in 1853, even carrying passengers across the Irish Sea was no longer viable. By an act of Parliament in 1859, ownership of the Chester and Holyhead Railway passed to the L&NWR.[16]

In December 1861 the directors of the L&NWR transacted with unseemly haste for the disposal of two of the steamers, the *Anglia* and the *Scotia*, to Liverpool shipping brokers Curry, Kellock, and Company. An agreement was drafted on December 19, and at 4 p.m. on Christmas Eve, Bramley, Moore, Liverpool agent for the L&NWR, sent a telegram to the company secretary, Charles Edward Stewart, at Euston Station in London requesting that he instruct his Holyhead shipping superintendent to hand over the vessels to Edward Bates, a Liverpool shipping magnate and an associate of Captain Bulloch. A letter received by Stewart on Christmas Day explained, "Mr. Bates has two vessels leaving port on Thursday and wishes the steamers that tow them to bring back the two he has purchased." The *Anglia* and the *Scotia* soon reemerged as blockade-runners.[17]

Ross Donnelly Mangles was the son of James Mangles of Woodbridge, near Guildford, Surrey, whose fortune had been made in banking and merchant shipping, his ships trading to India and transporting convicts and goods to the penal colony in New South Wales, Australia. Ross had a sister, Ellen, who was married to Sir James Stirling, the founding governor and commander in chief of Western Australia, and founder of the city of Perth and the port of Fremantle.

James Stirling was thirty-two when he married sixteen-year-old Ellen Mangles, and the couple had eleven children. Their fourth child, a daughter, was born on October 11, 1832, on board HMS *Sulphur* while the ship was four days out from Cape Town bound for England. When the vessel put in at St. Helena, the baby was christened Mary. Fate was holding a place for her within the footnotes of history.

Stirling came from a noble Scottish family that had already produced two admirals (his grandfather and an uncle) and had established an American connection by marrying into the Willing family of Philadelphia. His father, Andrew, had entered the world of commerce and in 1792 formed a partnership, Stirling, Hunters, and Company, which traded in London as a commission house, dealing in textiles and Scottish goods, from premises at 5 Bow Church Yard in the City. Over the years the business was dogged by the vicissitudes of trade (falling victim to the recession in 1825 with serious consequences), and the family's fortunes fluctuated as a result. James Stirling's brother, William, achieved rather more success in cotton, joining with Joseph Beckton of Manchester to trade as Stirling and Beckton. By May 1821 the pair had built and were operating a nine-story cotton-spinning mill at 41 Lower Mosley Street, Manchester, the city dubbed "Cottonopolis," with connections to Liverpool by canal and rail. Eventually, William formed a partnership with his twenty-six-year-old nephew Thomas Mayne Stirling to trade as W. & T. M. Stirling.[18]

In 1847, in command of the 120-gun ship of the line HMS *Howe*, Sir James Stirling had escorted the dowager queen Adelaide (Queen Victoria's aunt), who was convalescing after an illness, to Lisbon and then to the island of Madeira. While preparing to disembark, Adelaide was saved from falling overboard in a heavy swell by the prompt action of Stirling, who lost his ceremonial sword in the process. A year later Stirling was appointed her naval aide-de-camp. As such he had frequent audiences with Queen Victoria; but while he might have expected some preferment as a result of his royal connections and considerable public service in India and, particularly, Australia, it was not to be. As a boy, for a short time he had been one year below future foreign secretary and prime minister Lord John Russell (a friend of Stirling's father-in-law, James Mangles) at Westminster School, but when he appealed to Colonial Secretary Russell in 1841, privately hoping for some benefit, perhaps a baronetcy in lieu of further land compensation in the colony, no favors were forthcoming. He pursued his claim, to no avail, through correspondence with the Colonial Office, and was clearly feeling slighted when he wrote to Russell that "there is scarcely an instance amongst officers, similarly circumstanced, who have not received by your Lordship's intercession, honorary distinctions, pensions, or more profitable offices. I appeal to your Lordship's justice whether I ought to be permitted to retire from the Colonial Department after so long a connection without notice or reward." Russell's response, annotated to a dispatch, was, "Sir James Stirling is a very good and honourable man, but I do not know he is entitled to be made a Baronet. As to money, I thought he had large grants of land."[19]

In April 1858, two months after General Buckley had resigned his position as equerry to the Queen and two years after Victor Buckley had begun his Foreign Office career, James Stirling rented a house in fashionable Harley Street for the London season. Stirling's country estate was Belmont, near Havant in Hampshire, and he also leased properties on the Isle of Wight, close to Queen Victoria's beloved Osborne House, but James and Ellen Stirling now had two daughters of marriageable age who had not yet found husbands, and expensive though it was for the parents, the London season provided a young lady of standing with her formal "coming out" into society, marked by presentation at court. At the age of eighteen, Anna Stirling would soon be curtseying to Queen Victoria and entering the aristocratic marriage market. However, her older sister Mary, now twenty-five, was still unmarried, giving rise to concern within the family.[20]

The London society into which the Stirling girls were introduced had changed considerably since Queen Victoria had ascended the throne. The monarch and her consort, Prince Albert, set the mood for the country—one of sobriety and industriousness, with strict codes of conduct and a regard for morality. Gone was the extravagance and licentiousness that had marked the Regency period and the subsequent short reign of George IV.

In the sober Victorian spring of 1858, as Anna Stirling prepared for presentation at court, her parents knew that attendance at the Queen's Drawing

Rooms and at the season's fashionable balls and soirees would increase the likelihood of Mary finding a husband.[21] It may also have provided Mary's introduction to, or cemented an existing relationship with, Victor Buckley. Certainly, Osborne House on the Isle of Wight would have provided many opportunities for Sir James Stirling and General Edward Pery Buckley and their families to become acquainted, and they would have mixed in similar social circles. Mary was six years older than Victor, an unusual age difference for a love match; moreover, despite the standing of James Stirling in society (he had been promoted to vice admiral the previous year), the Stirling and Mangles families could not quite equal the aristocratic Buckleys with their impressive lineage and associations. The profitable opportunities afforded by the British East India Company, the industrial revolution, and the age of railways had begun to nudge the barriers between the aristocracy and an acceptable face of commerce. Yet while banks and other financial institutions could prudently woo members of the nobility to their boards, money made from manufacturing and "trade" remained stubbornly stigmatized. Whether or not this aspect of the Stirling and Mangles families was a consideration, or the age difference a concern, the marriage between Victor Buckley and Mary Stirling would not take place for eight years. In the meantime, the American Civil War and its ramifications in the Foreign Office would change the landscape of Anglo-American diplomacy.

In the summer of 1861 Capt. James Bulloch was being introduced to businessmen in Liverpool whose interests already lay with the South. First among those was a prominent local solicitor, Frederick Shepard Hull of the firm of Fletcher, Hull, and Stone, whose important legal contact in the Confederacy was Jefferson Davis' right-hand man, Judah P. Benjamin of Louisiana, a lawyer well versed in international maritime law. Hull was a man who clearly understood the problems ahead. He knew that Liverpool's links with the Southern states were deep rooted, that the continued prosperity of the textile industry in the "dark, satanic mills" of Lancashire depended on the free flow of cotton from the South, and that beyond those mills were hundreds of thousands of secondary workers whose livelihood also depended on the industry. Between them, the port of Liverpool and the northern mills formed the powerhouse of Britain, the textile valleys producing, it was said, sufficient cloth before ten o'clock each morning to satisfy the nation's requirements; after that, everything was for export, bolstering Great Britain's coffers. Hull was certain that the mill owners and the shipbuilders and bankers of Liverpool would throw their weight behind the South's cause. Two months earlier, the popular magazine *Punch* had echoed the sentiments of many:

Though with the North we sympathise
It must not be forgotten
That with the South we've stronger ties
Which are composed of cotton.[22]

The commercial community of Liverpool would gladly fly the Confederate flag from the rooftops and take personal pride in seeing warships being built for the South on Merseyside, but for Hull's new client there was one not insignificant obstacle. It came in the form of the Foreign Enlistment Act of 1819, a statute forbidding, under penalty of seizure, "any person in British territory . . . from equipping, furnishing, fitting out, arming (or attempting or assisting to do so) any vessel with the intent that such vessel should be used to commit hostilities against any state with which this country is at peace."[23] The law had never been properly tested in the English courts, but in time it would give rise to legal arguments between the most eminent lawyers in the land.

At the Foreign Office the daily newspapers were providing ample fuel for speculation. Bulloch's arrival in Liverpool as a Confederate agent had been exposed. His secret mission, imprudently confided within his half-sister's New York household, had been betrayed and made public knowledge. Those familiar with the provisions of the Foreign Enlistment Act might well have wondered what lay in store for Confederate plans to purchase arms and ships in Britain.

Bulloch's lawyer, Frederick Hull, grappled with the intricacies of the law and the interpretation of an act that appeared to prohibit his client's proposed activities—then sent a formal request to counsel for an opinion. The reply, taking into account the absence of precedent and the degree of evasiveness that could be employed, gave Bulloch, rightly or wrongly, the go-ahead to start building a navy.

CHAPTER 3

The Honorable Members for the United States

Charles Francis Adams, the new American minister to Britain, disembarked from the steamer *Niagara* at Liverpool on May 13, having suffered from persistent seasickness on the transatlantic voyage. He had, however, drawn comfort from reading Macauley's *History of England*, which reinforced his preconceptions about the nation's politics. While he suspected that Prime Minister Lord Palmerston might be hostile to the Union, he was optimistic that Foreign Secretary Lord John Russell, with his hitherto strong antislavery convictions, would be representative of the British people and their desire to support Lincoln's government.

Adams was sadly mistaken in his assessment of the country's mood, as was his more cynical son Henry, who accompanied him and later reflected (in the third person) on his own disappointment: "He had to learn that his ideas were the reverse of the truth, that in May 1861 no one in England, literally no one, doubted that Jefferson Davis had made, or would make, a nation, and nearly all were glad of it, though not often saying so."[1] Despite his slight stature, Charles Francis Adams was a diplomat of great bearing and a member of a dynastic American family that had produced two presidents. At fifty-five, he was younger than the two elderly statesmen whose prejudices he was already presuming, but the next four years would demand of him every vestige of diplomatic wisdom bequeathed to him by his distinguished ancestors.

Adams' disillusionment began immediately. Upon arriving in London with his family, he was greeted with an alarming announcement in the newspapers.

Just days earlier, Queen Victoria had effectively provided her government with the means to "sit on the fence" by issuing a proclamation of neutrality—"a bitter bit of marmalade for the minister's first breakfast."[2] Behind the decision, and Britain's negotiations with France to ensure joint neutrality, lay dismay at the blockade Abraham Lincoln had imposed over 3,500 miles of Southern coastline. Freedom of shipping was of paramount importance to maritime nations, and Lincoln's use of the term "blockade" did not go unnoticed—a nation closes its own ports but *blockades* those of an enemy. Thus interpreted, it appeared the Union was acknowledging that the Southern Confederacy was not part of the American nation, and that in turn enabled Britain to adopt a neutral stance and treat both sides as belligerents.

The indignation in Britain was further fueled by the fact that Lincoln had not yet proclaimed emancipation. The slavery issue, at least at the beginning of the war, seemed to be taking second place to Lincoln's determination to preserve the Union. For the present, the most prudent position for Britain—and France, which also depended heavily on the South's cotton—was one of neutrality while events in America developed.

Britain's neutrality proclamation had been made with some regard to Adams' pending arrival. Having the neutrality in place *before* he was presented at court avoided the inference that Britain was snubbing him, but the new minister failed to appreciate the nicety of the etiquette. His pique would persist, for if sensitivity to diplomatic relations had *not* been behind the timing of the announcement, the motive was certainly questionable, suggesting rashness on the part of the British government that smacked of partisanship. In the face of so much uncertainty, Adams decided to err on the side of caution and take a house in London on a monthly lease.[3] If he had any regrets for delaying his travel so that he could attend a son's wedding, however, he might have been gratified to learn that the two Confederate commissioners, William C. Yancey and Ambrose Dudley Mann, whose arrival in England had preceded his by several weeks, had fared no better at the hands of the foreign secretary. Brandishing the threat of King Cotton's powers of coercion only raised Lord Russell's hackles. Thereafter, he would "keep them at a proper distance," and the coveted recognition as a nation the Confederacy craved was to remain an elusive prize.[4]

Having taken an invidious position, refusing either to support the North or to recognize the South as anything other than a belligerent, the British government had to await developments. It was generally agreed that decisive victories on the battlefield would determine the South's chances of success, and while news was eagerly awaited, those politicians whose feelings ran high formed their own battle lines.

The usually eloquent Disraeli became taciturn. Parliament's witty orator would remain pragmatic about the Civil War, but both the North and South had their outspoken advocates in the House. It must sometimes have seemed to Palmerston that there was more than one American minister biting at his heels in London. John Bright, a Quaker MP and Rochdale mill owner, was now prepared to give the Union a voice in the House of Commons and carried on a considerable correspondence with Senator Charles Sumner, who read his letters aloud to Lincoln's cabinet.[5] Indeed, so respected was Bright for his unrelenting commitment and oratory power that his portrait hung in the American legation in London.

Aligned with Bright in Parliament were Quaker-born Yorkshireman William Forster, who had a wool-manufacturing business in Bradford, and Richard Cobden from Lancashire, who owned a calico-weaving factory in Bolton. Like their radical ally, Forster and Cobden spoke for the working masses and those of the textile mills in the north of England. There were now three politicians under the umbrella of "the Honourable Members for the United States."

Contrary to the South's belief that a cotton shortage would coerce the population into demanding that the government recognize the Confederacy as a nation, the working-class people of the textile valleys were prepared to stand by their distaste for slavery and suffer whatever hardship the war imposed on them if ultimately it led to emancipation. That their own labor was in danger of becoming nothing more than a commodity was not lost on them, and they identified with the Northern abolitionists on the principle.

While Bright, Forster, and Cobden, unusually for factory owners, stood for the working classes and the maintenance of the Union, other political heavyweights were arraigned against them. Most prominent was perhaps Robert Cecil—the later Prime Minister Lord Salisbury—who put aside his invective against Russell and dedicated himself and many of his extended, wealthy family to wholeheartedly supporting the South and bearing, as John Bright put it, "unsleeping ill-will towards the Americans."[6] Decidedly partisan too were cabinet members the Duke of Newcastle and William Ewart Gladstone, who was chancellor of the exchequer and whom the historian Brooks Adams would describe as "the most slippery of men."[7]

John Bright straightened his back and looked these formidable opponents in the eye. "*Privilege*," he threw at them, "thinks it has a great interest in this contest and every morning with blatant voice, it comes into our streets and curses the American Republic."[8]

It was not only the politicians who were cursing the American brand of republicanism. Queen Victoria had no liking for the American system, declaring thankfully after Charles Francis Adams had presented himself at court in elaborate attire instead of his legation's usual austere suit, "We shall have no more American funerals."[9] In accord with her feelings, the Prince of Wales would later write to his mother, "We have always been an aristocratic country and I hope we shall always remain so . . . unless we become so Americanized . . . and then the state of things will be quite according to Mr. Bright's views, who wishes only for the Sovereign and the People, and no class between."[10]

The Queen exerted considerable influence over foreign affairs, and the Foreign Office was the department in which she took the greatest interest. It was said that during a crisis in 1848, 28,000 dispatches were received at the Foreign Office, and every one passed through the Queen's hands.[11]

While London society was debating the divisiveness the Civil War was creating, Prime Minister Palmerston had to defend his stance on nonintervention, pointing out that both sides might resent interference by a foreign power. It was, he thought, in human nature that "the wiry edge must be taken off this appetite for conflict in arms before any real and widespread desire for peace by mutual concession can be looked for."[12]

The South's appetite for a navy was being satisfied in the meantime on Merseyside, where Captain Bulloch had wasted no time in commissioning his first cruisers. At the yard of William C. Miller and Sons he was able to take advantage of a fortunate coincidence. Miller, a former Royal Navy shipwright and naval instructor, "fortuitously" handed Bulloch a set of scale drawings for a Royal Navy gunboat that, with some modification, could be adapted to Bulloch's purpose.

Bulloch's requirements for a Confederate cruiser were specific. He wanted the gunboats built of wood rather than iron to facilitate ease of repair in remote ports. His ships would require speed, with the ability to cruise under steam or canvas, and they must be economical with coal, for that might prove difficult to obtain. He rightly anticipated that Confederate vessels would not be welcome in many pro-Union ports, and that access to some foreign ports would be restricted by international laws of neutrality. The cruisers would need the ability to survive long periods without re-coaling.

Miller's plans could not have suited Bulloch's purpose better. The design engineers were soon increasing the length of the ship, making provision for greater storage of coal and supplies, and modifying the rigging to improve sail strength. For expediency the actual contract for the building of the vessel would be between Bulloch and the engineering firm of Fawcett, Preston, and Company, also of Liverpool, which would make the engines for the ship and be the nominated recipient of all payments. Fraser, Trenholm would handle the financial dealings on Bulloch's behalf.[13] "Fossetts," as the company was affectionately known, also owned a foundry at which Blakely guns and other ordnance were manufactured. A gun reputedly made by Fawcett, Preston had been used in the defense of Fort Sumter, and Prioleau had been so impressed with the quality of the firm's weapons that he sent some of them to Charleston shortly before the war. The projectiles he shipped over were soon being used in the fateful bombardment of Fort Sumter, earning Fawcett, Preston the distinction of being behind the first shots on both sides that started the American Civil War.[14]

While Miller and Sons prepared to lay the keel for the gunboat, Bulloch addressed the problem of secrecy. As yet, his activities had not been challenged, but, ever cautious, he decided to lay a smoke screen to protect his ship. The recent political turmoil in Italy would create the perfect foil. It was also an opportunity for Bulloch to indulge in his fondness for wordplay by choosing an Italianate name for the ship to reflect her large spread of sail—the *Oreto*, anglicized from *orézzo*, meaning "a breath of wind or a gale." Having named his gunboat, he set in place an elaborate chain of misinformation. John Henry Thomas, local agent for Thomas Brothers of Palermo, Italy, was supervising the construction, and *his* name would appear as the ship's owner on her registration. It was a short step from that to suggest the vessel was in fact being built for the Italian government, a rumor that might be difficult to disprove given the political climate in Italy.

In time, the dockyard name for this first cruiser would give way to something more appropriate to the Southern states. She was destined to sail as the CSS *Florida*, but in the coming months she would retain her disguise and Miller and Sons would preserve its distance from the true nature of her construction.

Not so sensitive to possible implication in Confederate business was the shipyard of Laird Brothers across the Mersey at Birkenhead. The company's interest in the South had been public knowledge for some time; the firm of Fraser, Trenholm had been acting as a conduit for a possible venture between A. M. Weir of London, Laird Brothers, and George Alfred Trenholm's business in Charleston, South Carolina. A proposal had been put forward to build three iron ships to run between Charleston and Liverpool (each capable of carrying some four thousand bales of cotton) with half of the capital for the new shipping company being raised in Charleston and the other half in Great Britain. However, the plan relied somewhat optimistically on the Confederacy establishing itself without resort to war; the first shots in the harbor of Charleston doomed it to failure.[15]

There was, though, one highly sensitive aspect of Bulloch's proposed dealings with Laird Brothers. Although the company was now run by the brothers

William and John Jr. (joined by their brother Henry), their father had only recently retired from the business in favor of standing for Parliament for the newly created constituency of Birkenhead. It was political dynamite for John Laird Sr. to be adhering to the principles of neutrality in the Commons while his former company flirted with the penalties of the Foreign Enlistment Act. Bulloch would later describe in his memoirs how "a friend" who had taken him to their shipyard brought about his introduction to the Lairds. It was a rather disingenuous statement because events would later show that a coterie of businessmen had already begun orchestrating much of the Confederates' success in their shipping activities.[16]

The Lairds had a proud history of shipbuilding dating back to 1828 and had constructed some of the century's most renowned ships. The first iron vessels for the British Admiralty and the United States had been built at their yard, and a Lairds-built steamer, *Sirius* (chartered by the British and American Steam Navigation Company), had beaten Brunel's *Great Western* in a transatlantic race. They had supplied armed ships to the East India Company and had built the famous *Ma Roberts* steam launch for the explorer Dr. David Livingstone.

The African connection was instigated by John Laird Sr.'s younger brother Macgregor, who had also established an American association for Lairds, as a director with lawyer and businessman Junius Smith, in the British and American Steam Navigation Company. A deeply religious man, and an abolitionist, Macgregor joined an expedition to Africa in 1832 to assess missionary and trade possibilities. Although commercially a disaster, the expedition did prove that the Nile was navigable for trade. Macgregor Laird's knowledge of Africa and its trading potential were to be rewarded twenty years later with the managing directorship of an important new company.

The African Steam Ship Company was founded for political rather than commercial considerations, the British government wanting to establish its presence and also to develop alternatives to the slave trade. The company was incorporated by a royal charter on August 7, 1852, heralding a prosperous future for British interests in Africa. Its unusual liability status, aligned with a ten-year mail contract negotiated with the British government to carry mails to Madeira, Tenerife, and the West Coast of Africa, with a subsidy of some £21,250 per annum, quickly attracted investors. Under the auspicious chairmanship of Sir John Campbell, with members of the board including important and influential figures in banking and shipping, the shares were soon taken up.[17] The company's terminal port was London, with offices located at 79 Great Tower Street in the City, but each vessel would put in at Plymouth for mails, a system facilitated by the cooperation of the Great Western Railway.[18]

The company ordered five iron-screw steamers from John Laird's yard at Birkenhead, and, upon taking up his appointment as managing director of the African Steam Ship Company, Macgregor Laird sought a capable secretary to assist him. That secretary would become well acquainted with two generations of the Laird family—Macgregor's brothers William, Hamilton, and John (the future MP), as well as John Laird's sons, who were destined to take over the shipbuilding yard. William and Hamilton had been in business as coal merchants for some years, but they agreed to become the Liverpool agents for the African Steam Ship Company.[19] The secretary would follow the inevitable ebb and flow of the company's business as a £3 million profit in the first year vindicated Macgregor's commercial vision, and he would observe the decline in business in 1855 when, upon his employer's self-relegation to the board, control of the company passed into apparently less capable hands. The man Macgregor Laird chose for the job was Frederick William Bond. Since Bond's family was already supplying guns to the East India Company, for whom the Lairds were building ships, it was natural that they should also supply weapons to the African Steam Ship Company.

By 1855 the West African trade had deteriorated to such an extent that the directors were considering winding up the company. A rescue plan was implemented, making direct sailings from Liverpool rather than stopping in Plymouth, and this proved beneficial, although the effects of an economic downturn in 1858 compounded by accidents and litigation resulting from the loss of the vessel *Forerunner* were reflected in the company's subdued accounts. Macgregor Laird died at the age of fifty-two, just ten years after the formation of the African Steam Ship Company, and with his death in January 1861 came the changes to the Laird Company that would in time see John Laird Sr. depart for Westminster. The African Steam Ship Company too would see major changes, its future shaped in the years after the American Civil War by a curious twist of fate.

In the early summer of 1861, however, the Lairds' attention was focused on the contract they were about to sign with Captain Bulloch for construction of a magnificent 200-foot-long wooden ship. At over 1,000 tons she would be even bigger than the splendid 700-ton *Oreto*, and Bulloch considered her price tag of £47,500 to be more than reasonable for a vessel of 1,000 horsepower.

It was unusual for a successful shipbuilder such as Lairds to be designing and building a wooden cruiser in this new age of iron ships, but the company's dedication to the task resulted in a finished product made of the very best materials; carefully selected timbers were rejected if they fell short of expectations, and no expense was spared in perfecting Bulloch's ship. "She was as fine a vessel, and as well found, as could have been turned out of any dockyard in the kingdom, equal to any of Her Majesty's ships of corresponding class." So Bulloch proudly described his formidable cruiser with her tall, barque-rigged masts and her predatory intent. She was the 290th vessel to be laid on the stocks at Lairds and appeared as such in the company's order book, but "the 290" was to become more than a dockyard title. Long before she gained notoriety as the CSS *Alabama*, her numerical name would give rise to speculation and rumors. It would be suggested that 290 was in fact the number of wealthy pro-Confederate sympathizers who had contributed to her building costs, a myth that gained momentum as the mysterious vessel took shape.[20]

As before, Bulloch took care not to run afoul of the Foreign Enlistment Act. He signed the contract with Laird Brothers as a private individual, and the 290 would be built in readiness for her actual fitting out away from British waters. An appropriate reflection of the initiatives employed was to appear in the motto on the ship's wheel: *Aide toi et Dieu t'aidera*, "Help yourself and God will help you."

So far, Bulloch had been able to go about his business without interference, but all that was about to change. Charles Francis Adams was keen to put in place a system of surveillance to monitor the activities of Confederate agents, but even his determination was to be outshone by that of a fellow American, Henry Shelton Sanford.

The black-haired, eagle-eyed Sanford had served with the American legation in Paris between 1849 and 1854. Even among his peers he was considered an unlikeable person. In Paris he had become embroiled in a diplomatic row over the manner of his dress, choosing to present at the French court in a plain black suit, attire he considered to be appropriately representative of American republicanism. This unfortunate style, which earned him the nickname "Black Crow" and would certainly have been anathema to the British court, was subsequently dispensed with by the new minister, John Y. Mason, who reverted to flamboyant court dress.[21] In 1854, Sanford foolishly demanded the support of President Franklin Pierce's administration, assuming that the dispute would be settled in his favor; he received, by reply, a humiliating recall to the United States.[22]

Sanford had encountered Bulloch during the *Black Warrior* crisis in Cuba in 1854 and deemed him a very dangerous person. In these first months of the Civil War, from his new vantage point in the American legation in Belgium, he quickly assessed the threat posed by Bulloch's presence in England and set about creating an effective response.

Sanford's plan was approved by the U.S. consul in London, Freeman H. Morse, who hired a private detective, Ignatius Pollaky, for "thirty or forty days of close work" at a fee of £100. Morse soon reported to Sanford that Pollaky was "on the track," coordinating a network of spies and detectives who were following Huse and Bulloch daily. By July, Pollaky's costs were running at £150 per month for surveillance of Bulloch alone. Well aware of the surveillance, Bulloch arranged for letters to be addressed to him as Mr. Barnett at Hatchetts Hotel. It was a timely foil because Sanford was even bribing postmen, half a crown buying scrutiny of envelopes addressed to Bulloch, in the hope of ascertaining their place of origin. Sanford was becoming increasingly paranoid, but he reserved his special hatred for the man who represented the Confederate navy. He even devised a plan to kidnap Bulloch should he ever set foot on the Continent, suggesting he might be arrested "on some charge or other."[23]

Bulloch had originally hoped to buy naval supplies directly from the manufacturers, but, like Huse, he was to discover that trade was a closed shop in Britain. Use of "commission houses," or middlemen, such as Sinclair, Hamilton, and Company and the other major supplier, Isaac, Campbell, and Company, was mandatory. It was simply the way the British did business, with reciprocal commissions available to the Confederate agents for their introduction. Bulloch and Huse were making very substantial purchases of arms, ammunitions, and military and naval supplies. At the London Armoury Company, in particular, the tab was running high. Rifles cost £3 each, and Huse had been obliged to pay a deposit of £15,000 as security. The company's astuteness was more than matched by that of Samuel Isaac of Isaac, Campbell, and Company, who was fleecing the Confederate agents by maintaining two different sets of accounts.

Sanford's spying operations had raised the stakes in the battle of wits between the representatives of the South and the Union diplomats. Bulloch was soon feeling the pressure, and he wrote to Mallory in August:

> By far the greatest perplexity that has cramped my individual movements has arisen from a cause which you will doubtless be shocked to learn and which occasioned the utmost astonishment as well as chagrin. . . . Almost simultaneously with my arrival in England, there came in due course of mail a New York paper . . . in which my departure for Europe, with the precise service assigned to me, the total amount of money furnished, and even the banks and bankers through whom the credits were to be arranged was as minutely detailed as if the particulars had been furnished direct from the Treasury Department.[24]

Worse was to follow. Before long, the spies employed by Adams and Sanford would be supplying sufficient information for remonstrance to be made to the British government. If it were not already apparent to Archibald Hamilton and his associates that a mole in the Foreign Office would be a very useful ally, it soon would be. All the arms and munitions that Hamilton and Bond could supply were of no use to Bulloch and Huse if they could not be shipped from Britain and run through the blockade into the Southern states. Moreover, if the war were prolonged, the arms industry in Britain would benefit. The two men had a vested interest in being informed of the communications between the American legation and the Foreign Office.

At the moment, however, the Foreign Office clerks were somewhat preoccupied with a forthcoming upheaval. The Downing Street premises, with its ominous structural cracks and unpleasant surroundings, had at last been condemned, and the staff would move on August 27 to temporary offices in Whitehall Gardens. At that time, the clerks assembled for a photograph, sitting or standing before the shrouded lens of the camera. Some looked ill at ease, a few seemed grave, others posed stiffly. Young Victor Buckley stood prominently at the far right of the frame, the camera taking his tall, slim figure to advantage. His hair was fastidiously brushed, his jacket open to reveal a tailored waistcoat; the rim of a stovepipe top hat was balanced between his fingers, and a dandyish cane hung beneath it. With all the assurances of wealth, of his family's good name, and the aristocratic conscience on which the Foreign Office so heavily relied in choosing "gentlemen" to serve as its clerks, he looked the camera straight in the eye. A few feet away, in ponderous pose, sat his departmental friend Charles Abbott, pallid complexion and studious features concealed by a bushy beard. The bespectacled young man, also seated, was Thomas Sanderson, a friend who would one day be dubbed the Foreign Office "super-clerk."[25] The name of each clerk appeared beneath his own image in the developed photograph. All but two of the men were identified by surname only. The name of the handsome young man on the right had an initial added to read *V. Buckley*—a style of signature that would have a certain resonance in later years when it appeared in rather different circumstances.

In a world apart from the Foreign Office, two of Sanford's detectives were preparing to put *their* names to a damning document. Ignatius Pollaky and Edward Brennan had identified no fewer than seventeen "conspirators." Huse, of course, was duly noted, but at the top of the list was the name of Capt. James D. Bulloch. The detectives had identified the major companies with whom the Confederates were doing business and the likely ports from which their supplies would be shipped. In addition to watching the premises of the London Armoury Company, those of Bond's brother Edward, and the Barnetts' factory, they stationed themselves wherever the Confederate agents stayed or held their meetings.

Sanford was relishing his task now. "I am determined," he wrote to Secretary of State William Seward, "to get at the operations of these 'Commissioners' through their own papers. . . . How it will be done, whether through a pretty mistress, or an intelligent servant, or a spying landlord is nobody's business."[26]

CHAPTER 4

Money Will Accomplish Anything in England

"They are some of the most helpless and short sighted of men. They are like the people who held out their dishes and prayed that it might rain plum puddings." Such was Palmerston's opinion of the mill owners who, in the summer of 1861, had not yet experienced a shortage of cotton. "They think it is enough to open their mill gates, and that cotton will come of its own accord."[1] As yet, the complacency of the textile industry was going unpunished because the previous cotton harvest had been a bumper crop and Britain's warehouses were well stocked. The South's ill-founded policy of going into the war with an embargo on cotton exports as an example to Britain and France of what a shortage would mean to their economies was having no impact, and would soon prove to have been a rash move. King Cotton was not the bargaining chip Jefferson Davis and his cabinet had hoped it would be, for by the time the warehouses of Lancashire started to echo with the hollow sound of emptiness, Lincoln's blockade was becoming quite effective and only a trickle of cotton could find its way to Europe.

This stranglehold situation gave rise to an economic boom in other sectors of industry. Low-draft steamers in Britain suited to the shallow ports of the Southern states changed hands at exorbitant prices to be converted to blockade-runners. The order books of shipyards swelled with the demands of the speculative merchants, and wily sea captains with the skill and bravado to make a dash through the Union blockading fleet became wealthy men. Yet even before the dealers in futures had started amassing fortunes, Palmerston's experience as a statesman was proving its worth. Pressured by the lobbying of both sides in the Civil War, he maintained a cautious overview of the situation, his exasperation with the mill masters indicative of the problems he saw ahead.

Palmerston still enjoyed huge popularity among the people, and his pragmatic approach, at least in the months before either side baited John Bull with problems, seemed to the British public a satisfactory response to the issue. Privately, Palmerston harbored reservations about the Union's politicians. His biographer, Evelyn Ashley, would later confirm as much: "He entertained a feeling of contempt, and even of dislike, for many of the men who from time to time occupied public positions with the United States Government. He thought them deficient in honesty and offensive in tone, in short, not 'gentlemen.'"[2] Prudence and forbearance were to some extent helped by the deficiency in transatlantic communications; the telegraph system was not yet working, and news from America could take many days to reach Britain. Still, Palmerston and Russell bided their time behind the safety curtain of neutrality, waiting for that first outcome on the battlefield that might foreshadow America's destiny.

Much of Palmerston's popularity with the public stemmed from his personal charisma. An outspoken and apparently fearless aristocrat, and reputed to be something of a rake, he was of the age of Waterloo, of the generation whose attitudes were shaped by Wellington's making of history. It was Palmerston who instigated the recognition of "Waterloo man," the title by which every man who fought in the battle would be honored on the payroll of his regiment. This, he wrote, "would constantly keep alive in the minds of the soldiers of the Army the memory of this unexampled victory."[3]

It was an ethos that would certainly have found favor with General Edward Pery Buckley. In politics Buckley was, surprisingly perhaps, generally supportive of electoral reform, but when he spoke in the House he was at his most passionate when raising matters concerning the army or the royal family. If his stridently imposing figure cast any inhibiting shadow over Victor's career, it was as a devoted advocate of army concerns. Buckley's heart was still very much with the men in the field. He was also, perhaps, still grieving for his son Bat, who had lost his life in the Crimea and whose body was buried on Cathcart's Hill, Sebastopol. The war graves were an abiding concern to him, as was the well-being of the royal family. Weighed against such emotions, the comparatively quiescent lives of the young Foreign Office clerks must have paled into insignificance.

Among many of General Buckley's aristocratic contemporaries support for the Confederacy was steadily increasing. Robert Cecil's brother-in-law, Alexander Beresford Hope, was already delivering speeches on the war, illustrating one of his talks with a large map of America that the children from the school on his country estate had been instructed to draw. Beresford Hope was temporarily without a seat in Parliament, but with his enormous wealth and family connections, this was a fact that did not render him politically impotent or less respected. He had chaired the Select Committee on the Foreign Office Reconstruction in 1858 and would always be a powerful figure, buoyed by a fortune inherited from an ancestry of Dutch bankers and diamond merchants. His family would forever be associated with the famous Hope diamond and with providing financing for America's purchase of Louisiana from the French in 1803. A high churchman, Beresford Hope was also an influential figure in ecclesiastical circles, with a concern for the effects of the Civil War on the church in America. He was soon financing the publication of his own booklets, pamphlets, and, later, novels. The enormity of his wealth and his flamboyant style of entertaining, both at his country seat, Bedgebury Park, and at his London residence, had a magnetic effect on the wide circle of people who aspired to his acquaintance. All the prominent Confederates were welcome at his table, where his guests wined and dined in the splendor of high society. "I dined last night with Beresford Hope," wrote the Confederate financial agent James Spence. "Fifty two sat down and such a spread of gold plate it was."[4]

Spence himself was quite accustomed to fine dining. A wealthy Liverpool businessman and financial agent for the Confederacy, in 1861 he published a short book, *The American Union: An Examination of the Causes of the Civil War*, creating an effective piece of propaganda for the South with his contention that England was the natural ally of the South.[5]

Among Beresford Hope's present or later friends and correspondents were significant names of the period: the Duke of Newcastle (a cabinet member whose son would marry one of Beresford Hope's nieces) was related to Victor Buckley's mother and had accompanied the Prince of Wales in 1860 on his tour of Canada and America (when, coincidentally, the prince had been introduced to Bulloch's former father-in-law in Richmond, Virginia); Lord Wharncliffe (Edward Montague Stuart-Wortley), who owned estates in the West Riding of Yorkshire and in Cornwall, and whose travels in America had endeared to him the Southern way of life, would become president of the Manchester branch of the Southern Independence Association; and Chancellor of the Exchequer William Ewart Gladstone, who became one of the most vocal members of the government supporting the South. Gladstone was born in Rodney Street, Liverpool, to a wealthy family whose merchant interests included shipping. His father owned slaves in the West Indies, a fact sometimes seen as contributing to his pro-South rhetoric.[6]

Beresford Hope's American contacts included Jefferson Davis and Gen. Robert E. Lee, and he became close to the Confederate commissioners William Yancey and James Mason, the propaganda agent Henry Hotze, and Captain Bulloch. Arklow House, his opulent London home, was described as "one of the great meeting places or camping grounds at which . . . Confederates assembled"; and it became the London headquarters of the Southern Independence Association, whose influential members included aristocrats, clergy, and members of Parliament. Intriguingly, Beresford Hope had the ear of Palmerston while enjoying the acquaintance of Bulloch's legal adviser in Liverpool, Frederick Hull.

It was to Liverpool that Henry Sanford's spies were soon turning in their relentless pursuit of Bulloch and his associates. They jumped into hansom cabs in hot pursuit of their quarry and boarded the Liverpool-bound train in London close on Bulloch's heels. The false name Bulloch adopted for his correspondence was a tongue-in-cheek attempt to confuse the detectives intercepting his mail, but the lightheartedness with which he could treat the situation was not shared by his colleague Charles Prioleau, whose offices at Fraser, Trenholm were also under constant surveillance. Irritated by the intrusion into his privacy, Prioleau turned to the press for support. "One of the members of an influential Liverpool firm is watched as systematically and tenaciously as if he were known to be hatching some infernal plot which would annihilate President Lincoln and his whole cabinet in one blast," declared the *Evening Star.* "An ever and mysterious stranger in the person of a private detective is on his track."[7] Under the tantalizing headline "Political Espionage in Liverpool," the *Manchester Examiner* noted that on the city's Cotton Exchange the principal topic of conversation concerned the system of political espionage and terrorism exercised in connection with "gentlemen supposed to be directly or indirectly connected with the Southern States of America."[8]

In late June the number of subjects worthy of the detectives' scrutiny increased with the arrival in Liverpool of a Confederate naval officer, Lt. James Heyward North, and a forty-six-year-old army officer, Maj. Edward C. Anderson—both on missions for the Confederate government. Their arrival came as a surprise to Bulloch and Huse, who had established their own close and working relationships and were devoting the whole of their time to making the major purchases required for their respective naval and ordnance departments.

Lieutenant North was to prove a thorn in Bulloch's side. He had made the transatlantic crossing with his wife and young daughter and was already a source of annoyance to Anderson because of his apparent ineptness for the task ahead of him. The Confederate navy secretary was expecting diplomacy to win over the French government, and Mallory's instructions to North were to acquire one of France's coveted ironclad warships. A new breed of iron ship had been born with the French *Gloire* and the British *Warrior*, and Mallory's vision of naval victory comprised Bulloch's cruisers drawing out the blockading fleet while powerful ironclads pounded those Union vessels left along the Southern coast.

Mallory, however, was overly optimistic. He had underestimated the imbroglio of European politics that would not allow France to recognize the South as a nation and had failed to understand that the technology of ships such as the *Gloire* was jealously guarded lest the vessel pass at some future date into the hands of an unfriendly power. Mallory's plan was seriously flawed even before North's incompetence was proven.

Anderson's role was ostensibly an unpleasant one. Huse had never quite shaken off his "Yankee" image, and his presence in England representing the South remained disquieting to some in the Confederacy. Anderson's brief, apart from making purchases in Britain for the army, was to ascertain whether Jefferson Davis' appointed agent was indeed trustworthy or, as some suspected, was harboring divided loyalties. Indeed, Huse brought to his mission excellent credentials in arms purchasing, but he had also discovered the benefits of the British system of commission agents. One of the niceties of this practice for Huse was the appreciation shown by merchants who paid their own commission to those placing orders; in time he would be called upon to explain the purpose for which he had been retaining these sums.

Anderson's fears were quickly allayed, in part because, like Huse, he respected Bulloch's integrity and judgment of character. Between them, Bulloch and Prioleau convinced him of Huse's commitment to the Confederacy, and Anderson sent immediate assurances back to the government at Richmond. Anderson soon moved into Jermyn Street with Bulloch and Huse and was introduced to the Confederacy's main suppliers—Isaac, Campbell, and Company and the London Armoury Company.

To Archibald Hamilton and Frederick Bond, Anderson's arrival represented a significant increase in Confederate purchasing power and an opportunity not to be missed. Whether Corey McFarland was having second thoughts about the order he had placed with Bond's associates or was encountering problems with Barings—the British bank used by Lincoln's government—is unclear, but Samuel Isaac, a close associate of Hamilton and Bond, was soon having a private word with Anderson. He had "heard" that McFarland had not yet received his funds from the United States, and the deposit required to confirm his order for a "a very superior lot of Enfield rifles" had accordingly not yet been paid.

Anderson was inclined to take credit wherever possible for successes in the purchasing operations and recorded in his diary that he asked Samuel Isaac to call on the gun makers and to ascertain whether, if *they* paid the deposit, the Confederates could secure the order for themselves. In fact, the three Southern agents were temporarily in a position of financial embarrassment because their own remittances had not yet arrived from Richmond; but such was Anderson's eagerness to seize the opportunity that he immediately sought to borrow the ten thousand pounds demanded. In the event, funds did arrive in time from the South and, whether by design or good fortune, Anderson was able to congratulate himself on having deprived the North of the rifles. The drip feed of remittances from the government in Richmond was a perennial problem for the purchasing agents, who were constantly turning to Prioleau for support and, when finding him unaccommodating, were sometimes obliged to remind him that the Confederacy's credit was at risk. Fraser, Trenholm, and Company was earning substantial commissions from the vast sums of money it was handling on behalf of the South and consequently wielded a measure of power that it was at pains to protect.

By now, the purchases that Bulloch and Huse had already made were piling up in warehouses around the country and plans had to be made for their shipment to the Confederacy—a delicate task given Britain's neutrality. The answer to the problem came from Prioleau, who had a mutually advantageous proposition to put to his associates. Although ostensibly the banker for the Confederacy in Britain, Fraser, Trenholm's primary purpose was to maximize profits. The company was fitting out a steamer, the *Bermuda*, due to sail shortly with a cargo of goods that would bring a handsome return if successfully run into the South.

Prioleau suggested selling cargo space in the vessel to Bulloch, Huse, and Anderson, who, although keen to get their supplies across the Atlantic, balked somewhat at the high price demanded. With no alternatives, however, they soon capitulated, and Sinclair, Hamilton, and Company began coordinating the shipment on their behalf.

The men were at last becoming aware of the shrewdness of their suppliers. A Liverpool gun dealer, William Grazebrook, had just received a further order from Anderson for 17,000 muskets, but once the order had been confirmed he promptly disposed of the guns to a Union agent, presumably at a higher price. When the indignant Anderson demanded an explanation, Grazebrook artfully provided the excuse that the sale had been made by a subordinate, without his knowledge or approval. Anderson immediately consulted a lawyer (no doubt Bulloch's legal adviser, Frederick Hull), but he was advised that he could not let the matter go to court because that might compromise his position as an agent for the Confederacy. A settlement was eventually reached whereby Grazebrook—that "precious rascal," Anderson called him—paid five hundred pounds in compensation. Business with Grazebrook continued, however, with Huse soon placing an order for 550 short Enfield rifles. A mistrusting Anderson decided that an inspector should be called in to examine the weapons they were buying, "to meet the frauds of the gun dealers," and conveniently, Hamilton and Bond knew just the man for the job. John Southgate, an expert employed as "tower viewer" by the British government, would feign illness and take a period of sick leave enabling him to devote his time and skills to the Confederates' needs.[9]

Prioleau, in the meantime, was finding himself at the center of an inevitable dispute. A Fraser, Trenholm vessel, the *Thomas Watson*, had arrived in port with a valuable cargo of cotton a few weeks earlier, having sailed from the Cape Fear River, North Carolina, and run successfully through the blockade. The sight of her coming up the Mersey with the Confederate flag flying at her masthead elicited an immediate protest from acting U.S. consul Henry Whiting and an oath from seamen on board the U.S. vessels in port that they would "do violence" to Prioleau's captain if he ventured to hoist the flag on the coming Sunday.

The task of preserving the peace on the Mersey fell to the port admiral, and Major Anderson wrote in his journal that this elderly gentleman, accompanied by Mr. (A.) Hamilton, formerly of Savannah, called at the office of Fraser, Trenholm to ask Prioleau, as a personal favor, to avoid bloodshed by not permitting the Confederate flag to be flown on the coming Sunday.[10] Prioleau tactfully consented. Any resentment the Confederates might have felt at such a concession was quickly replaced by a feeling of schadenfreude when, on that Sunday, important news from America arrived by telegraph from Queenstown. The long-awaited battlefield victory had been secured, and to the delight of Huse and Anderson, the city's Reading Room was displaying large placards announcing the result of the battle of Bull Run (also known as Manassas). July 21, 1861, was now a date for posterity. News of the South's victory was soon spreading across Britain and giving credibility to the Confederacy as a fighting force. At Prioleau's country house, Allerton Hall, Anderson and Huse climbed to the rooftop and took charge of the flagpole. The Confederate flag was destined to fly after all on that Sunday.

Ebullient though the mood of the Confederates might have been, the Union spies were now working very effectively against them, gathering intelligence and conveying it to their superiors in London and to the acting U.S.

consul in Liverpool. Crates at a private warehouse on Merseyside that purported to contain earthenware were found to house a large order of rifles for the South from Grazebrook, and private detectives were now tenaciously tracking down the steamer Fraser, Trenholm had loading.

By August 9, Prioleau was genuinely worried that the identity of the *Bermuda* had been discovered, and for the moment his associates halted all shipments to the vessel, which was lying at West Hartlepool. Sanford's network of spies had provided enough information about the ship for the American minister to write a letter of protest to Lord Russell:

> It is stated to me that a new screw steamer called the *Bermuda*, ostensibly owned by the commercial house of Fraser, Trenholm and Co. of Liverpool, well known to consist in part of Americans in sympathy with the insurgents in the United States, is now lying at West Hartlepool, ready for sea. She is stated to carry English colors but to be commanded by a Frenchman . . . this steamer is armed with four guns, and she has for some time been taking in crates, cases and barrels, believed to contain arms and munitions of all kinds ordinarily used in carrying on war . . . her armament and cargo are of such nature as to render it morally certain that the merchants who claim to be the owners can have no intention of dispatching her on any errand of mercy or peace.[11]

To Adams' dismay, his protest seemed to fall on deaf ears at the Foreign Office; and even as he was penning his outrage, Bulloch was at Hartlepool hastening the vessel's loading. A few days later she sailed with her huge cargo—18 rifled pieces, 4 heavyweight seacoast guns, 6,500 Enfield rifles, more than 200,000 cartridges, and 180 barrels of gunpowder. In addition, the vessel's hold was packed with quinine, morphine, and other medical stores; 60,000 pairs of army shoes; and 20,000 blankets.

With the *Bermuda* safely away, the purchasing agents turned again to their work: inspecting the *Oreto* as she took shape at the yard of William C. Miller and Sons in Liverpool and refilling the warehouses with arms purchases, pausing only to congratulate themselves when Samuel Isaac learned that the Union agents had run out of funds, thus forfeiting a five-thousand-pound deposit paid for four thousand Enfield rifles and leaving the order wide open for a Confederate coup. When Anderson took stock of the situation, he admitted their purchases were "a long way ahead of our funds," but opportunities to outwit the Union agents continued to present themselves, and the Confederates ordered ever more. Anderson in particular was intoxicated by their success, and even more so by the unending generosity of their suppliers. The agents were regularly assured of the best box at the theater with tickets furnished by Isaac, who also accompanied them on an inspection tour of the *Warrior* and a visit to the Royal Arsenal. Not to be outdone, Hamilton and Bond provided expensive evening entertainments for their customers, and when Anderson caught sight of Corey McFarland entering the building of the London Armoury Company, his genial hosts were quick to reassure him. The following evening Bond took Huse and Anderson to Hamilton's country house, where several glasses of good wine drowned their annoyance and suspicions. "Our dinner was sumptuous," Anderson conceded, "the costliest wines being lavished upon us." His misgivings now soothed away, he added wryly, "Mr. Hamilton . . . in business haggles over a ha'penny, but in his hospitality is princely."[12]

The Confederates' extravagance in purchasing arms had not escaped the notice of the Union spies or the American minister. In his letters Adams spoke of "floods of money" that the Confederates wasted in their "voluminous intrigues," but in these early months of the war, the greatest sums were still to be expended in pursuit of intrigues as yet unimagined.[13]

As the summer drew to a close, one of the first such situations was about to materialize. The Confederate agents knew they could not afford to repeat the costly *Bermuda* exercise and must devise some other means of shipping their purchases to the South. Away from the prying eyes of the vigilant private detectives, a meeting was convened in the dim anteroom of the Angel Tavern, a hostelry near the Liverpool Exchange, and a plan was formulated. They would buy a vessel that could be loaded entirely with their own supplies and run into the South, thus cutting out the expensive middleman.

A few days later Bulloch was able to report a satisfactory purchase. With his talent for discretion, he employed the brothers Andrew and Thomas Byrne of Glasgow, who had business connections in New Orleans and were now actively trading with the Confederacy. The Byrne brothers were to acquire, on Bulloch's behalf, a newly built 800-ton steamer. The *Fingal*, built on the Clyde for the Highland trade, had made just two voyages to date, but her log showed an impressive speed of thirteen knots in the good weather she had been fortunate enough to encounter. Her dimensions were said to be exactly those of the beautiful Fingal's Cave in the Hebrides (227 feet long and 40 feet wide). Bulloch was delighted with her, later writing fondly that he found within her inventory of cabin stores "six dozen toddy glasses with ladles to match. Each glass had the capacity of about half a pint, and they were hard and thick and heavy enough to serve for grape shot, in case of need."[14]

The *Fingal* would remain at Glasgow until her cargo could be sent to Greenock, but Bulloch resolved to keep away from the ship for the time being, knowing his presence would be observed and might precipitate a more potent protest from Adams. Moreover, with his two cruisers still on their stocks on Merseyside and a persistent shortage of funds from Richmond hampering his purchases, the *Fingal* presented an opportunity for him to go to sea. He would personally take her across the Atlantic and run her in through the blockade to the port of Savannah, Georgia. His planned return a few weeks later was intended to coincide with the first of his cruisers, the *Oreto*, being ready for sea.

In London and Liverpool the spies were spending long hours in their unrelenting pursuit of the Confederate agents, arriving in Jermyn Street at 8 a.m. and not leaving until dusk, when the blinds at number 58 had been drawn. The pressure on their quarry was beginning to tell. At this time, feeling particularly harassed by the spies and annoyed that they were endeavoring to intercept his telegrams for information, Anderson recorded in his diary an apparent countercoup: "In the meantime, *I* had not been idle in establishing sources of information, and mine, I am inclined to think, were on higher and more authentic quarters. There was a gentleman holding a confidential position in the Foreign Office whose near kinsman was one of the most important contractors."

Anderson continued immodestly, "Knowing the importance of correct information in the business I was engaged in, I sent for Bd [Bond] and proposed to him to associate his relative as a partner in interest in our contract, making it certain to him that he should not be a loser. Money will accomplish anything in England. The bait took and every night before I retired to bed I was thoroughly apprised of all the American Ministers [*sic*] operations for the day, so far as they affected the interests I was representing."[15] The Foreign Office mole, it would seem, was in place.

Hamilton and Bond brought their trump card into play at a crucial time. Anderson was fed this information after the *Bermuda*'s satisfactory departure without hindrance while the Foreign Office prevaricated and Adams fumed—a situation that could provide the catalyst for an arrangement. Anderson had no reason, and probably no desire, to question the validity of Bond's claim to a close family relationship with someone in the Foreign Office, and indeed, he did not confide in his diary that he had done so. If such a boast was exaggerated, and at best related to a friendship or tenuous link, then the social circles that facilitated likely connections should at least be considered. Frederick Bond was living in Victoria Street, Westminster, an upper-class address (since its construction after slum clearance) close to the Houses of Parliament and the government offices in Whitehall. His social circle would certainly have included many affluent young men whose lives, like his, revolved around clubs, entertainments, and mutual acquaintances.

As if to seal his admission to the inner sanctum of their secret operations, two days later Hamilton and Bond took Anderson, with Huse and another

Confederate agent, Maj. C. J. Helm, to dine at Richardson's Hotel in Covent Garden. Despite the "dingy and dark" surroundings, the meal was, as always, "an excellent dinner, well served and with an abundant supply of wine of superior quality"—a prelude to the rest of the night when the party moved on to the Holborn Casino, where they remained until late, "enjoying the festivities and looking at the dancers."[16] The Holborn Casino was famous for its large, brilliantly lit hall, with myriad glittering gaslights festooning the ceiling above dancers spinning to the music of lively polkas and quadrilles. By reputation it was a disreputable night haunt and place of easy pickup. A contemporary observer commented, "The women are of course all prostitutes. They are for the most part pretty, and quietly, though expensively dressed."[17]

The American journalist Daniel Joseph Kirwan later wrote, "The Holborn Casino is frequented by loose livers and aristocratic idlers of the English capital. The women are generally the mistresses of men of leisure." The clientele numbered many younger men from prosperous professions, and the casino's owner was careful "to maintain the appearance, at least, of decorum."[18] In 1859 the Victorian social observer Arthur Joseph Munby wrote in his diary, "It is certain . . . that the clearance, so called, of the Haymarket and casinos produced a large and still flourishing crop of secret dens and night haunts all about."[19] Kirwan said of the most aristocratic visitor to London's nightlife, the Prince of Wales, that "long nights of dissipation and debauchery had seamed the once youthful and unwrinkled features." Of the Holborn Casino's counterpart, the Alhambra, he wrote, "The angels of the ballet are . . . content with stray Americans who have a reputation for reckless liberality."[20]

This was the London of Charles Dickens, a city with many layers—by day it throbbed with the energy and affluence of the mercantile classes; the shouts of street sellers; and the relentless clatter of horse-drawn carriages, omnibuses, and carts, set alongside the grim underbelly of rat catchers and scavengers, paupers, and pickpockets. It was estimated that there were up to 80,000 prostitutes in London, and by night they were evident in such haunts as the Haymarket, Regent Street, and Holborn. The darkness also facilitated garrotters who dragged their prey into side alleys, strangling and then robbing them. On a subsequent visit to the Haymarket (according to Kirwan "the republic of vice") Anderson would suspect he had been drugged.[21]

The method of drawing Anderson into a web of espionage involving the Foreign Office was consistent with the practice Hamilton and Bond had previously employed, apparently using Samuel Isaac to leak selected pieces of information to the Confederate agents; it may have been Isaac who made mention to Anderson of a convenient relationship between Bond and a "gentleman" in the Foreign Office. Bond himself appears to have avoided the compromising situation of making overtures to Anderson personally, but the Confederate agent's contention that money was no obstacle was surely a factor both salient and, probably, anticipated.

The Confederates had every reason to be in a celebratory mood. Despite the excellent intelligence gathered by the Union spies, and with or without prior knowledge of the Foreign Office's indifference to Adams' protest, they had successfully dispatched the *Bermuda.* Public opinion too had seemed to swing their way after the victory at Bull Run, although by the autumn John Bright was detecting the onset of apathy. "Public opinion is in a languid and confused state," he wrote to Senator Charles Sumner.[22] The upper classes in general would not have shared that view and would clearly have resented Bright's contention that British foreign policy was nothing but "a gigantic system of relief for the aristocracy," while those newspapers that reflected their mood were buoyed by the Confederate victory and accordingly increased their support for the South.

Palmerston, that most aristocratic of prime ministers, had privately rejoiced in the Union's defeat in Virginia. The news that the powerful republic was not invincible appealed to his sense of honor. He jokingly referred to the battle "at Bull Run or rather at Yankee's Run," but the jocular tone masked his true sense of caution. By October he was writing to Layard at the Foreign Office, "The operations of the war have as yet been too indecisive to warrant an acknowledgement of the southern union."[23] While Palmerston was of the generation of Waterloo men who might wish for a Union defeat to reinforce Britain's own powerful position in the world, however, he was too old and too wise a statesman to ignore the truth—that one battle did not win the war.

CHAPTER 5

Our Friend in the Foreign Office

Benjamin Moran, the secretary at the American legation in London, was not a contented man. Working long hours in the gloomy basement of 24 Portland Place, choosing to take few holidays because he trusted no one with his papers, and meticulous to the point of pedantry, his traits made him an irritating colleague. His social life was limited, the nature of his position keeping him forever in the shadow of the American minister; when a fellow secretary sought to introduce him to a party of attractive young dancers, he confided to his diary that he found the girls "rather fast."

Moran's journal was his release from the dullness of his daily life. At the end of each working day, after the last of a constant stream of visitors, passport applicants, and charity seekers had left the offices, Moran took out a leather-spined volume, opened the mottled paper cover, and began writing. Between 1857 and 1875 he filled forty-one volumes, waspishly confiding his personal frustrations and his innermost thoughts, painting for the reader a detailed picture of life at the legation and, at the same time, a candid pen portrait of himself.[1]

Moran was strangely well qualified when it came to portraits. An amateur artist himself (and a dilettante who attended most of the art exhibitions in London and met many famous artists of the day), he made a point of describing in his journal the physical features and characteristics of most of the important visitors to the legation in a way that only an artist can. These details, the minutiae of Moran's daily life, were a joy to him and constituted a unique legacy for his future readers.

Born in Pennsylvania in 1820, Moran had married an English woman ten years his senior, but their unhappy life together ended with her death in 1857. The remorseful widower referred to her often in his journal, having at last found some peace in her memory, but although his writings reveal an eye for every pretty woman he encountered, he never remarried. Instead, he sought solace in the freedom of speech his diary afforded him. Through its pages he could complain about the American minister attending auctions when he should be working, vent his resentment at the arrogance of Adams' son Henry, with whom he had a sharp clash of personalities, and reflect bitterly on Britain's attitude to the United States during the Civil War.

Moran was an admirer of the bellicose William Seward, whom British politicians mistrusted intensely. He was also fiercely patriotic, cynical when it came to observing the British aristocracy and their society, and miserable at the comparatively menial nature of his position, which often relegated him to standing on the periphery at Buckingham Palace Drawing Rooms while the American minister enjoyed the limelight. In his diary he emerges from those dark corners of ceremonial occasions as a man whose personal loyalty might have been bought with a few well-chosen tokens of respect. He would one day receive recognition that would elevate him from his humble situation, but in the autumn of 1861, the Victor Buckley affair was still some way ahead in what seemed to Moran to be a bleak and pointless future, with no end in sight to the drudgery that was his lot.

Life at the American legation was soon gingered by the arrival of the new U.S. consul for Liverpool, Thomas Haines Dudley. As was his custom, Moran scrutinized the newcomer, describing him in his journal as having "a fine head and remarkably intellectual countenance." The forty-two-year-old Dudley was a Quaker from New England, tall and thin with Lincolnian features fringed by a sharply pointed beard. A strident abolitionist, he had demonstrated considerable courage as a young man, earning his first lawyer's fee by disguising himself as a slave trader and journeying south to return a kidnapped young Negro mother and her three children to freedom. A steamboat explosion that had almost cost him his life left him with impaired health, but Dudley possessed seemingly boundless reserves of energy, which carried him to the heights of the Republican Party and to a pivotal role in Lincoln's government. In the autumn of 1861 he had turned down the offer of a diplomatic post in Japan in favor of Liverpool (for its better medical facilities), where he was to replace the acting consul, Henry Wilding.

In London, Adams was becoming increasingly irritated by Henry Sanford's control of the Union spies, and in particular by the adverse newspaper publicity, which inevitably seemed to reflect poorly on him. Adams wrote to Seward in Washington demanding that supervision of the surveillance system be transferred to Consul Freeman H. Morse in London and Consul Thomas Dudley in Liverpool, an arrangement that was to prove both efficient and highly beneficial to the Union's intelligence operation.

Dudley had arrived when Confederate morale was high and the British public, ever appreciative of a tale of maritime bravado, was still rejoicing at the latest news from America. Prioleau had been the first to hear of the safe arrival of the *Bermuda*; now the story of her unhindered departure from Hartlepool could be told. She had left port without pausing to obtain clearance papers, choosing instead to put into Falmouth in Cornwall where she could take on coal. The frustrated U.S. vice consul there, Alfred Fox, wrote hastily to Washington that although the *Bermuda* was ostensibly bound for Havana, no one doubted her true destination. Her captain, Eugene Tessier, had previously skippered another Fraser, Trenholm vessel, the *Emily St. Pierre*, and had intimate knowledge of the Southern ports. Henry Wilding had described him as "a most desperate fellow, capable of any venture," and he lived up to his reputation, guiding his ship past Union shipping to steam the blockade-runner into the port of Savannah.[2]

Prioleau could hardly contain his delight, and the sweet taste of success was to last well into the coming months. "I have reported to me on good authority," Dudley later wrote to Seward, "a statement made by Mr. Prioleau that he had made a fortune by the *Bermuda* venture and should send her again."[3]

Adams, too, was lamenting the blockade-runner's triumph, speaking of his "want of success in preventing the departure of that vessel," and regarding her dispatch with a cargo reported to contain seventy tons of gunpowder as "a most important agent in continuing the war."[4] He might have derived some small consolation had he known that, impressive though her cargo was, Confederate navy secretary Mallory was unable to conceal his dismay: "Her failure to bring us small arms has caused universal regret. Fifty thousand arms at this time would be worth untold millions to us."[5]

Bulloch, Huse, and Anderson were working with ever-increasing confidence now to fill the hold of the *Fingal* with the desperately needed arms. "The same parties are purchasing arms as fast as they can be made, and at high prices," Adams observed, going on to note, "Mr. Bulloch appears to be the most efficient agent engaged in these operations."[6]

Adams was right to be apprehensive. Expert stevedores would soon be packing every inch of the *Fingal*'s cargo space with what was to be the largest shipment of military and naval supplies ever to reach the Confederacy. For the South's War Department there were 10,000 Enfield rifles, 1 million ball cartridges, 2 million percussion caps, 3,000 cavalry sabres, material for clothing, and medical supplies. For the Navy Department, Bulloch was shipping 1,000 short rifles with cutlass bayonets, revolvers, ammunition, muzzle- and breech-loading rifled guns, 400 barrels of gunpowder, and a large quantity of seamen's clothing.

Samuel Isaac offered a chartered vessel, the *Colletis*, to ship the goods from London to Greenock in Scotland. The Confederate agents understood that Isaac was a man who "never lost sight of his profits," but after some haggling, during which he found himself able to reduce his price per square measure by seventy-five pounds, an agreement was reached. In the meantime, other supplies were being sent to Greenock by rail or transported by the removal company Pickfords.[7]

As the days slipped by, the spies in London and Scotland intensified their surveillance. They noted the departure of the *Colletis* from the Thames on September 29, but as yet the *Fingal* had not left Glasgow. On October 4 the commissioner of customs at Greenock received a letter from the Board of Customs in London. Enclosed was a copy of a letter received the previous day from the under-secretary of state for the Home Department. Marked "immediate," the letter stated: "I am directed by Secretary Sir George Grey to acquaint you that he has received an anonymous communication stating that a ship is about to sail (from Greenock it is believed) having on board 3000 rifles for the Southern States of America," and told him to "take what steps he may deem necessary." The collector reported back that the *Fingal*, which he imagined was the vessel alluded to, had not yet arrived at the port, although her agents had handed in a shipping bill for her, for Jamaica and Honduras, for the exportation of 7,800 guns and pistols. Pending the receipt of any orders from the board, the vessel would be detained, as also would be the steamer *Colletis*.[8]

It was Bulloch's intention to avoid full disclosure of the cargo and to have the *Colletis* transfer her load to the *Fingal* away from the dock, but two days later Anderson recorded in his diary that Bulloch had received a dispatch from one of the Byrne brothers to the effect that "by an order from the Foreign Office in London the *Fingal* would not be permitted to take in her cargo in the stream."[9]

While the *Colletis* proceeded to discharge her cargo at a shed in the harbor, the collector of customs studied a letter he had just received from London: "If the guns and pistols are shipped as a mercantile transaction for Jamaica and Honduras neither the ships nor their owners are to be detained or in any way interfered with."[10] Bulloch's smoke screen appeared to be working. When the *Fingal* at last arrived in Greenock and started loading, the collector reported back that this did appear to be a mercantile transaction.

The watchful Union men did not agree. William Cook, the U.S. consul in Glasgow, sent a dispatch to Washington with such particulars as he could "quickly get" of the steamer. He spoke highly of the private detective Brennan, who had now taken up residence at the Seamen's Home in Greenock, and was able to state that the customs officials indeed suspected that the vessel's intended destination was not for a lawful purpose, but had received no authority to detain her. Brennan had, "with considerable manoeuvring," succeeded in ascertaining particulars of the *Fingal*'s cargo from "an official source," and in a dispatch to agent Pollaky in London he revealed the alarming details.

In the meantime, the surveyor of customs, who had also examined the vessel, had scrutinized a copy of the *Fingal*'s certificate of registry. The insistence on landing the cargo of the *Colletis* rather than letting her tranship in the stream drew a complaint from Anderson that "this is done at the instance of the American minister (Adams) who is using every effort to head off our operation."[11] Temperatures were rising on both sides. "We shall go on loading however," Anderson continued, "and have determined as needed to declare the entire contents of the cargo of the *Colletis*, leaving Mr. Adams to make out ownership if he can."[12]

Anderson's arrogance was short lived. On October 10 he was writing in his diary, "This has been an anxious day for me. We have received information from a reliable authority that it became absolutely necessary to drop the *Fingal* down the river some miles to avoid the espionage and interference of Mr. Adams' spies: that many of our packages had been left behind, and the last shipment of 2000 muskets sent on from London had not been taken on board." Anderson went on to identify the source of the warning: "We had been advised by our friend in the Foreign Office that the American minister had obtained an order to send an official to Glasgow fully empowered to ascertain the ownership of the vessel and cargo."[13]

Bulloch, however, was soon ahead of his rivals. Upon receipt of the Foreign Office warning, he immediately sent a message to John Anderson, the British captain who would be taking the *Fingal* to sea. To comply with legal requirements, it was necessary for the captain to hold a British Board of Trade certificate, and Anderson was appropriately qualified. His response to Bulloch's urgent message was subsequently observed by the watching Brennan: "The *Fingal* hauled out of the Victoria Harbour where she had been loaded at 10.0 a.m. this day and dropped down to the tail of the bank where she came to an anchor . . . she is evidently waiting for somebody or thing as she has her fires banked up."[14]

The *Fingal* was in fact awaiting the arrival of John Low, a trusted friend of Bulloch's who was to oversee the vessel's departure from Scotland. Born in Aberdeen but raised in Liverpool, Low had gone to sea at an early age, but a near-fatal illness persuaded him to settle in Savannah, Georgia. There he enjoyed the patronage of a wealthy uncle, Andrew Low, who was also born in Scotland and had retained his British citizenship. Years earlier, Andrew Low had been a major investor in the SS *Savannah,* the first steamship to sail across the Atlantic to Liverpool, but the public's suspicion of steam-powered vessels had rendered the venture a financial disaster for the group of businessmen who backed it. Among them had been Bulloch's father, Low's close friend and a prominent resident of Savannah, for whom the failure sparked serious money problems. William Makepeace Thackery later described Andrew Low's house in Savannah as "the most comfortable quarters I have ever had in the United States."[15] Like Bulloch, Low was well acquainted with Robert E. Lee.

Although very successful in maritime business at the outbreak of the war, John Low immediately offered his services to the South, and his arrival in Liverpool came, as Bulloch put it, "at a very opportune time." Knowing that Low would be a stranger to the watching Union spies, he sent him to Greenock with instructions to the Byrne brothers to transfer ownership of the *Fingal* and her cargo, for one shilling sterling, to Mr. John Low, merchant, of Liverpool. The vessel was slipping down the river even as the officials were beginning their inquiries into the status of the mysterious Mr. Low.

Such was the urgency of the situation, however, that immediately upon Low's return to Liverpool, Bulloch dispatched him back to Greenock to take charge of the ship. At 8 a.m. on October 10, the *Fingal* was safely away. At the port Brennan could only make a hasty sketch of the vessel, hoping the picture might alert Union shipping. In London an embittered Morse wrote to Seward, "The last mail brings us the unpleasant intelligence that the steamer *Bermuda* has got into Savannah with a full cargo of powder for the rebels. Trusting that we shall not have to bear the mortification of hearing that a similar success has attended the *Fingal* also."[16]

Mortification in plenty lay ahead. The *Fingal*'s escape was the final straw for Adams' strained relationship with Henry Sanford and precipitated the termination of Sanford's operations in Britain. Henceforth, Adams, Morse, and Dudley would control the spying operation. They had clearly been outwitted by Bulloch, but as yet they had no reason to believe the ship's sudden departure had been facilitated by inside information, or that the Confederate agents had "a friend in the Foreign Office."

Bulloch's carefully lain plans to join the *Fingal* once she was away succeeded, but not without problems. Accompanied by Anderson, who was returning to the Confederacy now that his presence in England was no longer necessary, he dodged the Union detectives and made his way from Liverpool to Holyhead in north Wales, where a rendezvous had been arranged with the ship. Anderson confessed to being quite disappointed that at least one of the detectives, Matthew Maguire, had not followed them. Anderson described Maguire as "indefatigable in his attentions . . . an ugly, red headed villain," and wrote in his diary, "I determined to make an emigrant of Mr. MacG. if he ever attempted to follow me to Holyhead."[17]

Although she was out of the Clyde, inclement weather impeded the progress of the *Fingal* and two days passed before Bulloch and Anderson could join her. In the middle of the night, Bulloch was suddenly roused from bed at his hotel in Holyhead by the sight of John Low wearing a dripping sou'wester, lantern in hand, "loom[ing] like a huge octopus, or some other marine monster." He bore bad news. Caught in a fierce storm, the *Fingal* had struck an Austrian brig as she came into the outer harbor of Holyhead. Official inquiries and delays were inevitable, and the success of the whole operation seemed to hang in the balance.

Bulloch quickly penned instructions to Fraser, Trenholm to reach a financial settlement with the owners of the brig, and then turned to the *Fingal*. "I thought of the rifles and sabres in the hold," he later recalled, "and the ill-armed pickets on the Potomac, waiting and longing for them, and told the captain to weigh anchor at once." He and Anderson boarded, and the voyage began.[18]

The *Fingal* encountered only one major problem before making her run through the blockade. Captain Anderson had failed to check the supplies of fresh water, and Bulloch was obliged to put into port to replenish the tanks. Fortuitously, he found they were near the remote port of Praya, on the island of Terceira in the Azores. So isolated was the spot that Bulloch made a note to utilize its seclusion in the future for arming one of his cruisers.

The *Fingal* put into Bermuda and then turned her bow toward the southern coast of America. In the capable hands of her engineer, John McNair, "a silent, steady, reliable Scot, immovable and impassive as the Grampian Hills,"[19] her engines made a good eleven knots in the final run toward the coast. Befriended by a thick fog that concealed her from the blockading fleet, the *Fingal* was brought up the Savannah River, anchoring abreast of the city in the afternoon of November 12. "The men appeared to be a little disappointed at the pacific and commonplace termination of the adventure," Bulloch noted, but the people of Savannah thronged the riverside in jubilation at the arrival. The cobblestones beneath their feet on River Street had been brought from Liverpool over the years as ballast in ships, but on board the *Fingal* was just her large, precious cargo.[20]

Meanwhile, soon after her departure from the Clyde, officials had untangled the web of deceit surrounding the *Fingal*'s ownership, and their inquiries led eventually to the Confederate bankers in Liverpool. "It appears that the *Fingal* has been sold to a Liverpool house, Fraser Trenholm & Co.," wrote Morse on October 16. "If this be so she is in reality a Confederate ship, and will change her papers on arriving at some port in the rebel States and then turn pirate."[21]

In fact, no such notoriety lay in store for the *Fingal.* After consultations with the Navy Department in Richmond, Bulloch decided to run the *Fingal* back to Britain with a cargo of cotton that could be sold to help finance his purchases. Nor was his the rapid return to England he had planned. Thwarted by the tightened Union blockade, he was obliged to wait until February 1862 before running past the Union fleet on the steamer *Annie Childs*. In the meantime, the *Fingal* was put in dry dock at Savannah. Eventually converted to an ironclad and renamed the *Atlanta*, she met an ignominious end in June 1863 when she was captured by two Union monitors after a brief fifteen-minute battle.

While Bulloch remained in the Confederacy, anxious to return to England to resume his operations there, progress was continuing on the 290. Bulloch had made careful provision for the work to be overseen in his absence by Prioleau at Fraser, Trenholm and by his brother-in-law Seth Grosvenor Porter, following his policy of maintaining a very tight circle of reliable and trustworthy aides.[22] Bulloch's wife and their young children had arrived in Liverpool shortly before his departure on the *Fingal*, and in his absence Hattie Bulloch had moved the family out of the city to a cottage at Waterloo, on the banks of the Mersey.

It was to this domestic idyll that Bulloch returned when he arrived back in Liverpool on March 10. While he had been away, Huse had been making his own purchases of vessels for the Confederate Ordnance Department, the *Fingal* having set a very satisfactory precedent. With government-owned blockade-runners now fitting out to run arms swiftly to the South, the orders were flowing into the London Armoury Company and the other suppliers. Moreover, the Foreign Office tipoff that had facilitated the *Fingal*'s departure had apparently gone undetected. Bond still had his mole in place, and with Anderson gone and Bulloch out of the country for more than three months, his relationship with Huse no doubt strengthened, although the reciprocal commissions Huse was accepting from his suppliers were, unknown to him, already counting against him.

Huse's position in London was ideal from Bulloch's point of view. Close to the political and commercial pulse of the city, he was well placed while Bond maintained the espionage connection that had so proven its worth. Bulloch himself was to be preoccupied in Liverpool for the coming months with his two cruisers, the first of which, to his surprise, was now afloat on the Mersey, dangerously tantalizing Thomas Dudley and his spies.

While Bulloch had been away, public opinion toward the American war had been swinging toward the South, particularly in light of a political drama that occurred at the end of 1861 and brought Great Britain perilously close to war with the United States. The *Trent* affair had started on November 8 when the USS *San Jacinto* overhauled a British mail steamer, the *Trent*, on which two Confederate envoys, John Slidell and James Mason, were taking passage to Europe. The men were forcibly removed from the ship and subsequently imprisoned in Boston while an impassioned British press demanded that the outrage against one of Her Majesty's Royal Mail ships be avenged. Amid calls to dispatch the *Warrior*, Palmerston and Russell received advice from the law officers of the Crown (the senior of whom was Queen's Advocate Sir John Dorney Harding) confirming that Captain Wilkes of the *San Jacinto* had acted illegally and unjustifiably under international law.

Wilkes was fêted as a hero on his return to Washington, and Congress passed a resolution congratulating him. In the ensuing days, attitudes on both sides became more entrenched. Queen Victoria considered that the Americans had "behaved scandalously" and wished to be kept "fully informed" of all that passed in this "grave affair." Palmerston was said to have fumed to his colleagues, "You may stand for this but damned if I will." Nothing less than an apology and release of the envoys would satisfy the prime minister, and Russell was soon conceding, "It looks like war."[23]

Russell suspected that the aggressive William Seward would welcome war with Britain, and as a precaution, troops were quickly sent to Canada. Even John Bright and Richard Cobden, whose sympathies during the war were certainly with the Union, wrote an urgent note to Lincoln's adviser Charles Sumner advising the release of the commissioners. Britain, they recognized, would be inclined to join with the South if war came about. At the American legation in London, the minister's son Henry Adams considered the situation "hopeless."

The fact that there were no telegraphic means of communication across the Atlantic—and therefore long delays in transmitting correspondence—was later acknowledged to have been an advantage because it allowed tempers to cool on both sides. Prince Albert, however, played perhaps the most important role in averting disaster. At the end of November, as the Queen's consort lay dying of typhoid fever at Windsor Castle, Russell drew up a strongly worded ultimatum for the U.S. government. It was to be the last official document put before the prince, and his apparent suggestion for modifying the wording was deemed to provide an honorable loophole for Lincoln's cabinet to avert the war that seemed imminent. The British government, the dispatch stated, was willing to believe that the U.S. officer who committed the aggression was not acting in compliance with any authority from his government.

Palmerston, Russell, the cabinet, and the British public held their collective breath. So too did those proponents of the Confederate cause in Britain for whom the prospect of British recognition and support seemed imminent. It was not the first time, or the last, that Adams' ministerial position and that of the legation's dedicated secretary, Benjamin Moran, looked decidedly precarious.

Prince Albert died at Windsor on December 14, before the result of the conciliatory modification was known. The letters of John Bright and Richard Cobden urging moderation and release of the commissioners were read at a meeting of Lincoln's cabinet on Christmas Day, but no agreement was reached. Two days later, the writer Anthony Trollope dined with Seward and Sumner in Washington. The cabinet had made its decision that afternoon, he was told, availing itself of the face-saving caveat. The Confederate commissioners would be released; there would be no war with Britain.

Relief swept over both countries. The protestations of John Bull had been born of outrage at Captain Wilkes' insult to the British flag, not out of any genuine desire to go to war with a friendly nation. The bitter memory of the Crimea was still fresh in the public's mind, and the agenda of Emperor Louis Napoleon in France remained a haunting uncertainty. In Washington, Lincoln had been well advised to deal with one war at a time.

Before long, the Confederates in Britain were suspecting that the crisis had actually harmed their cause. With the passing of time, the *Trent* affair, with its attendant froth of nationalism, faded away, overcome in importance by the loss of Prince Albert and the Queen's subsequent reclusion. The eventual arrival of the Confederate envoys in Britain was an anticlimax; even the pro-Confederate *Times* newspaper labeled them "worthless booty."[24] There was a sense that the scales were now tipping very slightly in favor of the North.

In February 1862, however, that shift in sympathy had not yet made its presence felt in Liverpool. Since taking up his post as consul there, Dudley had found himself in hostile territory. "The people here," he complained to Seward, "undoubtedly desire to see the Southern Confederacy established. Their sympathies for the South and dislike of the North are too apparent to be mistaken." Dudley was right. He would soon reflect that there were more Confederate flags flying over Liverpool than over Richmond, Virginia.[25]

He was accordingly not surprised to learn from his spies that the vessel known as the *Oreto* under construction at the yard of William C. Miller and Sons was a warship intended for the South. The entire shipping fraternity of Liverpool seemed to be aware of the Confederates' dealings, and when Dudley followed the chain of command, he discovered that Fawcett, Preston, and Company was paying Miller and Sons; and Fraser, Trenholm, in turn, was settling Fawcett, Preston's costs. Although Millers informed Dudley that the *Oreto* was being built for the Italian government, the Italian consul disclaimed all knowledge of the matter. Now, the twin-funneled, three-masted ship, ominously pierced with eight gun ports on either side, was languishing at anchor on the Mersey. And as if to add insult to injury, on the night of his return to Liverpool from the Confederacy, Bulloch dined with his wife on board.

CHAPTER 6

Choice Foreign Office Fiction

"Perplexing" was how Bulloch described the predicament in which he now found himself.[1] It had always been his intention to take command of the first cruiser he could get to sea, but during his enforced sojourn in the Confederacy he had come to realize that this would not be possible. Secretary Mallory appreciated the unique talents of the man he had chosen to represent the South's naval interests in Europe and had asked Bulloch to investigate the possibilities of building ironclad vessels in England or France, a task that would take some further time.

Before departing on the *Fingal*, Bulloch had taken the precaution of giving Prioleau authority to release the *Oreto* to the first available Confederate officer. In the early weeks of 1862, as the builders finished the vessel and pressed Fraser, Trenholm to take delivery, Prioleau turned to Lt. James North, the naval officer who had come to England with Anderson. Unfortunately, North was smarting from Bulloch's recent promotion to commander and indignant that Bulloch had refused to turn the ship over to him before leaving Britain. Apparently unable to conquer a tendency to irresoluteness, he confessed to the Confederate commissioner James Mason that he was at a loss to know what to do. Prioleau, mindful of the Foreign Enlistment Act and the need for haste, became exasperated with him and, following one heated disagreement, wrote pointedly, "In reply to your question, the reason why I think she may not take arms etc. on board is because she is perfectly well known to be a war vessel, built for the Confederate States."[2]

That was precisely the view of Dudley, who warned Adams in London that the *Oreto* had gun ports and when fully armed would be a formidable craft.

When overzealous spies reported wrongly that gun carriages had been taken on board, he felt he had sound evidence at last that a violation of the Foreign Enlistment Act had been committed. Dudley contacted Adams, who in turn made immediate representation to Lord Russell. The Foreign Office took prompt action, instructing the Treasury "to take such steps as may be right and proper." An agent was sent to inspect the ship, but his subsequent report did not support the complainants. While conceding that the *Oreto* was pierced for guns and had some of the character of a warship, the agent found no arms or gun carriages on board. When the surveyor of customs at Liverpool added to the doubts by saying he had no reason to disbelieve the builders' assertion that she was intended for the Italian government, the conclusion reached was that the *Oreto*'s owners had not broken the law and the ship could not be seized.

The U.S. government's fears regarding the *Oreto*'s future had been heightened by events at sea during the last few months, when Confederate naval power had begun to have an impact on Yankee shipping. At the beginning of the war, a former U.S. naval officer, Cdr. Raphael Semmes, converted an aging steam vessel—"a dismantled packet ship" that he had found rotting at New Orleans—and took command of the first Confederate corsair. The CSS *Sumter*, under Semmes' fearless and skillful captaincy, harassed commercial shipping on a scale that belied the steamer's inadequacies, capturing and burning a New England sailing ship off the coast of Cuba within three days of running through the blockade and getting to sea. Semmes was denounced throughout the North as a pirate, but his subsequent captures were only a taste of what the notoriously daring commander had in store for the Union. To Semmes' dismay, however, when he took "seven prizes of war" into port at Cuba, the authorities returned them to their owners. Henceforth, Semmes decided, captured ships would be burned.

Union warships hurried to search out "the pirate Semmes," who was not having the total success he wished for his cruise. The *Sumter*'s need for coal made frequent costly and risky stopovers unavoidable, and Semmes found himself having to pay excessive prices for the essential fuel. He was able to elude Union gunboats only by spreading disinformation about his movements.

Damaged by a storm while crossing the Atlantic, the *Sumter* eventually limped into the port of Cádiz, where she received a cool reception from Spanish officials. Semmes then steamed toward Gibraltar, pausing to take two more prizes along the way. The *Sumter* was more welcome in the British-owned refuge, but while Semmes awaited funds requisitioned from Fraser, Trenholm to pay for repairs, the USS *Tuscarora* arrived in the bay, quickly followed by another warship, the USS *Kearsarge*. "He is out of coal and out of credit," U.S. naval officer David Dixon Porter had remarked prematurely the previous summer. Now it was true.[3]

Semmes' communications with the Confederacy had been nonexistent during his voyage. Only in December 1861 did he learn from British newspapers supplied by a Liverpool vessel that there was another Confederate cruiser at sea, the *Nashville*, a steamer on which the ill-fated commissioners Mason and Slidell had originally intended taking passage.The *Nashville* steamed across the Atlantic, earning the admiration of the Confederacy and the awe of the British public by capturing and burning a Yankee clipper, the *Harvey Birch*, off the coast of Ireland. Her subsequent arrival at Southampton with the Confederate flag flying at her masthead sparked considerable excitement and persuaded frightened transatlantic shippers to order their vessels to remain in port.

Anticipating a protest from Adams, the British government sought the advice of the law officers of the Crown. It was unequivocal: British neutrality would not be breached by the *Nashville*'s presence in Southampton to carry out essential repairs, provided she did not take on any armaments or increase her fighting strength. As a commissioned ship of war belonging to a recognized belligerent, the *Nashville* could claim those legal rights. To Adams' chagrin, the law officers also found that the steamer had been in international waters when she destroyed the *Harvey Birch* and had therefore not violated British neutrality. It was not the news Adams wanted to hear, although he could draw some comfort from Russell's assurance that the government would adopt whatever measures it thought necessary to maintain its strict neutrality.

The *Nashville*'s commander, Lt. Robert B. Pegram, maintained cordial relations with the authorities in Southampton. On learning of the death of Prince Albert, he ordered the Confederate flag to be flown at half-mast. Russell was true to his word, however, and the steamer's fitting out was closely monitored. "The authorities are dreadfully afraid of doing something to incur the wrath of the Yankees," Pegram wrote dejectedly to Lieutenant North.[4]

While Pegram fretted over not being allowed to take on certain equipment, Gideon Welles sent a message to Cdr. Tunis A. M. Craven of the USS *Tuscarora* with orders to proceed without delay to the English coast. On January 8, as Pegram was making his final preparations to leave, the formidable Union warship entered Southampton and anchored close to the *Nashville*. The crews of the two vessels were soon coming to blows in the bars and taverns ashore. When Craven decided to avail himself of "the twenty-four-hour rule," by which the first of two belligerents leaving a neutral port was accorded that amount of time before the other vessel could sail, Pegram suspected a trap: the *Tuscarora* would simply wait for him outside Southampton harbor.

Pegram made an impassioned plea to the Duke of Somerset (the standoff causing the Foreign Office to review the twenty-four-hour rule), and on February 3 a British navy frigate, HMS *Shannon*, escorted the *Nashville* out. The frigate returned shortly afterward to take up a position alongside the Union vessel, blockading her in port for the twenty-four hours that were so vital to Pegram.[5] It was later claimed the *Nashville*'s captain sent a message, "Catch me if you can!" as his ship steamed past the *Tuscarora*. Certainly there was considerable wounded pride on the *Tuscarora* that day. "The whole transaction appears to me, Sir," Craven wrote to Welles, "to have a strong impress of collusion on the part of the authorities to effect the escape of the privateer."[6]

Bulloch had hoped to find an officer on the *Nashville* who could captain the *Oreto*, but by the time he confronted the problem of his new cruiser afloat on the Mersey, that warship was already out of reach of communication. Semmes was still blockaded with the *Sumter* in Gibraltar, and Lieutenant North, who could no longer bring himself to even speak to Bulloch, was writing a whiny letter to the Confederate navy secretary, characteristically excusing his lack of initiative in the affair.

As mid-March approached, Bulloch decided to assign command of the *Oreto* to a friend and former fellow officer in the U.S. Navy, Lt. John Newland Maffitt, who would be at Nassau in the Bahamas blockade-running for the Confederate government. Maffitt was a dashing officer whose charismatic personality made him popular with the ladies, but more important, Bulloch knew him to possess the courage and shrewdness required to take command of his warship. Again Bulloch selected John Low to oversee the vessel's safe passage to Nassau, where he would seek out Maffitt and deliver to him the crucial orders. Low would appear as a passenger on the *Oreto*'s roster while an Englishman, James Alexander Duguid (son-in-law of William Miller, who built the ship), would fulfill the legal requirement of holding the requisite Board of Trade master's certificate and appear as captain of the vessel. As usual, Bulloch held his cards close to his chest, keeping his operations within the "family" of close and trusted associates on whose integrity he could rely.

For a while the attention of Dudley and Adams had been diverted by something of a red herring. Dudley had correctly surmised that if the *Oreto* was indeed a Confederate ship, Bulloch must be planning to arm and equip her outside British waters. He was heartened to learn from his spies that his bête noir, Fraser, Trenholm's *Bermuda*, was being loaded with arms, and surveillance on that vessel was accordingly intensified. In the meantime, Hamilton and Bond were at work coordinating the loading of the real tender. In port at Hartlepool, the *Bermuda*'s sister ship, the *Bahama*, was receiving the *Oreto*'s arms and equipment, including a substantial amount of guns and munitions from the foundry of Fawcett, Preston, and Company, delivered by Pickfords.

Adams was becoming acutely frustrated with the apparent lack of cooperation from the Foreign Office. Russell had confirmed to him in late February that the *Oreto* was being built for the Italian government, adding confidentially that she had been ordered by the firm of Thomas and Company of Palermo. It was a remarkably effective piece of disinformation on the part of Bulloch. "The story is choice Foreign Office fiction," Benjamin Moran wrote in his journal. "I don't believe a word of it, nor does Lord Russell."[7]

February 28 was, according to Moran, "a cold and cheerless day," the more so because, not satisfied with Russell's assurances, Adams had sent his secretary to the office of the Italian minister, where he learned that the minister's secretary knew nothing of the *Oreto*. She was not intended for the Italian government, Moran reported to his chief; and that, he added, was the truth.

Again Adams nudged the Foreign Office, and a telegram was sent to Sir James Hudson, the British consul at Turin, asking him to ascertain whether the *Oreto* was indeed for the Italians. Hudson posed the question to Minister for Foreign Affairs Signor Ricasoli, but a reply was not immediately forthcoming. As fate would have it, the Italian ministry was in the throes of change, and a delay in replying was inevitable. A despondent Adams neglected to push the Foreign Office for an answer, and Russell himself saw no reason to put pressure on the Italian government. There must, however, have been some tension in the Foreign Office because the reply was expected at any time. It would later be alleged as part of the American case against Great Britain (in which the *Oreto* situation was described as "a farce") that the Foreign Office had received notification of the falsehood within sufficient time to intercede but, strangely, had not acted.

On March 22 the *Oreto* was ready to sail. She was temporarily renamed *Manassas* in honor of the Confederate victory, but Bulloch had already agreed with Mallory that she was to be named after the navy secretary's home state and become the CSS *Florida*. She was an impressive sight as she made ready to sail. Her twin smokestacks were hinged so they could be folded down to disguise her character, and her large capacity to carry sail meant that she would not rely too heavily on coal.

Dudley watched from shore as Bulloch took a party of visitors on board. They might have been embarking on another trial run. The consul must have hoped as much, for he knew that despite all the evidence he had amassed, his protestations to the government had so far come to nothing. He recalled how the *Annie Childs*, the steamer that had brought Bulloch back across the

Atlantic from the Southern states, had been observed to dip her Confederate flag by way of salute at the sight of the vessel, and how the *Oreto*, in response, had dipped her own colors. While Dudley watched helplessly a crowd of well-wishers thronged the quayside, cheering and waving at the ship. It was not another trial run; the passengers were brought back in a boat shortly afterward and the warship slipped unimpeded down the Mersey.

On March 25 the Foreign Office officially received Hudson's telegram in reply to its question, confirming what Adams and Dudley had known all along—the *Oreto* had not been built for the Italian government. But it was too late; the CSS *Florida* was on her way to the Bahamas.

There is no evidence that Victor Buckley played a part in the escape of the *Oreto*. Since Anderson had returned to the Confederacy no one, as far as is known, was keeping a diary incriminating a member of the Foreign Office; yet a viable contact was to emerge. If the state of relations between the American legation and the Foreign Office was still being leaked to the Confederate agents, and if, as the Americans were later to assert, the government was aware before the departure of the *Oreto* that she was not intended for the Italian government, there was undoubtedly a role for Buckley to play.

By that time a new figure had appeared on the scene whose name was subsequently to be linked to Buckley's. Henry Hotze had arrived in England during the latter part of the previous year carrying important dispatches from the Confederate government and, with his valuable experience of munitions, orders to check on arms shipments. Huse would certainly have introduced him to Hamilton and Bond at the London Armoury Company.

Bulloch, who was arranging for the loading of the *Fingal* when Huse brought Hotze from London, joined the two men for a "secret conference" in Liverpool accompanied by Bulloch's close friend Andrew Low, who had arrived from the South that August and was actively engaged in assisting Bulloch. His nephew, John Low, was the friend with whom Bulloch would sail on the *Fingal*. Anderson recorded in his diary that the men remained in conversation in his quarters until after one o'clock, and "the next day when near dinnertime I asked after Mr. Hotze and going to his room found that in order to avoid observation he had remained in his bed the entire day."[8]

Hotze left Liverpool the following day, carrying dispatches and coded signals for the Confederate government, and returned to London, where Samuel Isaac procured a passport for him to travel to the Continent. Hotze had planned to visit friends in Switzerland and travel from there to New York, and then make his way down to Richmond. While in London he met Confederate commissioners William L. Yancey, Ambrose Dudley Mann, and

Pierre A. Rost, who impressed upon him the urgent need for the South's case to be appropriately represented in Britain and France. Their efforts to garner sufficient support and pave the way for recognition of the South had so far been ineffectual, but Hotze warmed to the concept of a propaganda campaign aimed at the core of the British establishment and took the seed of an idea with him when he returned to the Confederacy.

Hotze was born in Zurich on September 2, 1833, into a family with a strong military past; his great-uncle was a renowned general, and his father, a captain of the Swiss Guard of Charles X, had played an important role in the country's 1830 revolution. At the age of sixteen he moved to the United States—first to New Orleans, and then, in 1855, to Mobile, Alabama, where he became a naturalized citizen. The product of a Jesuit education, Hotze developed an interest in anthropology that led to his translating into English Arthur de Gobineau's *Essai sur l'inégalité des races humaines.* Hotze's adaptation of the three volumes into a single book, *The Moral and Intellectual Diversity of Races*, revealed his own racial views that would have found ample support in the Deep South. "A human being whom God has created with a Negro's skull and general physique," Hotze wrote, "can never equal one with a Newton's or Humboldt's cranial development."[9]

Hotze became a popular figure in the affluent and genteel society of Mobile. His instinctive understanding of European culture and attitudes earned him kudos from his many admirers, and he would soon develop the knack of applying that wisdom to assessing the problems facing the Confederacy in Great Britain. In 1858 Hotze had been appointed a member of a delegation sent by the city of Mobile to the Southern Commercial Convention in Montgomery, where a rousing debate took place on the issue of reopening the slave trade.[10] Meetings with influential Southerners paved his way for advancement, and when Gen. Elisha Y. Fair of Alabama took up the post of minister to Belgium, Hotze was appointed secretary to the American legation in Brussels.

En route to his post he managed to annoy Benjamin Moran at the London legation, who (mistaking his nationality) wrote testily in his diary, "Gen'l. Fair paid us a visit in company with a young German by the name of Hotze, whom he is taking to Belgium as his attaché. This person is stupid in addition to being a foreigner, and ought not to be permitted to occupy the post he goes to fill."[11]

Hotze's appointment was in any event destined to be brief because Congress failed to appropriate funds for his post. Nonetheless, before returning to the South he maximized his experience in Brussels by serving as chargé d'affaires in addition to performing his duties as secretary.[12] Upon his return to Alabama, Hotze joined the *Mobile Register*, a newspaper of which John Forsyth was the influential and politically well-respected editor, as an associate editor. Hotze benefited from Forsyth's professional talents, but he had his own connections, and when the war broke out he became a member of the elite and aristocratic Mobile Cadets. Despite eyesight problems that would plague him for the rest of his life, he served in this prestigious company of the Confederate army for three months. In August 1861 the War Department decided to send him on the special mission to Europe to ascertain whether the Confederate agents had received the $1 million sent to purchase war materiel, and to seek assurance for Secretary of War Leroy Pope Walker that there would be no delays in the receipt of munitions.

By the time Hotze had returned to Richmond in the late fall of 1861, his fruitful meetings in Liverpool and London having convinced him of his potential to aid the Southern cause on the other side of the Atlantic, there had been changes in the Confederate government. The secretary of state was now Robert T. Hunter, and Judah P. Benjamin, the "brains of the Confederacy," had been installed as secretary of war, a preliminary to other senior positions he would occupy.

Hotze presented an audacious plan to Benjamin and Hunter: he proposed setting up a propaganda offensive in England, harnessing the power of the press to get the South's message across. Although he would initially write articles himself, he would educate English writers in a favorable interpretation of the Confederacy and persuade them to place their editorials in newspapers, the incentive being the collection of their usual fee, which ranged from two to ten guineas.[13] The propaganda, Hotze believed, would be self-perpetuating; in effect he would be "multiplying himself" to achieve Southern influence in the press.

At only twenty-nine, Hotze carried a daunting responsibility for the Confederacy when he arrived back in England toward the end of February 1862, officially as a commercial agent paid what seemed to him a derisory $1,500 per year, with a further scant $750 for expenses. It would be no small task to sway public opinion in favor of the South in Britain and Europe. By coincidence, he arrived on board the same steamer that belatedly brought the Confederate commissioners James Mason and John Slidell back to England after the *Trent* affair. Great Britain's renewed avowal to maintain its neutrality was the first obstacle in Hotze's path as he took up residence in London. Soon he opened a commercial agency at 17 Savile Row in a property owned by Dr. Richard King, founder of the Ethnological Society of London, which occupied the drawing room floor. In light of Hotze's reputation as an anthropologist, it was probably no coincidence that he was acquainted with Dr. King. Their offices became an important base for Confederates in London.

The climate of British neutrality that greeted Hotze did not unduly faze him. He was shrewd and resourceful as well as sophisticated and intellectual, and his pathway to the power-wielding aristocracy would be facilitated by the Confederate commissioners and smoothed by the friendship of the Confederacy's influential supporters. Certainly his progress was rapid. He reported to Secretary of State Hunter, "I have been fortunate enough to gain almost immediate access to a higher social sphere, giving me a wider range of influence and immeasurably greater facilities for usefulness other than I hoped to attain in so short a period of time."[14] He dined with such prominent pro-Southern politicians as Chancellor of the Exchequer William Gladstone and assisted the Confederate sympathizer Lord George Campbell, "one of our most zealous friends," in writing his speech to Parliament against the blockade.[15]

Hotze was quick to appreciate that the return of small favors and the cultivation of the right contacts would open doors for him. He was said to be a master at dispensing good cigars and choice whiskey at the proper moment. He was certainly well aware of his personal charisma and was able to exploit his subtle combination of Southern charm and European insouciance that appealed to many of the aristocracy.

Henry Adams, the American minister's son and secretary, was not finding the aristocracy at all welcoming, but Drawing Rooms and society functions were a necessary part of his father's everyday life. It was only a matter of time before Charles Francis Adams would be introduced in London's fashionable parlors to a young man who worked in the department of the Foreign Office that dealt with American matters. When that meeting took place, Adams could not have guessed at the intrigue developing. Victor Buckley betrayed no personal opinions and behaved with the good manners of the aristocracy's social code; Adams and his wife and daughter found no fault with his youthful charm.

The clubs and drawing rooms of London society would undoubtedly have provided fertile ground for Hotze to develop and mature friendships with young men such as Victor Buckley. Their acquaintance certainly formed part of the later evidence against Buckley. Eventually Hotze would deal with the gun trade in Britain and France, and in London he found that affluent arms suppliers such as Hamilton and Bond, with whom he shared considerable experience in the arms industry, were comfortable movers and shakers in the world of generous hospitality as it greased the formation of acquaintances and mutual interests. It was undoubtedly in the financial interests of Hamilton and Bond to maintain a mole in the Foreign Office, and Hotze was a natural ally in that effort.

Hotze modified his accent as he settled into society (Huse had also mistaken him for a German), and with his persuasive intellectual arguments and easy social graces he epitomized the British upper-class vision of Southern aristocracy and presented the Southern point of view in a way that many would find alluring. A Southern observer commented, "He has made quite a reputation in political circles and is in a fair way to become a European celebrity."[16] An esteemed guest at social events, he contrived to be popular, it was said, not only with fellow journalists but also among the highborn gentry, one contemporary describing him as "a born conspirator."[17] Moreover, his beguiling image was potentially appealing, and a contrast to a daily life governed by the strict protocol of the Foreign Office.

It was said of Hotze that he designed and purchased guns, discussed military strategy, and took a keen interest in economics and government. He might have arrived in England as a simple courier, but he would go on to establish "the mysterious mail service of Mr. Hotze," which conveyed important dispatches to the Confederate government.[18] Hotze's name appeared in correspondence in connection with drafts for various agents abroad, and a suspicion would later arise that he was not just acting as a paymaster but also operating a spy ring, contacting and paying off men whose names the Confederate commissioners in London either did not know or did not care to mention.[19] Felix Senac, the Confederate navy paymaster and Hotze's future father-in-law, would arrive in England the following year to join Bulloch in Liverpool, and Senac's daughter, Ruby, would be presented to Queen Victoria.[20]

Events suggest that a friendship did develop between Hotze and Victor Buckley, and Hotze was undoubtedly the most trustworthy conduit for information. That the two men apparently struck up a close acquaintance is not surprising. Buckley would have observed Hotze as he eased his way cautiously into society and cultivated contacts while preparing to launch his propaganda campaign.

That opportunity soon presented itself; Hotze achieved something of a coup by writing an editorial in support of the Confederacy and its right to recognition and having it appear as a leader in the *London Post*, a paper considered to be the mouthpiece of the prime minister, Lord Palmerston. The "special trust and confidence in his abilities" expressed in the Confederate secretary of state's appointment of Hotze as "commercial agent" was vindicated. He achieved the credibility he needed to write for almost any newspaper, and he did so by exercising restraint. He studiously maintained an "English point of view . . . not advancing too far beyond recognized public opinion . . . a little timidity of a first step on untried ground."[21]

Hotze's name cropped up ever more frequently in London's fashionable clubs and coffee houses, but when the novelty of the young intellectual's presence began inevitably to subside, so too did his initial euphoria and his own sense of satisfaction. He began to realize that he had been partly blinded to public opinion in general by allowing himself to be courted and promoted by those most ardent Confederate supporters. "Most of us here," he wrote to Robert Hunter, "have been too rapid in our conclusions and too sanguine in our expectations as regards the policy of Europe, and especially England."[22] Hotze had now assessed two of the heavyweights in the political arena and wrote with some pique, "There are but two men of weight in both houses of Parliament who are our declared foes—Earl Russell, who has lately made himself the apologist of the Federal Government in the House of Lords, and Mr. Bright in the Commons, who, I am happy to say, represents or leads no party but himself."[23]

It did not take long, however, for Hotze to find an appropriate remedy for the insidious indifference of the public. He would fight the propaganda war in the most effective way, by producing his own newspaper, its writers carefully selected and "educated" as to the purpose and style of the publication, whose format would mirror that with which the British were most comfortable. Hotze had identified a fertile ground for his propaganda; in the gentlemen's clubs of London, lubricated by fine port amid the trappings of comfort, the social elite digested the daily reports from America presented in fastidiously ironed newspapers such as *The Times*. Hotze planned to create a paper that would slip seamlessly into these reading rooms—and beyond—to reach its target audience.

The first edition of the *Index* appeared on May 1, 1862, and its physical appearance rendered it very much at home in the hands of City merchants and in private clubs. Its name, set in familiar one-inch Gothic letters, instilled confidence, and Hotze included an innocuous subtitle—*a Weekly Journal of Politics, Literature and News*. The paper measured a conventional ten by thirteen inches, and each edition included advertisements, shipping notices, sales of Confederate bonds, intelligence on the cotton and dry goods market, and the latest news from the South; the editorial content was supplemented by articles promoting recognition of the Confederacy. Hotze's indefatigable energy was manifest in the range of issues covered: military science, politics, international law, religion, ethics, and an atrocity story of the depredations allegedly committed by black soldiers in the Mississippi Valley.[24] He also included court reports and "news of high society spiced with gossip column items concerning celebrities or near royalty."[25]

An effective piece of pro-Union news that emanated from Merseyside in the summer of 1862 would certainly not have been included in the pages of the *Index*. On July 4 the purser on Brunel's *Great Eastern*, steaming from New

York to Liverpool, refused to trim the grand saloon with the Stars and Stripes for a ship's ball. When angry passengers hammered on the British captain's door demanding satisfaction, Captain Walter Paton sent a boy to the flag locker for the biggest British and American colors on board, personally climbed a ladder in the saloon, and nailed the flags to the ceiling. The purser was discharged when the ship docked in Liverpool, and Paton, later described by the *New York Times* as "gentlemanly and patriot[ic]," ensured that the news was promptly sent to the New York papers.[26]

Hotze published the *Index* in an office at 13 Bouverie Street, Fleet Street. It sold in London for six pennies per copy, and there was a subscription price of twenty-six shillings per annum, or thirty shillings payable in advance if posted. In the early days of the paper Hotze struggled financially, experiencing the problem common to all Confederate agents—inadequate and often infrequent funds from the South—but he obtained financial assistance from two wealthy Southerners, Augustus Peter Wetter of Savannah and Henry O. Brewer, a shipping and commission merchant from New York and Mobile. Brewer, who knew Hotze from Mobile, would later enter into a partnership with bankers Emile Erlanger and Company of Paris and J. H. Schröder and Company of Manchester to form the European Trading Company and purchase blockade-runners, notably the Lairds'-built *Denbigh*. His financial dealings would include, to his ultimate detriment, the sale of Confederate bonds.

Before long Hotze was visiting both Houses of Parliament, socializing with their members, and dining at a private dinner table with Gladstone, enjoying "several hours of conversation." In August he wrote to Secretary of State Benjamin, "Thanks to friends, whom without ciphers, it may not now be prudent to name, I could form a sufficiently correct opinion of the arguments which had most weight with the cabinet and to these from week to week I devoted myself." Reinforcing his connections, he added, "Just as I close this, a reliable friend steps in to inform me that there have been three successive cabinet meetings . . . and that each time the cabinet was evenly divided, Mr. Gladstone leading the party in favor of recognition."[27]

Hotze's reports to Richmond were becoming increasingly confident, and despite the intermittent nature of receipts from the Confederacy he was able to prop up the production costs of the *Index* with generous private contributions. For the moment, at least, his list of subscribers was growing, and among them would appear the name of Victor Buckley.

CHAPTER 7

The *Enrica* Is Launched and the *Florida* Is Freed

It had been a spring of mixed fortunes for the Confederacy and its agents, and also for the textile mills of Lancashire. The bountiful harvest of cotton that had sustained the factories the previous summer was almost exhausted, and the rattle of the Lancashire looms was giving way to ominous silence. The Stirling family's mill in Lower Mosley Street, Manchester, was no exception, and Thomas Mayne Stirling was grappling with the serious consequences of the cotton famine. In April Hotze described the situation in a letter to Secretary of State Robert Hunter: "The cotton famine, so long predicated and so unaccountably delayed, has at last overtaken the land, with all its train of destitution and ruin."[1]

While speculators were making fortunes on the trickle of cotton brought in by blockade-runners (prices rose to their highest in January 1862), mill workers were facing poverty. As the warehouse stocks dwindled, so too did the last vestige of sympathy the workers might have felt for the South. The war was becoming a wedge creating an ever-widening divide within the British class system.

The Confederacy was dealt a blow in April with the fall of New Orleans, a vital port for access and defense of the Mississippi, and elsewhere its armies were still on the defensive. That lack of success, however, did little to nudge the inclination of the British government toward the North. Although tempers had cooled since the *Trent* affair, acrimonious exchanges took place in the House of Commons between Palmerston and Bright until well into February, the radical

MP accusing the government of "ferocious gestures" in having sent troops to Canada.[2]

If the American legation hoped for a more conciliatory mood now, it was to be disappointed as news from America placed further strain on the uneasy relations between Palmerston and Adams. The commander of the occupying army at New Orleans was Gen. Benjamin Butler, a former Massachusetts lawyer who was so incensed at the hostility shown his troops by the women of the city that he issued a proclamation: any woman insulting an officer or soldier of the U.S. Army would be treated as "a woman of the town plying her vocation" and imprisoned in the house of correction with common prostitutes.

Butler's ploy, although it stopped the spitting and insults, presented the perfect propaganda opportunity for Southern supporters in Britain, who interpreted the decree as carte blanche for the soldiers to commit rape. Palmerston too chose to regard Butler's decree in that light and wrote a personal, strongly worded letter to Adams: "I will venture to say that no example can be found in the History of Civilized Nations till the publication of this order . . . of so infamous an act."[3]

Adams, sensing that Palmerston was seeking to pick a quarrel, demanded to know whether the letter was a personal one or an official communication, while Russell, who had not been consulted by the prime minister before the protest was penned, was naturally annoyed at his exclusion from so sensitive a foreign issue. Pride on all sides was eventually salvaged by the news that Lincoln had replaced Butler at New Orleans, but a period of coolness followed during which Adams and his wife were not invited to Lady Palmerston's receptions.

Toward the end of April Fraser, Trenholm's ship *Bermuda* fell victim to a Union warship, her log incriminating her with its records of previous blockade-running. The capture of the *Bermuda* represented a substantial financial loss to Prioleau and came as devastating news to the Confederacy because she was carrying a cargo of heavy artillery and desperately needed munitions.

On Merseyside, at least, things were again going well for Bulloch. Although progress on the 290 had been frustratingly slow, the vessel was living up to his expectations. She was of outstanding quality and would, in the words of her future captain, sit upon the water "with the lightness and grace of a swan."[4] A ship so magnificent inevitably attracted great interest as she took shape, and the common knowledge that she was being built for the South had been brought to the attention of Thomas Dudley on his arrival in Liverpool the previous autumn by the acting consul, Henry Wilding.

Dudley assigned Matthew Maguire, the "ugly, read-headed villain" who had so irked Anderson, to infiltrate Laird Brothers' yard and to direct special attention to Bulloch, who, although endeavoring to keep away from his ship, was unnerved by the constant surveillance. With Laird Brothers seriously behind schedule, he admitted to being "in want of professional aid." The arrival of another Confederate officer, Lt. John Randolph Hamilton (who, as John Low had been, was unknown to the Union spies), provided Bulloch with both the assistance and the breathing space he required. Bulloch again sought the advice of Frederick Hull, who assured him he was doing nothing illegal in building his cruiser and should "maintain a quiet reserve" while hastening to complete the ship and get her away as soon as possible.

By April 4 the reports of the Union spies had become so alarming that Dudley wrote to Seward in Washington to voice his fears. No expense was being spared in the vessel's construction, he pointed out, and he had good reason to believe that she was for the Confederacy. No one in Liverpool who observed the mysterious 290 taking shape would have disagreed. The vessel was almost ready for her official launch, and already the Lairds were muddying the water with an intriguing piece of disinformation designed to confuse the American consul. Suggestions had been put about that the vessel was being built for a Spanish company, but when General John Burgoyne of the British army visited the shipyard, Henry Laird told him that the 290 was actually for the Spanish government. Dudley conveyed the news promptly to Adams in London, who, in a repeat of the *Oreto* suspicions, sent Moran to call on the Spanish embassy. In a reply distinctly déjà vu, he was assured the ship was not being built for Spain.

The launch of the future CSS *Alabama* (named for the home state of Henry Hotze) took place on May 14. A light rain had been falling, but the gray sky was giving way to a pale sun as the party assembled for the occasion in the offices of Laird Brothers overlooking the dock where the vessel awaited her launch. True to tradition, a lady officiated the ceremony. In resolutely concealing her name in his memoirs, Bulloch created an enduring mystery that tantalized and frustrated researchers for more than 150 years as they pondered a riddle and sought to establish her identity.

"The Spanish language," Bulloch wrote, "provided a flexible and mellifluous equivalent for the Christian name of the lady who served the office, and when the ship got free of the blocks and glided down the way, she had been christened *Enrica*."[5] Historians agree that the name Henrietta is a flexible equivalent of Enrica, proposing as possible namesakes Bulloch's wife, Harriott, and Harriet, the wife of his friend John Low, who would serve as fourth lieutenant on the ship.[6]

Bulloch noted that the ceremony went smoothly and "the lady fulfilled it in a comely manner, little knowing that she was constructively taking part in a Great Civil War, and wholly unconscious that she was helping to make work for five eminent statesmen at Geneva ten years after." In this statement, however, he was being guileful, for he added, with a familiarity perhaps betraying the closeness of their friendship and his confidence in her allegiance, "I hope her conscience has never upbraided her since, and that she has not felt in any way responsible for the bill of £3,000,000, which Her Most Gracious Majesty had to pay on account of the *Alabama* Claims."[7]

An examination of a spy's report of the event, and of Bulloch's associates on the occasion, reveals the most likely identity of the mystery lady. A detective hired by Consul Dudley had enlisted Richard Broderick, a shipwright working for Lairds, as an informant, and his report of the proceedings provides a vital clue that unlocks the secret of the name *Enrica*.

Then, as now, an invitation to launch a ship was considered an honor—one Bulloch was in a position to bestow, perhaps as a mark of gratitude or respect to the lady's husband or family. The detective's presentation to Dudley of Broderick's report reveals that "on the day of the launch of the gunboat 'No. 290' Captain Bullock [*sic*] and his wife, with several American gentlemen, were in attendance. Captain Bullock's wife was in one of the office windows, with other ladies. . . . [He] also states that one of the gentlemen who was present was tall, stout and wore red whiskers. . . . Captain Butcher is a young man, with light whiskers and a beard and is for the present in command of her and is appointing and shipping the crew."[8]

In choosing a lady to launch his warship, Bulloch might well have considered the niece of one of his most ardent supporters, Alexander Beresford Hope, for the same day, May 14, had been her twentieth birthday. Henriette was the daughter of Captain Adrian Hope and his French wife, Countess Emile Melanie Mathilde Rapp, whose father was one of Napoleon's generals. After the acrimonious divorce of her parents she went to live with her uncle and aunt (Lady Mildred, sister of Robert Cecil) at their estate, Bedgebury Park, in Kent. In time she became active in the family's support for the Confederacy, even helping to raise funds for Southern prisoners at a charitable event in Liverpool.

However grateful Bulloch may have been for Beresford Hope's support, though, there was another person whose closeness exceeded that of all others, and he was central to the success of the future CSS *Alabama* getting to sea as a warship. He had also played a vital role thus far in Bulloch's activities, and yet history books give his name but a comparatively cursory mention. He was the one man in whose discretion Bulloch—and the Laird family—could have absolute confidence and was no doubt "the friend" who had accompanied Bulloch to the shipyard soon after his arrival in England. Provided with funds from the Confederate government, he was the man who had acquired the vessel that would act as a tender for the *Alabama*, and he had already orchestrated the purchase of the arms that ship would deliver at a planned rendezvous away from British waters. But Archibald Hamilton's connection to the launch of the *Enrica* had roots far deeper than these acquisitions.

Hamilton numbered among his Scottish ancestors the famous clan leader and Jacobite hero Rob Roy MacGregor—immortalized by Sir Walter Scott in his novel *Rob Roy*. His grandfather, John Hamilton, was one of the merchant princes who emerged in Greenock during the eighteenth century to establish considerable wealth as a result of the port's shipbuilding and engagement in the "tri-angular trade." It was a prosperity founded on shipping, sugar, tobacco, banking, and other benefits of the slave trade, as well as trade with the Americas, all of which were also creating vast fortunes in ports such as Bristol and Liverpool. John Hamilton's son Hugh, who followed in his footsteps as a merchant and banker, married twice. Hugh's first wife was Menzies Sinclair, the daughter of Robert Sinclair, who was listed as a trader in London in *Kelly's Post Office Directory* of 1799. Archibald Hamilton was their son.

The firm of Sinclair, Hamilton, and Company that Archibald formed with his brother Robert in 1854 was a family affair. Robert was to marry a relative, Mary Sinclair, in 1861, while a cousin, John James Hamilton, the son of Hugh's stepbrother Lewis Gellie Hamilton, participated in the business with three-eighths of the capital. Lewis Gellie Hamilton had moved to the Spanish island of Tenerife in 1819, and the family became extremely prosperous as merchants. Among their business interests they bred cochineal insects (for the dye used in the manufacture of the distinctive British "Red Coat" army uniforms), produced and exported wine from their own bodegas, and opened a wine merchants business in London in Trinity Square, Tower Hill. When Santa Cruz de Tenerife became the island's main port, they founded a successful shipping agency, which in 1839 led to Hamilton y Compañía being awarded the prestigious agency for Lloyds Shipping Register. A lucrative Spanish-British commercial connection was well established.[9]

By the mid-nineteenth century the Canary Islands (in particular Tenerife and Madeira) also provided an essential coaling and trading stopover for ships running to and from the African coast. There was an important family connection to that trade as well, for which reference must be made again to the family of John Hamilton. His sister Mary married Gregor Macgregor, a member of one of Scotland's aristocratic families and a grandson of Rob Roy MacGregor.[10]

In 1824 John's brother, William Hamilton, who moved from Greenock to Liverpool with two friends, John Forsyth and William Laird, was seeking orders for his family's rope and sail-making business. Astutely, the friends identified opportunities and soon decided to invest in the purchase of a sandy area of land on the banks of the river Mersey for which they paid just a few hundred pounds. Later it would become Birkenhead. In letters published in the *Liverpool Albion*, William Hamilton proposed the construction of docks to be entered by a ship canal from the mouth of the river Dee, thus avoiding the banks at the mouth of the Mersey, a suggestion that alerted the Liverpool Corporation to the importance of the land and prompted it to offer £20,000 for part of the foreshores.[11] The men also conceived a grandiose residential square in the architecture of that (Georgian) period, and this materialized as Birkenhead's magnificent Hamilton Square.

The commercial plans of Hamilton's associate William Laird changed when he recognized the potential for an ironworks that would make boilers (clearly the future of ships lay in steam rather than sail), and he opened a manufactory in Wallasey Pool, Birkenhead. The Birkenhead Ironworks business expanded rapidly, and Laird's son John joined the firm. In time, John Laird would be elected the first member of Parliament for Birkenhead, and his name would become synonymous with the building of the *Alabama*. The Lairds built their first ship in 1829, and in 1857 the yard was moved to Monks Ferry. Thus the famous Lairds' shipyard had become rooted on Merseyside. In the meantime, John Laird's younger brother, Macgregor Laird, had founded the African Steam Ship Company, for which, of course, Tenerife became a stopover.

In 1804 William Laird had married Agnes Macgregor, the daughter of Gregor Macgregor and Mary Hamilton, and this created a relationship of some significance to Bulloch, for the man singled out by Broderick at the launch of the *Enrica* as being "tall, stout with red whiskers" fits the description of Archibald Hamilton, who was second cousin of John Laird Sr. and of Macgregor Laird. John Laird Sr. was the grandnephew of Archibald's grandfather John Hamilton.

In a contemporary sepia photograph, Archibald appears affluent and self-assured. Stout and sporting the muttonchop whiskers fashionable at the time, he is seated with an ivory-topped cane in his hand. His hair, like that of his famous ancestor Rob Roy MacGregor, appears to be red. He was a man who kept his secrets well, as did his close business associate Frederick William Bond, Macgregor Laird's secretary at the African Steam Ship Company before he brought his expert knowledge of arms to the London Armoury Company. Conveniently, Archibald's business connections to the Spanish island of Tenerife could provide the source of the rumor that the suspicious ship being built by Lairds was for a Spanish company.

As one of the City's affluent and influential merchants, Archibald Hamilton mixed with the upper echelons of society. In London he was a director of the Highland Society, of which Prince Albert had been patron; he served as president of the Grampian Club (of which His Royal Highness the Prince of Wales was patron), and joined the Ethnological Society as well as the Kent Archaeological Society, in which Alexander Beresford Hope was also active.

There emerges a sense of "the clan," the closeness of a Scottish coterie whose success depended on the highest level of trust and which facilitated Bulloch's rapid introductions to both society and shipbuilding in Britain. While Bulloch was descended from the Scottish warrior king Robert the Bruce, Archibald Hamilton's pedigree was fused with Scotland's commercial aristocracy and the wealth it engendered. Privy to and an integral part of this Scottish-born trust was undoubtedly Archibald's wife.

Henrietta Newton Duncan Hamilton was born in 1828, the daughter of Alexander Duncan, a tenant farmer in Linlithgowshire, and his wife, Margaret (née Newton).[12] Henrietta, known in the family as Harriet, married Archibald in London in 1850. In 1846 her sister Isabella had married John Scott, a Liverpool merchant in the East India Trade.[13] If the presence of her husband was indeed confirmed by Broderick's description, then Henrietta Hamilton certainly presents the most likely candidate for the prestigious role of launching the *Alabama* and being the elusive Enrica. In his later description of the launch of the 290, Bulloch stated that the name "stuck to her for some time, and continued to be the term used when mentioning her in the Consular affidavits and in the diplomatic correspondence, until the frequent reports of her performance afloat gave great notoriety and distinction to her now historical name of *Alabama*."

Although Bulloch was still planning to take command of the *Enrica* himself, he needed a captain holding the necessary certificate to take her out of British waters, and consulted a reliable friend, George Barnett, a shipping agent with the Cunard Line, in that regard. Through Barnett he was to renew an old acquaintance and find the right man for the job.[14]

Bulloch had first met Mathew James Butcher in Havana in the fall of 1857. In his early twenties at that time, Butcher had spent most of his life at sea. Originally from Great Yarmouth, Norfolk, his family had moved to Liverpool, where he signed ship's articles shortly before his eleventh birthday. His career rapidly progressed, and by the age of twenty-four he had become first officer on the Cunard vessel *Karnak*. He had also been granted his master's certificate, although his youth seemed to preclude him from the coveted captaincy of a ship. It was a frustration Bulloch understood, his own experiences in the U.S.

Navy having suggested that men were promoted according to age rather than ability. Butcher was an ambitious and energetic man who boasted proudly of his membership in the Royal Naval Reserves, in which he was training in gunnery and command.

When Butcher answered George Barnett's summons to his office on business "of a special nature" he suspected what lay ahead. A steamer, he was told, "which might be adapted to war purposes," was being built for a foreign government whose agents needed the services of an English officer. His duty would be to take command, have her fitted out according to instructions, procure a crew, and proceed with her to a designated place. With the job came the promise of "a very liberal remuneration" (said to be three thousand pounds) and a commission in the foreign navy, if desired.[15] Butcher later stated, "I at once felt quite sure that the government alluded to was the Confederate, and I said that I would gladly take charge of the vessel."[16] The following day he was reunited with Bulloch before being taken to the Lairds' shipyard to inspect his future, albeit brief, command. Admission to such confidences as surrounded the 290/*Enrica* naturally involved considerable trust. Bulloch maintained a policy of telling people only what he thought they needed to know, but to Mathew Butcher he was obliged to reveal the most sensitive of information, knowing that one careless word to the wrong person might precipitate seizure of the future warship.

Bulloch's faith in the young man was to be vindicated. "Captain Butcher fulfilled all the requirements of the offices he engaged to perform," he later stated, "not only with tact, judgment and discretion, but with that nice and discriminating fidelity which marks the man of true honesty. . . . It was manifestly necessary to confide to him more than what appeared on the surface." It was, as Bulloch also reflected, "a prodigious trust."[17]

While Butcher took control of the fitting out at Lairds, Bulloch turned again to Hamilton and Bond in London. Union spies were now more active than ever, and the precariousness of the *Enrica*'s position rendered it vital that a tight circle of security be maintained. Bulloch knew that after the *Fingal*'s escape and the duplicity involved in the departure of the *Florida*, it needed only a marginal shift in the attitude of the government for Russell to view the spies' reports of Confederate intent differently. And if there were any serious suggestion that the building of the 290/*Enrica* in any way violated the Foreign Enlistment Act, seizure of the vessel would be inevitable pending consideration of the untested law.

That circle of security was soon in place. Only Bulloch, Butcher, Prioleau, and the Lairds knew the full story on Merseyside, and knowledge of it in

London was confined to Huse, Hamilton, Bond, and Hotze–with their Foreign Office mole apparently alerted to the necessity of again providing vital inside information.

Through his merchant arm of Sinclair, Hamilton, and Company Archibald Hamilton had purchased the *Agrippina*, a bark built in Scarborough in 1830 that had recently sailed into London from Gibraltar with a cargo of ordnance supplies for the British government. The *Agrippina* was ideally suited to be the tender Bulloch needed to arm the 290, with Hamilton orchestrating her lading. The "fitting out and arming" that British law expressly prohibited would take place in the safety of the little bay Bulloch had so fortuitously encountered with the *Fingal* at Terceira in the Azores.

Hamilton, who would remain the ostensible owner, entered the *Agrippina* out from London to Demerara loaded with 350 tons of coal, the transaction going unnoticed by Adams' spies. "She attracted no special notice," Bulloch observed with satisfaction, "and no suspicion whilst loading in the London docks. It was easy to regulate the forwarding of the cargo and the lading so as to fit in with the movements of the 290 in Liverpool, without creating the suspicion that there was any connection between the two vessels."[18]

The Foreign Office, in the meantime, was still dealing with the backlash from the *Florida* affair. Although Russell was obliged to admit that the vessel had not been bound for Italy, he continued to insist that the Americans should bear the burden of proof that she was a warship, pointing out to Adams and Dudley that no evidence had been furnished of any vessel receiving hostile or warlike equipment in British waters that had afterward been used against the United States. Although factual, that statement did not placate the frustrated American minister.

In the Bahamas, however, things were not going smoothly for the *Florida*. Still officially known by her dockyard name, *Oreto*, to Bulloch and his cohorts she was the *Florida*, and now the true character of the cruiser was about to be legally determined.[19] Upon her arrival in Nassau the U.S. consul, Samuel Whiting, had assumed her to be just another blockade-runner. Two weeks later, however, with her crew suspiciously denied shore leave, he reached a different conclusion and protested to the authorities that the ship was being armed in British waters and should be seized.

When the *Florida*'s tender, the *Bahama*, arrived with her armaments, John Low judiciously had the cargo stored in a bonded warehouse; but problems lay ahead. Lt. John Newland Maffitt duly arrived and was eager to take charge of the *Florida* in accordance with Bulloch's instructions, but the slow process of communication between Richmond and England had Mallory still believing that Lieutenant North had taken command. While this confusion was being resolved, Maffitt was obliged to await further orders from Richmond—a delay that was to prove costly.

In a rash move, the captain of HMS *Bulldog*, who had been assigned to keep watch on the vessel, seized the *Florida* in the belief that she was contravening the Foreign Enlistment Act. Her subsequent release was but a temporary reprieve while evidence was being gathered against her. Disgruntled members of the crew testified before a local magistrate that the ship's articles had been broken when the vessel headed for Nassau instead of Palermo; and Captain Duguid, fearing that the observant Commander H. D. Hinckley of HMS *Greyhound* had seen shells being loaded on the vessel, incriminated himself by promptly ordering their removal.[20]

The *Florida* was seized again, and while Maffitt discreetly kept his distance awaiting the outcome, court proceedings commenced in the colony's Vice-Admiralty court. From his comfortable quarters at the fashionable Royal Victoria Hotel, Maffitt followed reports of the hearing, describing a former third officer who testified the ship was "a perfect man of war" as a "low, dirty Liverpool dock rat."[21]

Maffitt need not have worried. The Foreign Enlistment Act had come up against formidable opposition—the very high degree of Confederate sympathy in Nassau, which pervaded the judiciary. The court relied heavily on the previous findings of the Liverpool port authorities that had allowed the ship to sail, and in the summation he issued at the beginning of August, the judge, Justice Lees, stated: "The evidence connecting the *Oreto* with the Confederate States of America as a vessel to be used in the service to cruise against the United States is but slight." To the fury of the U.S. consul, he finally damned the American case by adding, "Had there been a Confederate flag on board the *Oreto*, I should not consider it as very powerful evidence."[22] The court cheered. Samuel Whiting, who already complained of being victimized in the streets with taunts of "Mr. Lincoln's spy," retreated to lick his wounds while Maffitt went to inspect his now badly deteriorated cruiser. In the waters around Nassau, no less than twelve Union warships were standing ready to put an early end to her career.

Shortly after the *Florida* left Liverpool, Cdr. Raphael Semmes had finally abandoned the no longer serviceable *Sumter* at Gibraltar and traveled to England. Bulloch's instructions to Maffitt were by then on their way to Nassau, and there remained only the command of the *Enrica* to offer this able captain. Bulloch took the train to London, where Semmes was being wined and dined in some style, his notoriety gaining him an adulation that appealed to his vanity. "Much bon hommie [*sic*]," was how Semmes summed up the hospitality of such figures as James Mason (described by a later historian as a man who "exemplified the more bucolic aspects of the Southern character") and a group of enthusiastic sympathizers that included the Reverend Francis W. Tremlett of Belsize Park in north London.[23] Tremlett's efforts on behalf of the Southern states in England would earn him the title "the Confederate Parson," but ironically, the Newfoundland-born clergyman had studied for his degree in Boston, at the heart of the American abolitionist movement. He had personally helped to finance the building of St. Peter's Church, Belsize Park, of which he was now the incumbent.

At his meeting with Semmes toward the end of April, Bulloch dutifully offered up the *Enrica*.The magnanimous offer to relinquish his treasured ship was doubtless painful, his own ambition to command her having fueled his energies as he worked tirelessly in Britain for the Confederacy. He was more than relieved when Semmes, in deference to his fellow officer, declined the offer.

Despite his determination to see action with this splendid cruiser, Bulloch was also harboring reservations about the effectiveness of the South's naval policy of destroying captured ships. Less susceptible than Semmes to the excessive passions of London society, he wrote to Mallory, "The feeling everywhere in Europe is strongly against the simple destruction of private property at sea . . . the cruise of the *Sumter*, although evincing great energy, skill and tact on the part of Captain Semmes, has resulted in no profit but, on the contrary, has tended to excite some feeling against us among the commercial classes in Europe."[24] These words might have been construed as jealousy or as reflecting the demoralizing realization that the abandonment of the *Sumter* in Gibraltar was yet another problem that he personally would have to confront, but the perceptive Bulloch was also mindful of the delicate balance of government policy that could destroy his mission at a stroke. "The British Government seems more determined than ever to preserve its neutrality," he told Mallory, "and the chances of getting a vessel to sea in anything like fighting condition are next to impossible."[25]

Bulloch, however, had been sent to Europe to achieve the impossible, and once he had seen Semmes depart for the Confederacy on the *Melita*, a steamer owned by Isaac, Campbell, and Company on which he and Huse were sending another enormous cargo of arms and supplies, he returned to the task of getting his second cruiser to sea against increasing odds. He had to do so in the unpleasant shadow of political backbiting among his own colleagues.

Bulloch's successful run into the South with the *Fingal* had earned him promotion to commander, a move that invoked immediate hostility among some other officers. "Rank is everything to me," Lieutenant North wrote bitterly to Mallory on learning of the commission, "and that rank has been taken away from me." Regarding Bulloch as nothing more than a civilian, North's resentment spilled over: "I am not aware of anything I have done to merit such treatment from the department unless it is my inactivity since my arrival here, which God alone knows no one can deplore more deeply than myself."[26]

The Navy Department soon soothed North's agitation with a similar promotion to the rank of commander, but elsewhere jealousy continued to fester. Huse was again finding himself the target of dislike, unable to dispel the mistrust of the senior officers. The gossip among Confederates in Europe, one naval officer wrote to North, was that Huse might be recalled.[27] Huse tried to ignore the unpleasantness, and his enthusiasm for his dealings with Hamilton and Bond continued unabated. At the beginning of the war he had boldly claimed to his superiors, "This establishment is in some respects superior to every other musket manufactory in the world," and now he wrote no less effusively to the War Department, "The rifles of the London Armoury Company are so greatly superior to all others that I have made an effort to control all that they can make within the next three years."[28] Given the original assurances that the company would let him have all the arms it could manufacture, it was evidence perhaps that Huse was being tantalized with a subtle degree of uncertainty.

A degree of uncertainty was also plaguing the Lairds at Birkenhead. Constant surveillance by Union spies and the watchfulness of customs house officials dictated caution, and they had suggested to Bulloch that the bolts for the broadside guns on his ship not be installed. It was a minor concession for him to make, however, given the speed with which work on the vessel was now progressing.

No sooner had her official launch taken place than the *Enrica* was hauled by two tugs to the graving dock, where she was warped in and placed upon blocks. A great derrick was lowering the first pieces of machinery on board even before she was secured in her berth. Supervision of the machinery became the responsibility of John McNair, the Scottish engineer Bulloch had met on the *Fingal*, and by mid-June the ship was ready for a trial run. A quiet Sunday afternoon was chosen for steaming her down to the Formby Lighthouse and back, and Prioleau, the Lairds, and the brothers Thomas and Andrew Byrne joined Bulloch for the cruise.

A week later Adams wrote to the Foreign Office, reminding Russell that, notwithstanding the assurances of the Liverpool customs that she was not a warship, the *Florida* had gone to Nassau and was "engaged in completing her armament, provisioning and crew, for the purpose of carrying on war against the United States." The gauntlet was about to be thrown down in the battle to stop the *Enrica*. "I am now under the painful necessity," Adams continued, "of apprising your Lordship that a new and still more powerful war-steamer is nearly ready for departure from the port of Liverpool on the same errand. The parties engaged in the enterprise are persons well known at Liverpool to be agents and officers of the insurgents of the United States."[29]

A spiral of events had begun in which there were many vested interests, each cautioned by the prospect of failure and the knowledge that contravention of the Foreign Enlistment Act carried a penalty not just of forfeiture of the vessel but of imprisonment for the guilty parties. Against such a threat, each of the people involved had his own considerations. For Mathew Butcher there was the promise of money and adventure; for the Lairds, their pride and commercial integrity were at stake; and for Hamilton and Bond in London there was the continued success of their lucrative arms and maritime dealings. For the ubiquitous Henry Hotze, the forthcoming challenge would satisfy his innate adventurousness; and for Bulloch, the *Enrica*, with her anticipated prowess, represented the measure of his achievements as a Confederate agent. Russell's obligation to maintain Britain's neutrality was about to be tested, and for a young clerk in the Foreign Office, the forthcoming battle of wits for possession of a Confederate warship might present a tempting opportunity to assist the South's agents. It might also ensure mention of his name in the footnotes of history.

In the meantime, Earl Russell replied coolly to the American minister that the matter would be referred to "the proper department of Her Majesty's government."[30]

CHAPTER 8

Intended for a Ship of War

With characteristic determination Thomas Dudley set about mounting a powerful case against the 290. Although information on the activities at Birkenhead could be obtained at a price, the Lairds had now tightened their security, and bribery alone did not produce concrete evidence. All too often Dudley's informants wished to remain anonymous, leaving him with little more than hearsay evidence. His breakthrough finally came when Matthew Maguire managed to gain access to the vessel and compiled a detailed internal description of her.

In the meantime, the shipwright Richard Broderick shadowed Mathew Butcher as he moved about the ship and soon learned of his career with Cunard. Broderick also found out that Butcher and a shipping agent, George Barnett, were appointing and shipping a crew, some of whom Butcher was recruiting from the Royal Naval Reserves. Broderick was offered six pounds per month to ship as carpenter's mate but demanded seven. Further, because no one was prepared to reveal the identity of the owners, he asked for a guarantee that his wages would be paid. John Laird Jr., according to Broderick, smiled at the request and replied that he had no doubt it would be "all right."[1]

Maguire watched Bulloch arrive at the yard and noted that when he gave orders to the men, they saluted him. Butcher, he concluded, might be the nominal captain of the 290, but Bulloch was undoubtedly going to command her as a warship. Unfortunately for Bulloch, nothing could be further from the truth. The continuing problem of command confusion brought about by poor communications with Richmond had become a debacle that would severely wound his morale and dash his dreams of getting to sea.

Secretary of the Navy Mallory, unaware that the *Florida* had been assigned to Maffitt, wrote two letters to Bulloch. In the first he stated he had written to Semmes with orders to take command of the larger of the two cruisers, and to North to take the other ship. His subsequent letter announced that he had formally given command of the second vessel to Semmes, who would be furnished with $100,000 to fund his cruise. The letters did not reach Bulloch in Liverpool until June 11 and, coming as they did the day before he was to take the 290 on a trial, filled him with dismay.

Mallory's second letter presented Bulloch with an unpalatable option. In instructing Semmes to transfer his command to the second vessel, he had used the words "if he should deem expedient to do so."[2] Mallory was unaware that Semmes had declined Bulloch's offer of the ship in London and had set off for Nassau, en route to the Confederacy. Bulloch had become indispensable to the Confederate government in his present role ("Your services in England are so important at this time," Mallory wrote), and, buoyed by a recent battle between the *Monitor* and the *Virginia*, the navy secretary wanted his agent to concentrate on building ironclads.[3] The praise was cold comfort for Bulloch in face of the fact that North must now be offered his magnificent ship.

Mallory's decision not to allow Bulloch a naval command had shocked and disappointed him, the more so because the *Enrica*—as he now referred to the future *Alabama*—was the sum of his ambitions. "Every aspiration of my heart is bound up in her," he had once confided to North.[4] Relations between the two men were still strained, and true to form, North did not accede to Bulloch's request for a meeting. Instead he wrote on June 26 that he was ready to assume command of the vessel. The following day Bulloch took the painful step of formally and officially transferring command of the ship to him.

Fate, however, had no place for the truculent North in a story that was to become a legend. Unknown to both men, Mallory had confirmed his orders to Semmes to take command of the *Enrica*.When he reached Nassau, Semmes found that Capt. George T. Sinclair had recently arrived from the South bearing the navy secretary's letter; Maffitt had the pleasure of handing it to him. Semmes replied immediately to Mallory, explaining the circumstances of his departure from London, and then set about assembling his officers—men who had served with him on the *Sumter* and were used to the strict yet effective command of "Beeswax Semmes" with his eccentric curled and waxed moustache and his deep-rooted hatred of Yankees.

From his meeting with Bulloch in London, Semmes was well aware of the delicate situation regarding the ship and wrote suggesting that she should be hurried off as quickly as possible to a rendezvous without waiting for his arrival.

Until an opportunity presented itself to return to England, he was obliged to remain at Nassau, where the *Florida* was still under seizure and where time could be passed in an agreeable social life with Maffitt and other Confederate officers and "some very pretty and musical ladies whose husbands and brothers were engaged in the business of running the blockade." He later reflected that he spent "several anxious weeks" awaiting a Europe-bound vessel.[5]

On July 8 news of Semmes' command at last reached Bulloch, who wrote, not without some satisfaction, to North, advising him of the change of plan. An angry response from North evoked a further letter in which Bulloch betrayed some of his anguish: "It seems from all the information I have that Commander Semmes is more fortunate than either of us."[6]

The increasing effectiveness of Dudley's spying operations gave Bulloch little time to dwell on his personal disappointment. Matthew Maguire had gained the confidence of a youth from the Southern states who went by the name of Robinson. Claiming to have come from New Orleans, the young man had arrived in Liverpool on the blockade-runner *Julie Usher* and confided to his new friend that the captain and officers had spoken of a gunboat being built for the South at Lairds, financed by Fraser, Trenholm and to be commanded by Commander Bulloch.

There were further allegations, supported by Lairds' foreman, that a sailmaker and a gunner from the *Sumter* passing through Liverpool had spoken of Lairds building a gunboat for the South. To those reports Dudley could add his own knowledge that, on the day of the 290's trial run, all of those allowed on board were Confederate sympathizers. In a letter to Lord Russell on June 23, enclosing Dudley's report on the war steamer, Adams revealed a bitter irony: "The vessel has been built and launched from the dock-yard of persons, one of whom is now sitting as a member of the House of Commons."[7] That statement would haunt John Laird Sr. for the rest of his life.

Dudley was inclined to make a formal application to the collector of customs at Liverpool, but Adams, perhaps feeling more confident now in the calm that followed the storm of the General Butler quarrel, thought a direct approach by him to the Foreign Office might secure seizure of the vessel. Dudley's evidence was therefore duly submitted, and Adams waited hopefully for "the proper department" to respond. For his part, Russell appreciated the urgency of the situation and immediately referred the matter to the relevant parties. On receipt of Adams' letter on June 24, he sent a note with instructions to Edmund Hammond, the permanent under-secretary of state for foreign affairs. The following day Hammond wrote to the lords commissioners of the Treasury, enclosing a copy of Adams' letter with a request that they instigate inquiries. He also wrote to the law officers of the Crown, requesting that they consider the papers and provide Lord Russell with their observations.

The law officers of the Crown comprised a trio of distinguished lawyers: William Atherton (attorney general), Roundell Palmer (solicitor general, later Lord Selborne), and the Queen's advocate, Sir John Dorney Harding, QC—who was apparently indisposed. In his absence, on June 30, Atherton and Palmer sent their considered opinion to Russell. The specter of the Foreign Enlistment Act was about to raise its head. They responded:

> If the representation to Her Majesty's government by Mr. Adams is in accordance with the facts, the building and equipment of the steamer in question is a manifest violation of the Foreign Enlistment Act, and steps ought to be taken to put that Act in force and to prevent the vessel from going to sea. The report of the United States Consul at Liverpool inclosed by Mr. Adams, besides suggesting other grounds of reasonable suspicion, contains a direct assertion that the foreman of Messrs. Laird, the builders, has stated that the vessel is intended as a privateer for the service of the government of the Southern States; and, if the character of the vessel and her equipment be such as the same report describes them to be, it seems evident that she must be intended for some warlike purpose. Under these circumstances, we think that proper steps should be taken under the direction of Her Majesty's government, by the authorities at Liverpool, to ascertain the truth, and that, if sufficient evidence can be obtained to justify proceedings under the foreign enlistment act, such proceedings should be taken as early as possible.[8]

The report was no doubt received with considerable interest and speculation when it arrived at the Foreign Office, but alarming though it must have been to Russell, he was careful not to convey its contents to Adams. The law officers had provided him with a diplomatic caveat in their concluding words: "In the meantime, Mr. Adams ought, we think, to be informed that Her Majesty's government are proceeding to investigate the case; but that the course which they eventually take must necessarily depend upon the nature and sufficiency of any evidence of a breach of the law which they may be enabled to obtain."[9]

Russell's subsequent communication to Adams on July 4 consequently enclosed a copy of a report requisitioned from the commissioners of customs. That report, to the Treasury, contained no forebodings but, on the contrary, related the findings of the collector of customs at Liverpool, Samuel Price Edwards, who confirmed:

> Officers have at all times free access to the building-yards of the Messrs. Lairds at Birkenhead, where the vessel is lying; and that there has been no

> attempt on the part of the builders to disguise what is more apparent, that she is intended for a ship of war . . . she has several powder canisters on board but, as yet, neither guns nor carriages, and that the current report in regards to the vessel is that she has been built for a foreign government, which is not denied by the Messrs. Laird, with whom the surveyor has conferred, but they do not appear disposed to reply to any questions respecting the destination of the vessel after she leaves Liverpool.[10]

The commissioners of customs had also consulted their solicitor, who did not consider there to be sufficient grounds to warrant the detention of the vessel. The U.S. consul, he suggested, should submit such evidence as he possessed to the customs collector at Liverpool, who would thereupon take such measures as the provisions of the Foreign Enlistment Act would require. Without the production of full and sufficient evidence to justify their proceedings, he warned, the seizing officers might entail on themselves and on the government very serious consequences.[11]

Dudley lost no time in setting out his evidence. On July 9 he and Vice Consul Henry Wilding presented a petition to the collector of customs outlining the facts as he knew them to be: "That Captain Bulloch is in Liverpool, that he is an officer of the Confederate Navy; that he was sent over here for the express purpose of fitting out privateers and sending over munitions of war; that he transacts his business at the office of Fraser Trenholm & Co; that he has been all the time in communication with Fawcett Preston & Co. who fitted out the *Oreto*, and with the Lairds, who are fitting out this vessel; that he goes almost daily on board the gun-boat and seems to be recognised as in authority." Dudley's pen scratched furiously away at his final piece of damning evidence: "A Mr. Blair of Paradise Street, in this town, who furnished the cabins of the Laird gun-boat, has also stated that all the fittings and furniture were selected by Captain Bulloch, and were subject to his approval, although paid for by Mr. Laird."[12]

The U.S. consul might have considered these facts pertinent, but the collector did not. "I may observe," Samuel Price Edwards wrote the next day, "that I am respectfully of the opinion the statement made by you is not such as could be acted upon by the officers of the revenue, unless legally substantiated by evidence."[13]

Customs surveyor Edward Morgan reinspected the vessel and found her to be, as regards her armament, in the same state as his original report described. Having pondered over Dudley's statement, the Board of Customs decided to seek the advice of their solicitor, Felix J. Hamel. When the collection of papers arrived on his desk, Hamel concluded there was "only one proper way of looking at the question": Dudley's evidence was mostly hearsay, the witnesses were not forthcoming or even named, and there was nothing amounting to a prima facie proof sufficient to justify seizure.[14]

In the meantime, Dudley had watched in alarm as the 290 was taken out of the Lairds' yard and into the Great Float at Birkenhead. There could be no mistaking the fact that she was being prepared to sail; five hundred tons of coal was stowed below and supplies were being taken on board.[15]

So far, Dudley had protected the identity of his informants and detectives. However, when Adams learned of Hamel's response to his statement of July 9, he promptly directed Dudley to engage a lawyer and supply sworn affidavits to support his case.[16] Dudley's legal adviser in Liverpool was Andrew Tucker Squarey of Duncan, Squarey, and Mackinnon, who had represented the consulate before. Squarey had the sea in his blood, his forebears having been active in shipping to Newfoundland, and he had considerable experience in maritime law. The firm's offices were located a few doors away, and it was to this well-qualified lawyer that Dudley now turned.

Squarey decided immediately to seek counsel's opinion and sent a copy of Dudley's complaints to the learned counsel Sir Robert Collier, QC, who was in Worcester at the time, engaged on the Western Circuit. Collier was an eminent barrister who was also a member of Parliament, counsel to the fleet, and judge advocate of the Admiralty. Squarey could not have chosen a more able and respected lawyer.

As one would expect at that level of society, Collier had close acquaintances in government. Among them was Russell's under-secretary of state, Austen Henry Layard. Collier was a gifted artist who would one day exhibit at the Royal Academy, and Layard, an avid collector of the arts, affectionately described him as "a capital amateur artist who does not, however, wish to endanger his professional reputation by letting the solicitors into the secret of his accomplishments."[17] Layard himself had a wide circle of friends and acquaintances whose political persuasions spanned both antagonists in the war. Closest among them was William Gregory, an MP who was a strong proponent of recognition of the South but whose motion in the Commons in February to have the blockade declared ineffective had been removed without a vote. The press had facetiously dubbed Layard "the Ninevah Bull" and "the MP for Ninevah," while political enemies called him "Mr. Lie-Hard" for his passionate yet inaccurate speeches that were sometimes the result of recurring bouts of malaria. But Layard had learned the cost of too much outspokenness. Queen Victoria protested emphatically to Palmerston that she did not want Layard in a diplomatic post because, "In the contact with foreign countries we should be respresented by a thorough gentleman."[18] Palmerston, whom Layard described as "the kindest and most considerate of chiefs in the House of Commons," rose swiftly in defense of his chosen official, stating him to be very able and active minded. Layard had shown himself to be a very good man of departmental business when under-secretary to Lord Granville at the Foreign Office, Palmerston pointed out, and "his manners in personal intercourse are conciliatory and agreeable."[19]

In this highly charged period Layard was indeed being called upon to be conciliatory, appeasing Palmerston and Russell by keeping his radical opinions to himself. Still, if the views of his friend John Bright on the Civil War had found favor with him, he would not have been gratified by the contents of a note he had received the previous October from Palmerston: "It is in the highest degree likely that the North will not be able to subdue the South, and it is no doubt certain that if the Southern union is established as an independent State, it would afford a valuable and extensive market for British manufactures."[20] If protection of British trade were indeed one of the key elements behind the government's response to the Americans, Layard would never betray that fact. Like Palmerston, he would err on the side of caution and keep his own counsel.

On examining the papers sent to him by Squarey, Sir Robert Collier reached a very different conclusion from that of the solicitor to the Board of Customs. The evidence that the vessel was being fitted out in contravention of the Foreign Enlistment Act was, he decided, almost conclusive, and in his learned opinion (dated July 16), he went on to say, "As the matter is represented to me to be urgent, I advise that the principal officer of the customs of Liverpool be immediately applied to . . . it would appear proper at the same time to lay a statement of the fact before the secretary of state for foreign affairs, coupled with a request that Her Majesty's Government would direct the vessel to be seized, or ratify her seizure if it has been made. If the matter were not urgent," he concluded, "I should advise no further steps being taken until it was known whether or not the government thought fit to interfere; but inasmuch as the government might not unreasonably take some little time to determine what course to pursue, during which time the vessel might escape, I advise the more prompt remedy."[21]

Desirable though it might be to sound out the government on its willingness to intervene, Squarey decided to lose no time in securing formal depositions to substantiate his case. On Monday, July 21, he and Dudley went to the office of Samuel Price Edwards to formally request that the 290 be seized under the provisions of the Foreign Enlistment Act and to present him with six depositions together with their deponents, who were ready to officially swear the documents. The witnesses were a diverse group. They included William Passmore, a seaman who had served on HMS *Terrible* during the Crimean War; John de Costa, a shipping master; Allen S. Clare, an articled clerk; Henry Wilding, the vice consul; Wilding's detective, Matthew Maguire; and Dudley, whose deposition provided an informative sketch of Bulloch's activities.

In his affidavit, Passmore (who was retained as a spy by Dudley and paid two pounds, ten shillings for "board and wages") testified that Mathew Butcher had told him the vessel was for the Confederate States and that the crew would fight for the South, a provocative claim that seemed to bring into play the issue of foreign enlistment.

That same day the depositions were handed to the Board of Customs' solicitors, James O'Dowd and his superior, Felix Hamel, but the two men were still of the opinion that the evidence was insufficient, a view that was supported by the commissioners of customs in London, although their subsequent letter to the Treasury dated July 22 reflected the urgency that they attached to the matter. If the Treasury had any doubt on the subject, they wrote, the opinion of the law officers of the Crown should be taken.

In the next twenty-four hours events were to move apace. O'Dowd had informed Squarey that instructions had been forwarded (on the 22nd) to the collector at Liverpool not to exercise the power of the act as the facts disclosed in the affidavits were not sufficient to justify seizing the ship. Squarey now spelled out the stance of his client in no uncertain terms:

> On behalf of the government of the United States I now respectfully request that this matter, which I need not point out to you involves consequences of the greatest possible description, may be re-considered by the Board of Customs, on the further evidence now adduced. The gunboat now lies in Birkenhead docks ready for sea in all respects, with a crew of fifty men on board. She may sail at any time and I trust the urgency of the case will excuse the course I have adopted of sending these papers direct to the Board, instead of transmitting them through the Collector at Liverpool, and the request that I now venture to make, that the matter may receive immediate attention.[22]

In the meantime, to expedite matters Secretary to the Treasury George A. Hamilton sent the package immediately to Layard at the Foreign Office with a note: "As the communication may be considered pressing, I send it to you unofficially to save time. Perhaps you will ascertain from Lord Russell whether it is his wish that we should take the opinion of the law officers as to the case of this vessel. It is stated that she is nearly ready for sea."[23] Hamilton's all-important package arrived at the Foreign Office the following day, July 23, and Layard gave it his immediate attention. It is reasonable to suppose that so too might Victor Buckley.

The momentum between the Treasury and the Foreign Office would certainly have been appreciated by Squarey, who was also in London that day, in consultation with Adams prior to making his way to the Foreign Office. He wrote later to Adams, "I beg to inform you that I saw Mr. Laird at the Foreign office after leaving you this afternoon, and ascertained from him that the papers forwarded by you in reference to the gunboat 290 were submitted yesterday to the law officers of the crown for their opinion. The opinion had not, up to the time of my seeing Mr. Laird, been received, but he promised upon my representation of the extreme urgency of the case, to send for it at once. Mr. Laird was not disposed to discuss the matter, nor did he read Mr. Collier's opinion."[24]

CHAPTER 9

Information from a Private and Most Reliable Source

"I had the means of knowing with well nigh absolute certainty what was the state of the negotiations between the United States minister and Her Majesty's government."[1] Bulloch was under considerable pressure to get his ship completed and safely out to sea, and the knowledge passed on by the informant he refers to in his memoirs must have spurred him on. The confusion over command had created a serious delay. Had his original plans run smoothly, Bulloch would have been at sea with her by July, but he had been obliged to wait for news of Semmes' intentions, for confirmation even that his fellow officer had received Mallory's orders and would be returning to England.

Now the situation had become critical and the pace was quickening. As the Lairds' shipyard became the target of increased vigilance by the customs authorities, Bulloch could at least be satisfied that in the Birkenhead dock his ship would soon be ready to sail. The *Agrippina* in London, like the *Enrica* on Merseyside, awaited word from Semmes. Bulloch was reluctant to dispatch both ships to a rendezvous where a passing U.S. cruiser might chance upon them. For the moment, and as long as he had reliable inside information on which to base his judgment, Britain's Foreign Enlistment Act was the lesser of the two evils. And so the fate of the 290/*Enrica,* in the words of Dudley "a most formidable and dangerous warship which, if not stopped, would do great damage to American commerce," hung in the balance while, unknown to all the parties, a bizarre set of circumstances was evolving in London.[2]

Russell had indeed sanctioned sending the law officers of the Crown the six depositions furnished by Adams, and Layard himself had instructed his clerk to effect the dispatch on the same day, July 23, the papers being marked "immediate." The government was apparently defying its customary bureaucracy to ensure that the matter was dealt with urgently.

The accepted version of events has always been that no one was aware that the senior of the law officers, Queen's Advocate Sir John Harding, had suffered a mental breakdown, and that his wife (later described as "a better wife than subject") was at pains to conceal the fact. If this were indeed true, her reasons for doing so have never been established, although one possibility suggested is that she was endeavoring to protect her husband's pension.[3]

All the law officers were apparently in London at the time, and it was either to Sir John Harding's residence in town or his chambers that the package would have been delivered. The events that followed, and Harding's alleged culpability, were to provide much fuel for speculation and recriminations, and the circumstances of his absence at so a crucial a time would be debated for many years without resolution.

The parties involved in the drama later appeared to be of the same mind that Harding *was* in London and that all the papers delivered to him lay unopened. Whether or not he was out of town at the crucial time became academic because he never recovered from the insanity on which turned the events of late July. Harding was to defend himself later, and to unburden himself to friends, but the mental breakdown that resulted in his being committed to a lunatic asylum obscured his words, and the drift of time obscured the facts.

John Dorney Harding was born on June 13, 1809, the son of Rev. John Harding of Rockfield, Monmouthshire. The family had a noble ancestry dating back to Hardicanute (King of England, 1040–42). Somewhat ironically for the *Alabama* debacle, the family arms were three greyhounds courant, granted in the time of Edward I to commemorate the rapid and hazardous carrying of intelligence to the king, the greyhound being a symbol of speed.[4]

As a boy, Harding attended Charterhouse School. His personality may have foreshadowed future problems, for he was described by one of his schoolfellows as "having been an interesting, excitable and talkative fellow, precocious and weakly, evidently conscious that his tongue would have to make up for the want of bodily strength; and his physical frame seemed unequal to sustain the flights of his mind and the elations of his mercurial temperament."[5]

Privately tutored by Thomas Arnold, Harding went up to Oriel College, Oxford, to read classics. Among his friends he numbered William Wilberforce's son Henry and the future John Cardinal Newman. Another close friend was Archibald Campbell Tait, later Bishop of London and Archbishop of Canterbury. He maintained an interest in ecclesiastics and history; his prize-winning *Essay on the Influence of Welsh Tradition upon European Literature*, published in 1839, is still read today.[6]

Harding became a barrister-at-law and was admitted to the Inner Temple in 1835. He practiced as an advocate in Doctors' Commons, an archaic establishment that journalist Daniel Kirwan called "one of the queerest old rookeries in London." Its idiosyncrasies appealed to Charles Dickens, who described it in *David Copperfield* as "a lazy old nook near St. Paul's Churchyard . . . where they administer what is called ecclesiastical law. . . . It's a place that has an ancient monopoly in suits about people's wills and people's marriages, and disputes among ships and boats."[7] Located within a ten-minute walk of the Foreign Office, Doctors' Commons was officially dissolved in 1857, but the chambers were still active in the summer of 1862.

In 1849 Harding married Isabella Wyld, whose late father had been rector of Blunsdon St. Andrew, Wiltshire. Isabella's sister, Diana, married John Tyrrell, a barrister of Lincoln's Inn Fields. After his death Diana married Rev. William Hastings Martin Atkins of Farley Castle, Swallowfield, Berkshire, who, as a boy at Rugby School, had been a close friend of Roundell Palmer—later solicitor general under Palmerston and, with Harding, one of the law officers of the Crown.

The coveted position of Queen's advocate general was awarded to Harding in 1852 upon the recommendation of Lord Derby; that same year a knighthood was conferred upon him. He took silk in 1859 and, in addition to his ecclesiastical expertise, advised successive British governments on complex international and maritime issues arising from the Italian and Russian wars, the *Charles et Georges* dispute, and, vitally, Palmerston's administration during the *Trent* affair.[8] He and the other law officers had already advised the government on matters arising from Confederate naval activities in Great Britain, and now his expert consideration of the case against the 290 was the desired, requisite conclusion to the efforts of Adams, Dudley, and Squarey.

During the afternoon of Wednesday, July 23, Squarey was granted an interview with Layard at the Foreign Office. With time running out, Adams had prevailed on him to make this personal representation of the urgency involved, and Squarey arrived with two more depositions obtained on Merseyside. The first, sworn by Edward Roberts, a ship's carpenter, testified to the warlike character of the 290; the second, by Robert Taylor from Mobile, Alabama, who had sailed on blockade-runners, claimed that Mathew Butcher had hired him for his seaman's knowledge of the Gulf ports. The boatswain, he claimed, had reminded the men that this was not a merchant ship but a man-of-war.[9]

These two fresh depositions alone, however, did not represent the full force of the Americans' determination. Adams and Dudley had also sought a further opinion from Sir Robert Collier, who had seen all eight sworn affidavits. When Squarey produced that opinion (dated that same day, July 23), Layard diplomatically declined to read it. It was, he knew, a potentially crucial interpretation of the situation, one for which he was not the appropriate recipient. Had he broken with protocol and inspected the document, Layard might have been disturbed by its contents, the words coming as they did from such an eminent barrister. Collier stated:

> I am of the opinion that the Collector of Customs would be justified in detaining the vessel. Indeed, I should think it his duty to detain her; and that if, after the application which has been made to him, supported by the evidence which has been laid before me, he allows the vessel to leave Liverpool, he will incur a heavy responsibility. . . . It appears difficult to make out a stronger case of the infringement of the Foreign-Enlistment Act which, if not enforced on this occasion, is little better than a dead letter. It well deserves consideration whether, if the vessel be allowed to escape, the Federal Government would not have serious grounds for remonstrance.[10]

No one, until now, had taken the contentious and ambiguous Foreign Enlistment Act of 1819 by the horns and defined its application. The legislation had its roots in the Napoleonic Wars and the Latin American wars for independence; given the naval order and contemporary warfare in the mid-1860s, however, certain aspects of the act might seem obsolete. Collier thought otherwise, and the very existence of his learned opinion, based on all the evidence amassed, and worthy of personal representation to Layard, was in itself dangerously potent.

Reluctantly accepting that Layard would not read the document, Squarey went on to inquire of the progress with the law officers. The papers had been sent to them, he was assured, but no reply was yet forthcoming. With the further assurance that Layard would chase up a response, the interview came to an end and Squarey returned to his hotel in Covent Garden to send copies of the new depositions and Collier's further opinion to the Board of Customs.

Squarey's papers arrived at the Board of Customs at 3:45 p.m. and were quickly read by the solicitor, who felt the affidavits did not materially strengthen the Union's case. He did not agree with Collier, but in deference to Collier's eminence he recommended that the lords of the Treasury be asked to submit the papers to the law officers of the Crown. With striking rapidity, by 5:30 p.m. the documents were on their way from the Treasury to Layard, sent unofficially to expedite matters. An accompanying note illustrated the degree of urgency: "You may probably like to send the opinion of the law officers direct to the Commissioners of Customs, if it is an object to save time. We can put the matter right officially afterwards."[11]

When Layard, who was in the Commons at the time, received the package, he immediately attached his own note, addressed to Russell: "Shall I send this at once to the law officers?" Russell replied unhesitatingly, "Yes, at once." That same evening, according to the accepted sequence of events, the current bundle of documents was sent to the law officers to join the package already lying on Harding's desk while his distraught wife kept her silence.

The following day, Thursday, July 24, Adams formally dispatched copies of the papers, including Collier's second opinion, which Squarey had sent to the Board of Customs (who had bounced them on to the Treasury), to Russell. The thrust of the wording of Adams' covering letter seemed to presage an end game. "*In order that I may complete the evidence* in the case of the vessel now fitting out in Liverpool . . . [i]n the view which I have taken of this extraordinary proceeding as a violation of the Enlistment Act, I am happy to find myself sustained by the opinion of an eminent lawyer of Great Britain, a copy of which I do myself the honor likewise to transmit."[12]

For some reason unexplained, this latest dispatch took rather longer than might have been expected to reach its destination. In the meantime a ninth affidavit had been obtained, from Henry Redden, a seaman whose evidence supported the existing depositions. That was received at the Board of Customs on the 25th, characteristically dismissed by the solicitor, then sent on to the Treasury, which immediately forwarded it to the Foreign Office, which in turn dispatched it on the 26th to add to the papers awaiting Harding's attention.

Dudley had returned to Liverpool on the 23rd, and Squarey joined him two days later, both men frustrated that no action had been taken to seize the ship. On Saturday, July 26, while Squarey was writing to the Board of Customs pleading for a decision, a further, fateful twist in the events was occurring in London. The package containing the two depositions and Collier's second opinion that Adams had sent directly to the Foreign Office on Thursday the 24th was only just now arriving.[13] It would appear that the opinion itself—with Collier's finding that there was a clear infringement of the Foreign Enlistment Act and the warning that if the vessel were to escape, the U.S. government might have grounds for remonstrance—had not, until now, been available to the Foreign Office clerks.

The law officer Sir Roundell Palmer stated later (as Lord Selborne) that these supplementary depositions (which were enclosed with Collier's second opinion) had been marked as received at the Foreign Office on the 26th, but could not have been delivered at the chambers of the attorney general (Sir William Atherton) until after the usual hours of business on that day (Saturday). Furthermore, if they were then delivered, they remained there unopened (as would generally happen with papers so left, if no special means were used to prevent it) until the Monday morning.[14] Future historians would recognize that the timing opened a window of opportunity for someone to anticipate the likely outcome.[15]

The Foreign Office department (which now dealt with Siam, Japan, Mexico, China, Central America, the Mosquito Coast, and the United States) opened officially at noon and closed at 6 p.m. Those expected to be present that Saturday would be head of the department, Sir Francis Beilby Alston; Charles Abbott; Edward Gifford; and Victor Buckley. The strength and importance of Collier's opinion was not to be underestimated and its likely impact would be quickly noted. The inference was undoubtedly that with the weight of so much sworn evidence and now the unequivocal opinion of one of the most eminent lawyers in the land, the law officers of the Crown must recommend detention of the vessel.

Adams certainly held that view. He wrote later of the events to Seward in Washington, "I myself have little doubt that her sudden departure was occasioned by a notion, obtained somehow or other, that such a proceeding was impending."[16] Adams' secretary, Benjamin Moran, shared that suspicion, believing that the government actually knew of Harding's indisposition and that the failure to delegate the task to other lawyers sooner smacked of high-level connivance. Part of the American case against Great Britain would later include the observation that Harding's unexplained absence had not prevented the other two law officers, William Atherton and Roundell Palmer, from delivering their first opinion on June 30 without his counsel; the delay was inexplicable. Harding would later make a statement that, if containing some grains of truth, would certainly have given credence to Moran's contention. Whatever the individual views of Adams and Moran at the time, however, they would both later believe that Victor Buckley was the actual source of the betrayal.

On that all-important Saturday, with Hamilton, Bond, Huse, and Hotze sharing the anxiety Bulloch was suffering on Merseyside, a telegram was sent from London. "I received information from a private and most reliable source," Bulloch later revealed, "that it would not be safe to leave the ship in Liverpool for another forty-eight hours."[17]

Those crucial "forty-eight hours" would have placed the moment of danger on Monday, the 28th, when the wheels of government would grind into action once more. Six years later, when the chronology was examined and recorded in Hansard, it was stated in the Commons that Palmer, acting as attorney general, had received the documents only *after* they had been sent to Harding:

> Unfortunately, at that very moment the then Queen's Advocate was suffering from a severe malady, from which, it was to be feared, he never recovered, and the result was that long delay. That fact had not hitherto been stated in the House, chiefly through the kind reserve of the Hon. and learned Member for Richmond. . . . On the 28th, the papers reached the Attorney General, who at once gave his opinion, and orders were sent to stop the vessel on the next day. Unfortunately, before the order arrived, or was executed, the builders got wind of it, and the *Alabama* got away.[18]

Russell later stated, "Almost while Sir Roundell Palmer and Sir William Atherton were considering the papers, the *Alabama* left her dock." Adams' younger son, Brooks, would later focus on those words to reason "that the adverse decision must have been betrayed before it could have been drafted."[19]

Sir John Harding's own version of the events differs from the accepted chronology. It was later claimed that he told a friend, "They won't give me a case"; and after the *Alabama* had sailed he explained that he had been anxiously expecting a communication from the government for a whole week before, and that the expectation had unsettled and unnerved him for other business.[20] He stated that he had stayed in his chambers later than usual on the critical Saturday in the expectation of hearing at last from the government and had then gone to his house in the country. Returning on Monday, when he was engaged to appear in court, he found a large bundle of documents in a big envelope that had been dropped into his letterbox on Saturday evening, without even an accompanying note. To all appearance, he stated, every letter, every remonstrance, and every affidavit, as fast as it had arrived from Liverpool, had been piled in a pigeonhole till four or five o'clock on Saturday, when the minister, on taking his own departure for the country, had directed a clerk to tie up the whole heap and carry it to Harding's chambers in Doctors' Commons. Harding further stated that "the people of the *Alabama* and their confederates among the authorities at Liverpool understood the ways of Her Majesty's Ministers, and the ship sailed accordingly early on Sunday (29th July 1862), when nothing could be done to stop it till the middle of the next day, as those concerned very well knew."[21] The date and day were not correct.

The friend to whom this statement was alleged to have been made was Thomas Mozley, Harding's contemporary at Oriel College, Oxford, who was also a barrister specializing in the Admiralty and ecclesiastical courts. Both men had been leading figures in the Oxford movement, which promoted High Church of England beliefs, and the recollection was included in a book of Mozley's reminiscences.[22] It was a version later to be hotly contested by prominent figures of the period and by such critics as the Anglo-Welsh lawyer Sir Henry James, who put forward the theatrical explanation that Harding had been "reposing on the banks of the River Wye" on his country estate in Monmouthshire, and that his opinion, wrapped in a brown paper parcel, "was followed by some enterprising persons connected with the Confederate States, and before the papers reached London, their contents were known to the agents of the Southern States."[23]

Harding's own version of events, of course, must be viewed in the light of his serious mental illness. Writing from Dartmouth to his friend Archibald Campbell Tait, Bishop of London, in December, Harding stated: "On June 28th, without any warning or notice I was forcibly and treacherously seized by Wm. Martin Atkins who married Lady H's sister, and whose guest I was, (with Lady H's concurrence) and placed in strict solitary confinement, with two keepers in a private house in the Regent's Park." Harding made charges that "Lady H., by the advice of the Doctors and some injudicious friends, intercepted and destroyed all my letters, including one to your Lordship, asking for the spiritual comfort of a visit from some clergyman personally known to me—all legal advice was cut off." Harding contended that he was "rescued" by Mr. Scott Russell, who sent him to stay in Devonshire. A famous naval architect, John Scott Russell was noted for his development of steam engines; his shipyard built Isambard Kingdom Brunel's *Great Eastern*.[24]

Harding went on to declare, "Mr. Scott Russell and others are of the opinion that I never was of 'unsound mind,' but that I was excited from mistreatment." He referred to one of his "so called delusions," and expressed a regret at troubling Tait "with this cozy and sad story," adding, "but I cannot allow a 'cloud' or 'mystery' to hang over my soul." Somewhat poignantly, he confessed, "I fell in the discharge of my duty in that state of life."[25]

Harding thus claimed to have been confined two days prior to the issuance of his fellow law officers' first report on June 30, at which time, it had been said, his absence was due to his indisposition. Had he confused this with the following month, the event would have occurred at the crucial time—Monday, July 28. On either date, in such social circles, it is most likely that his fellow law officers, and indeed, Russell and Palmerston, would have known of or anticipated his inability to attend to his work.

In time, Harding was admitted to Sandywell Park Lunatic Asylum at Dowdeswell, near Cheltenham, under the supervision of the renowned physician Dr. William Henry Octavius Sankey, lecturer on mental diseases at University College, London, and the author of *Lectures on Mental Diseases*. He remained at Sandywell for the few years of life left to him.

When he wrote his memoirs Bulloch scrupulously protected those who had aided him, his reticence sometimes leading him to distort the truth. He was certainly protective of the Lairds and disingenuously recorded going into their office on receipt of the warning and advising them that he wished to have a thorough all-day trial of the ship.

Captain Mathew Butcher later recalled that he had just reached home on the Saturday afternoon when a note was brought from the Lairds requesting his immediate attendance at their offices. "I lost no time in getting there," he wrote, "as I felt sure that some intimation must have been received from London of intended action on the part of the government. At their offices, Mr. L. told everyone assembled he had just received a telegram from London warning that no time should be lost in getting the vessel away from Liverpool as the American Minister, Mr. Adams, had laid such evidence of the ship being intended for war purposes before the officials of the government as had decided them upon taking immediate steps to prevent her departure."[26]

The specific mention of Adams hints that it was indeed the package that he had sent personally to the Foreign Office that triggered the alarm. That intimation would later be made in Parliament when, in answer to a question on the United States and the Foreign Enlistment Act, Earl Russell stated ambiguously, "It appeared that the representations of the American Minister had merely the effect of warning the owners that it was necessary she should sail at once."[27] The words of the ship's future captain, Raphael Semmes, substantiate this contention: "Fortunately for the Confederate vessel her friends were equally on the watch, and tidings of the projected seizure were promptly conveyed to Birkenhead."[28] Butcher's account of what took place was written some twenty years later, but in essence, the timeline appears to be correct. After a consultation between those present (one or more of the Laird brothers, Bulloch, the engineer McNair, and Butcher) it was decided to work "night and day" to finish the essential preparations for the ship's departure.

Semmes would later boast that the Lairds were better informed of the secret thoughts and actions of the highest officials than those officials were informed of one another's.[29] The remark suggests that the connection of Frederick Bond and, more particularly, Archibald Hamilton to the Lairds was the conduit to the Foreign Office mole, but the actual sender of the crucial telegram that Saturday remains a mystery. If, as subsequent events suggest, Henry Hotze was made aware of the government's impending anticipated decision by Victor

Buckley, then it is likely that Hotze forwarded the warning, either directly or via Hamilton or Bond. But the telegram itself, with so much other evidence surrounding the mystery, has been lost in time.

While the hours were ticking away, Dudley had engaged a photographer to take a picture of the ship that could be sent to vigilant Union vessels, but the other ships lying around her blocked his view. Already the cruiser was getting the better of her adversaries. "I hope for the best," Dudley wrote to Seward, "but I am prepared for the worst. I have done about all that I can do to stop this vessel."[30]

In London, Adams was remaining hopeful and had formally retained Collier to represent the Union's case in the event that the government suddenly ordered seizure. As a further precaution, he sent a message to Cdr. Tunis Craven of the USS *Tuscarora* (he of the unfortunate run-in with the CSS *Nashville*) instructing him to leave Southampton, where he was in port, and prepare to intercept the Confederate vessel should she try to flee.

Mathew Butcher quickly set to work shipping more hands. Bulloch's trusted friend John Low, who had returned from Nassau, leaving the *Florida*'s fate hanging in the balance, was now preparing to sail again, and chief engineer John McNair, who had so impressed Bulloch on the *Fingal*, was in charge of the engines. Extra tons of coal were taken on board, and in the afternoon Dudley's spy William Passmore observed "seamen, say thirty in number . . . coming down Canning Street from the ship, playing 'Dixie's Land' on a fife, concertina and cornopean [*sic*] and they all took the 4:30 Woodside boat for Liverpool."[31] According to Passmore, the strains of the South's anthem could still be heard as the ferry crossed the Mersey.

On the morning of Monday, July 28, with no further ominous tidings forthcoming from London, the *Enrica* was brought out of her dock on the tide, taken in tow by a steamer, and came to anchor in the river off Seacombe while preparations were made for leaving the harbor the next day. The following morning the decks were cleared and the ship partially dressed with flags before, at 9 a.m., a small party of visitors came on board for a further "trial run." Bulloch and his wife greeted the guests while Dudley's spies watched impotently, scanning the visitors' faces in the hope of identifying them. John Laird Sr., it was said, was one of those present with his daughter and other members of the family. Andrew Byrne was again on board, and with him was Lt. Arthur Sinclair, the Confederate naval officer who had earlier brought Bulloch the crushing news of Semmes' appointment to command the vessel. Among the crinolines and fancy bonnets could be found Mrs. North with her husband, to whom Bulloch had extended the hand of friendship by invitation to this most unusual of parties. Also on board were a party of riggers and additional engineers to ensure the preparedness of the ship.

As the *Enrica* proceeded down the channel in the capable hands of Liverpool pilot George Bond, Collector of Customs Samuel Price Edwards was "conveniently" in another part of the port and had no reason, therefore, to be suspicious. Bulloch and his wife entertained their guests with music and good food while the ship ran several times between the bell buoy and the lightship. The weather conditions, after a dull start, became perfect—fine and clear with only a light wind from the northwest—and there was a mood of conviviality that lasted until 5 p.m. when, just after tea, Bulloch completed the charade by announcing to his guests that a further, overnight trial was proving necessary. He would accompany them back to Liverpool on board a steam tug, the *Hercules*, which he had engaged to lie within sight of the vessel throughout the day in case her services were needed.

The pilot remained on board to carry out Bulloch's next plan, and under the command of young Captain Butcher, with John Low at his side, the future CSS *Alabama* steamed toward Moelfre Bay, a secluded spot on the Isle of Anglesey, north Wales. There she remained as darkness fell, refusing communication with local trading boats that came out to offer their wares, lying silent in the sanctuary of the little bay.

Bulloch had already sent a telegram to Archibald Hamilton telling him to dispatch the *Agrippina* forthwith. Hamilton sent orders to the tender's Scottish captain, Alexander McQueen, that were not to be opened until all hands were on board and the ship was practically ready to sail. Those orders directed him, with his cargo of coal, cannon (including a 100-pounder Blakely rifle), arms, and uniforms, to the port of Praya, Terceira. If he should find another vessel there, the two were to communicate using a coded flag signal. The *Enrica* would identify the *Agrippina* by her black hull with a yellow bead along the sides and would stop a white English ensign to the main rigging, after which Captain McQueen could answer with his number and then communicate freely.[32]

While Bulloch's elaborate pretense had been taking place on Merseyside, the government's legal advice system had been suddenly marshaled into action. On Monday, July 28, if later accounts are to be believed, the realization had at last dawned that Sir John Harding was not attending to his duties; but it was not until that evening that Atherton and Roundell Palmer met in the earl marshal's room in the House of Lords with the bundle of papers they had retrieved.

The two men considered the papers and reached the inevitable conclusion. The testimony of the four sailors, taken with the character and structure of the vessel, made it reasonably clear that she was intended for military use against the United States by the Confederacy. They did not overlook the fact that neither guns nor ammunition had been taken on board, and anticipated a Confederate defense that would argue the proper construction of the words "equip, furnish, fit out or arm" in the Foreign Enlistment Act, which related to the rendering of a vessel "presently fit to engage in hostilities." "We think, however," the law officers wrote, "that such a narrow construction ought not to be adopted . . . we therefore recommend that, without loss of time, the vessel be seized by the proper authorities."

In a show of what was later described as "masterly inactivity," the government seemed to abandon its earlier sense of urgency once the law officers rendered their advice.[33] The opinion was received at the Foreign Office the following day, July 29, as the *Enrica* was completing her pleasure cruise on the Mersey, but was not forwarded to the Treasury until the 30th. Upon receipt of it, Layard sent a memorandum to Russell: "You will see by the papers I send that the gunboat which has been fitting out for the Confederates at Liverpool left that port this morning. This afternoon we received the law officers' opinion stating that we should stop her. The papers were sent to the law officers with an instruction that they were of urgent importance."[34]

No such importance was attached to the document at the Treasury, where it languished for some further hours before the Board of Trade was at last instructed to have the vessel seized. On July 31 orders were telegraphed to the collectors of Liverpool and Cork, and on the next day to customs officers at Beaumaris and Holyhead. Squarey had anticipated that the vessel would put in at Queenstown, and on August 2 a letter ordering detention of the 290, should she indeed put in there, was sent to the collector at Cork.

In fact, nothing could have been further from Bulloch's intentions as he meticulously planned the ship's escape from British waters. At 7 a.m. on the 30th he arrived at the Woodside landing stage to meet the tug *Hercules* and thirty or forty men whom the shipping master had been instructed to engage, ostensibly for a voyage to the Bahamas and possibly Havana. The tug was there, as were various other stores destined for the *Enrica*, but to Bulloch's dismay, the seamen were not alone. Hanging determinedly on their arms were the "ladies of the port," who were intent on upholding the tradition of having one month's pay in advance on behalf of their men. Bulloch protested, but the shipping master pointed out it was "all or none." With his ship still in danger, Bulloch hurried them all on board, pausing only to take a telegram handed to him.

He had already anticipated that his vessel would be expected to come down St. George's Channel, perhaps putting into Queenstown, as she made her way to the Atlantic. The contents of the telegram confirmed his decision to send her up and around the northern coast of Ireland instead. It was a judicious move in the light of the message that had come from Southampton: a contact Bulloch had been maintaining there had telegraphed that the USS *Tuscarora* had left port for Queenstown.

After a brief inspection by customs officials, the tug *Hercules* conveyed Bulloch and the ship's future crew to Moelfre Bay, where, on board the Confederate cruiser, the men and their ladies were treated to a hearty meal washed down with a generous quantity of grog. In a suitably contented mood, most of the men agreed to ship for a run, say, to Havana, and each in turn stepped into the cabin to sign ship's articles, his lady taking possession of the one month's advance pay. Shortly before midnight, with Bulloch impatient to get his vessel away, the ladies were transferred to the *Hercules* and returned to Liverpool.

Bulloch again employed the skills of pilot Bond to take the *Enrica* "north about," and at 2:30 a.m. on July 31 the *Enrica* got under way and steamed out of the bay into the Irish Sea. By evening she was hugging the Irish coast. The engines were stopped at 6 p.m. off the Giant's Causeway so that Bulloch and Bond could hail a passing fishing boat to take them ashore. That night, in the dining room of their hotel, they sipped the best Coleraine malt whiskey, jubilant at the success of their venture yet apprehensive for the safety of the ship "buffeting her way around that rugged coast of Ireland."[35]

Upon his return to Liverpool, Bulloch was to learn with satisfaction that his ploy had indeed fooled the *Tuscarora*. She had come off Port Lynas on August 1 and then put her nose into Moelfre Bay—"but found nothing there to engage her special attention."[36] Captain Butcher was now well on his way to the Azores.

Liverpool had become a hotbed of rumor and innuendo. The master of the *Hercules* had been obliged to sign a sworn statement refuting Dudley's allegations that the 290 had been armed, and Samuel Price Edwards would never dispel the public's belief that he had been paid a substantial bribe by the Confederates to be absent from his post on the morning of July 29.

The situation was no more favorable to the Union in London. Palmerston called a meeting of his cabinet ministers to consider a dispatch drawn up by Russell that ordered detention of the 290 should she put into a British-owned port. Only one member of the cabinet, the Duke of Argyll, voted for the proposal (his conscience earning him a later accolade from *Vanity Fair* magazine, "God Bless the Duke of Argyll").[37] But his was the lone voice in favor of seizing the 290, Russell's draft prompting what the duke later recalled as "a perfect insurrection."[38] Gladstone, in particular, was "vehement" against it, and the plan was quickly dropped. The telegrams already sent to Liverpool and the other ports represented the sum of the government's resolve to lock the stable door after the horse had bolted.

At the American legation, Adams was feeling bruised and humiliated, his morale at its lowest point so far in his unenviable diplomatic position. He was prepared, he confided in Moran, to let the South go, though adding in good conscience, not until the abolition of slavery.

On August 1 Adams had a meeting with Russell. It was the beginning of a long postmortem into what had actually happened. The foreign secretary laid the blame entirely at the door of Sir John Harding, whose illness, he told the American minister, had caused the delay, but Adams was not entirely satisfied with the explanation. Doubts and rumors fueled his suspicions, and before long he would be diplomatically fending off suggestions that he was making specific allegations. Summoned to an interview with the foreign secretary in the autumn, he found Russell complaining of remarks made by John Bright insinuating that the warning had come from Russell himself. "It seemed to me," Adams wrote to Seward, "a little as if he suspected that Mr. Bright had heard this from me."[39]

While politicians argued and debated the government's actions, at the port of Praya on the island of Terceira the *Enrica* was undergoing her final transformation into the warship of Bulloch's dreams. Commander Semmes had arrived in Liverpool just days after her hurried departure, and after a short stay during which he assembled officers who had served with him on the *Sumter*, he and Bulloch embarked on Fraser, Trenholm's *Bahama*, captained by Eugene Tessier, bound for the Azores. In the bay of Porto Praya they found their ship with her tender, the *Agrippina*; already the arms and equipment that Archibald Hamilton had shipped were being transferred to the cruiser. On the morning of Sunday, August 24, with the ship's battery now complete and her bunkers well coaled, the vessel steamed slowly off land. Once out of Portuguese waters, Semmes mounted a gun carriage on the quarterdeck and read out the commission he had received from the Confederate Navy Department. He then formally commissioned the ship CSS *Alabama*. A salute was fired, and the Confederate flag was hoisted as the men cheered and the ship's band struck up "Dixie."

"She is as fine a vessel as ever floated," Semmes told the assembled men. Whetting their appetite with the prospect of prize money and a dubious assurance that those who were in the Royal Naval Reserve would have their papers signed when he put into port, he declared, "We are going to burn, sink and destroy the commerce of the United States." In the negotiations that followed, the naval reservists would receive twice the amount they would have achieved in the Royal Navy, along with the incentive of the prize money.[40]

Bulloch and Butcher took their leave of Semmes and returned to Liverpool on the *Bahama*, leaving the *Alabama* to fulfill Adams' worst fears. Just eleven days later she made her first capture, an unfortunate Massachusetts whaling ship fooled by the false U.S. colors the *Alabama* was flying. After the crew removed stores and provisions from the vessel she became a bonfire on the waves, a procedure that was to become something of a habit for the *Alabama*. She would ruthlessly pursue and destroy American commercial shipping, departing from the practice only twice: to battle with and sink a warship of the U.S. Navy itself, the USS *Hatteras*, and to engage, fatefully and finally, the USS *Kearsarge*. In the meantime, Hamilton's ship, the *Agrippina*, would continue to serve as her tender, Semmes alluding to her whiskey-loving captain when he warmed to the sight of "my old Scotch collier."

The *Alabama* would have a major impact on American maritime commerce. Ship owners swiftly deserted the U.S. flag, choosing to re-register in a neutral country. Those who were unwise enough to try to "cover" their cargoes or supply defective legal testimony asserting their neutrality fell foul of Semmes' formidable experience as a maritime lawyer.

In January 1863 the CSS *Florida* would join the *Alabama* on the high seas. Released at last from Nassau, Maffitt had battled yellow fever and the blockading fleet to run his ship into the Confederacy. Weak from the disease that almost claimed his life, he faced the Union gunboats blockading the port in the knowledge that many of the *Florida*'s armaments were still in the warehouses of Nassau. His ship was quite helpless, but he courageously put aside his grief at losing his step-son in the yellow fever outbreak, sent the crew below, and limped up on deck beside a few officers to bring her into Mobile under punishing heavy fire. The *Florida* was repaired and armed, and in due course the fearless Maffitt unleashed his own retribution on the commercial vessels of the United States.

Henry Hotze's description of the devastation in the cotton industry during that summer of 1862 was indeed correct. Liverpool and Manchester, with their more diverse economies, had been faring better than the mill towns, but even they were now suffering, and the manufacturing districts of Lancashire, starved of cotton, were reduced to a level of poverty unimagined in the days before the war. John Bright, through correspondence with Senator Charles Sumner, was able to persuade Lincoln to send grain to the distressed cotton districts of Lancashire, and in the autumn of 1862 three large ships sailed for England. The *Alabama* took the *Brilliant*, however, and Semmes burned the ship and her cargo.[41]

A relief committee was set up in almost every town in the distressed areas, with money raised to help the poor. Thrifty mill workers had saved in the good times, but with no end to the cotton famine in sight, their savings had dwindled to nothing. Workers in secondary industries suffered too from the slump and abject poverty had engulfed the industrial, and industrious, towns and cities as the spinning, weaving, and bleaching machinery fell silent. Homelessness, starvation, and debt pervaded the lives of the mill operatives, who scratched out an existence in grim slum dwellings, often relying on soup kitchens and handouts to survive.

Even as the *Alabama* had been slipping out of the Mersey on July 29, the *Liverpool Mercury* had been reporting that public subscriptions were to be raised to help the distressed cotton-manufacturing areas. By November more than 200,000 people were receiving aid from relief committees.[42] Yet the workers remained overwhelmingly in support of the Northern states. That December, following a public meeting in the Manchester Free Trade Hall, a letter was sent to Abraham Lincoln telling him that "the vast progress which you have made in the short space of twenty months fills us all with hope . . . that the erasure of that foul blot on Civilisation and Christianity—chattel slavery—during your Presidency will cause the name of Abraham Lincoln to be honoured and revered by posterity." In his moving response, the president said that he regarded their "precise utterances as an instance of sublime Christian heroism."[43]

The merchants and manufacturers, however, were largely still resolute in their support of the Confederacy. John Bright remained an exception, despite the fact that his own mill in Rochdale was forced to close its doors. For some businesses the blockade and its resultant cotton famine would be a disaster from which there could be no recovery; the Stirling family's mill in Manchester was one of those failing. It is not known whether Thomas Mayne Stirling supported the South, although most of his contemporaries certainly did. Nor is it known whether his cousin Mary hoped for a Confederate victory. What is certain, however, is that in the summer of 1862 the romance between the young Foreign Office clerk Victor Buckley and Mary Stirling blossomed.

CHAPTER 10

Everlasting Infamy

As reports of the *Alabama*'s activities started to reach London, the British government was firming its official stance on the cruiser's escape. Fortified by news of recent Confederate victories, Palmerston could afford to take the moral high ground. Governmental pride would remain intact as long as the only issue at stake was not Britain's adherence to its neutrality, but whether the provisions of the Foreign Enlistment Act had been violated. Following that line of reasoning, the path of blame always led, conveniently and gratifyingly, straight to the door of the delinquent Sir John Harding and his ill-timed bout of insanity.

The extent of the internal inquiries made by the Foreign Office is difficult to determine because when detailed information was required for Britain's defense to America's claims, "secret archives" were created and measures put in place to mitigate the level of exposure.[1] It was natural that there should be a policy of closing ranks.

Palmerston was well aware that if the North won the war, the United States would make enormous demands against Great Britain for reparation. The seeds of recompense were sown the moment the *Alabama* slipped out of the Mersey, and from that day on, the Americans would keep the prospect of such a claim high on their agenda. For the present, however, Britain had to await the outcome of the war. During the autumn of 1862 the British and French governments flirted briefly with the idea of joint mediation between the two sides, but once again official recognition of its independence slipped through the fingers of the Confederacy. Debates and deliberations served only to conclude that neither the North nor the South was achieving sustainable success on the battlefield. It seemed almost inevitable that the conflict would have to be fought out to the bitter end, and the side with the most stamina and advantages would claim the ultimate prize.

Rashly anticipating that intervention favorable to the South would take place, Gladstone made a speech after a banquet at Newcastle Town Hall on October 7. His injudicious words, which he later blamed on the "heat of the American struggle," would taunt him for the rest of his political career: "There is no doubt that Jefferson Davis and the other leaders of the South have made an army; they are making, it appears, a navy; and . . . they have made a nation."[2] Gladstone's speech created something of a sensation and initially gave false hope to many Confederates.[3] Earlier that year he had predicted confidently to Hotze that the war would end speedily in the acknowledged independence of the South.[4] Now, in the cold light of the morning after the Newcastle banquet, his remarks met with dismay from his government colleagues, who considered them an abuse of his ministerial position. Palmerston's cool prudence prevailed, however, and the prospect of British and French intervention faded into maintenance of the status quo, leaving the echo of the chancellor's remarks to assume the character of an embarrassing misjudgment.

Other speeches were soon to arouse both public interest and political indignation. In March 1863 Bright made his famous "privilege" speech at the opening of the Trade Unions of London meeting at St. James' Hall, referring to "men sitting among our legislators, who will build and equip corsair ships to prey upon the commerce of a friendly power . . . who, for the sake of the glittering profit which sometimes waits on crime, are content to cover themselves with everlasting infamy."[5]

The following evening in the Commons (in a debate on a motion by the radical Forster) John Laird felt compelled to respond, presuming the remark to have been applied to him. "I would rather be handed down to posterity as the builder of a dozen *Alabamas*," he thundered, "than as the man who applies himself deliberately to set class against class." It was a raw moment in what one of Adams' sons would later describe as "aristocracy's contest with democracy," and one sadly missed by Benjamin Moran, who had hastened to the Commons only to be turned away by the doorkeeper.[6]

Laird also stated to the House that his shipyard had been approached by representatives of the Northern states but had refused to build vessels for them. That, he contended, was the reason for the Union's hostility toward him. Loud cheers from the benches accompanied Laird's defense of his actions, but while his oratory might have provided a moment of elation, it also deprived him of any chance of a knighthood.

For the beleaguered finances of the Confederates in England there was a light on the horizon at last. Huse had been working closely with John Slidell, who was now the Confederacy's emissary in Paris and had used his social connections to secure French support for the South. Among the European nobility with whom Slidell was acquainted was a young Jewish banker, Baron Frédéric Emile d'Erlanger, Frankfurt-born son of Baron Raphael Von Erlanger. The Erlanger banking empire included offices in Paris and, later, London. To Slidell's delight, a love match developed between his daughter Mathilde and the wealthy thirty-year-old Emile, whose first marriage had ended in divorce. Their courtship sealed his relations with the Erlangers, and the couple's marriage in 1864 would assure Slidell of a seat at the table of Europe's financial aristocracy. It was said that the influential banker had "a direct line to the Foreign Office."[7]

Erlanger was a powerful figure whose opinions held some sway with Louis Napoleon, and through him Slidell hoped France might be persuaded to recognize the Confederacy, albeit without Britain's collaboration. In the hope of such political favors Slidell entertained a proposal from Emile Erlanger for a complex loan which, although not particularly favorable to the South, would provide badly needed funds for the purchasing agents.

By the end of 1862 Huse's debts had become exceedingly pressing. To date he had received more than $3 million, but that amount, as J. Gorgas, the colonel in chief of ordnance in Richmond, noted, was "wholly inadequate to his wants." Huse was in debt to the tune of almost £6 million, and the prospect of a loan arranged through Slidell was most appealing.

Erlanger's original proposal was dismissed by the astute Confederate secretary of state, Judah P. Benjamin, who jibbed at the huge profits that would accrue to the banking house, but, supporting Slidell's hope that political advantages could be gained from a deal with Erlanger, he agreed to revised terms. Erlanger was to advance a loan of $15 million at an interest rate of 7 percent, bonds to be sold at 77 points, and each one backed by a promise to exchange at face value for cotton at 12 cents a pound. Since redemption of the bonds depended on the ability to transport cotton out of the blockaded Southern ports, there was a degree of optimism involved, although Erlanger himself also had a financial finger in the pie of blockade-running.

Not surprisingly, Adams was annoyed at the apparent indifference of the British government when, on March 18, 1863, the bonds were offered for sale in England—in Liverpool by Fraser, Trenholm and on the London market by J. H. Schroeder and Company. He would have been even more agitated had he known that the Confederate Navy Department, spurred by the successes of the *Alabama* and *Florida*, had earmarked £3 million of the loan for Bulloch to acquire similar warships.

At first, the bond issue (also available in Paris, Amsterdam, and Frankfurt) was three times oversubscribed in London. The promise of such an imminent fortune falling into Huse's hands presented an opportunity Hamilton and Bond felt they could not miss. "I have had an offer of sale from the London Armoury Company of their entire plant," Huse wrote to Colonel Gorgas.[8]

In truth, Hamilton and Bond were already sensing the cool winds of recession in the gun-making business. The North was now manufacturing almost all its own weapons, and competition for Southern contracts would become intense as British manufacturers found their machinery increasingly standing idle. Moreover, the war was dragging on and the Confederate agents were carping about lack of funds. It was time to bow out.

Unfortunately for the London Armoury Company, and even more so for those City speculators who had staked their money, the euphoria that attended the bond issue quickly subsided. By the summer, when news of Gettysburg and Vicksburg reached England, the fate of the Erlanger loan was sealed. The prospect of the scheme becoming one of history's "extraordinary popular delusions and the madness of crowds" waned rather more quickly than anyone expected.[9] Soon, proceeds from the first issue were propping up the quotations to prevent the market from completely collapsing.

It was disquieting news for the City and for major investors, among whom numbered some of the most influential Confederate sympathizers. At the American legation, Benjamin Moran delighted in watching the bond values plummet. However, Britain's economy had been enjoying a period of boom that was peaking at that time, and, historically, a downturn would almost inevitably follow soon. Frederick Bond's name did not appear on the published list of people who personally invested in the Erlanger scheme, but Archibald Hamilton was certainly mentioned. Sinclair, Hamilton, and Company was left at the end of the day with five bonds on which the owners were fortunate enough to have their interest paid up; many others sustained heavy losses.

As the Confederate bond market was crashing around his ears, Huse was also experiencing personal problems. Yet again his integrity was being questioned by his superiors, who now had evidence with which to confront him. Samuel Isaac had imprudently offered Commander North a cash incentive—the division of a 5 percent commission on goods purchased by Isaac, Campbell, and Company. North righteously refused and reported the offer to a senior quartermaster. Soon Huse was obliged to admit to having benefited from the commission system, although he claimed he intended using the funds to establish a military library in the South. The whole business left an unpleasant taste, with the financial agent William Crenshaw complaining that Huse was determined "his orders should be executed by his friends."[10] Such squabbling did little to help the momentum so essential in Huse's purchasing operations. Second only to Bulloch in energy, he had made a valuable contribution to the South. But if Huse had cause for complaint in the spring of 1863, Bulloch would fare no better as the British government was stepping in to curtail his operations. There would be no more *Alabamas*.

Misfortune was also to strike one of the earliest protagonists in the story. With the prospect of Confederate funds quickly evaporating, and the experience of a boom turning to bust in the years 1857–58 dictating that they might be overexposed to an economic downturn, the seasoned businessmen Hamilton and Bond decided the time was right to invoke the surrender clause in their lease. In the deepening arms recession (poor sales at a gun makers' fair in London had foreshadowed the coming slump for manufacturers), the costly premises of the London Armoury Company in Bermondsey, once so worthy of a florid description in the prospectus, were now becoming a liability. The business could be moved to its less expensive manufactory at Victoria Mills, Bow. Accordingly, the lease was terminated and the potential white elephant restored to its owner. Although he did not know it yet, the esteemed gun maker Robert Adams had taken the first steps on the road to bankruptcy.

Samuel Walters' "CSS Alabama at Sea." Before it was known as the *Alabama,* the ship went under the pseudonyms "290" and "Enrica." (Williamson Art Gallery and Museum, Birkenhead; Wirral Museums Service)

James D. Bulloch, working as a Confederate naval agent, secured funding and oversaw the *Alabama*'s construction. (Century Magazine)

Bulloch settled in Liverpool after the Civil War where he became a much respected figure. (Courtesy of Jim Elliott, great grandson of James D. Bulloch)

The Foreign Office clerks assembled at the time of their temporary move to Whitehall in August 1861. (Courtesy of the FCO)

(left) Victor Buckley was a clerk in the department of the Foreign Office that dealt with American matters. (By kind permission of Ed Buckley)

(below) Mary Stirling, daughter of Admiral Sir James Stirling, founder and governor of Western Australia, married Victor Buckley. (From the Stirling History Collection, WA)

Sir John Dorney Harding D.C.L., QC was the Queen's advocate whose absence at the crucial time facilitated the Alabama's escape from British waters. (Artist's impression. "John Stamp"/ Author's collection)

Archibald Hamilton, merchant and arms expert, was the head of the London Armoury Company and of Sinclair, Hamilton & Co. (Courtesy of Teresa Hamilton Moore)

Henrietta "Enrica" Hamilton became part of an enduring mystery. (Artist's impression. "John Stamp"/ Author's collection)

Frederick William Bond was manager of the London Armoury Company and later Managing Director of the African Steam Ship Company. (Artist's impression. "John Stamp"/ Author's collection)

Benjamin Moran, secretary at the American legation in London, was determined to solve the mystery of the *Alabama*'s escape. (Pennsylvania Historical Society)

(right) Henry Hotze, Confederate agent and arms expert, wooed the aristocracy with his effective propaganda campaign for the South. (Courtesy of The History Museum of Mobile, Alabama)

(below) Joshua Nunn, deputy United States consul in London, posed for this photograph in his Masonic regalia. (Courtesy of the Joshua Nunn Lodge No. 2154)

Francis Bicknell Carpenter was photographed with his painting, "International Arbitration"—the Treaty of Washington, which was later presented to Queen Victoria but has since disappeared. (Courtesy of A. George Scherer III, great-great-grandson of Francis B. Carpenter)

The offices of the African Steam Ship Company featured in a book by Arthur Conan Doyle. (Photograph, 1870s, by Henry Dixon. © The British Library Board Tab. 700.b.3 111)

The combat between the CSS *Alabama*, and USS *Kearsarge* off Cherbourg, June 19, 1864, resulted in the sinking of the most notorious Confederate cruiser. (Colored engraving. Author's collection)

CHAPTER 11

Humble Submission to Yankee Bullying

When the yard of William C. Millers and Sons was seen to be constructing another vessel, ostensibly for Fawcett, Preston, and Company, the whole transaction seemed to U.S. consul Thomas Dudley's spies to be a repeat of the *Oreto* affair. Launched on March 7, 1863, and given the name of the future Princess of Wales, who had arrived in London for her wedding the day before, the *Alexandra*, a trim 300-ton, 124-foot-long vessel, had all the makings of a small gunboat. When she was towed into Toxteth Dock for fitting out, Dudley determined to do everything possible to prevent her joining her consorts on the high seas and began collecting statements and depositions with which to build a case against her. However, when he traveled to London and called on Queen's Counsel Sir Robert Collier, whose words had previously carried such sway, he was disappointed. Moran reported in his journal, "He has been to see Mr. Collier who gave such a decided opinion about the '290'; but that gentleman has been bought up by the Government for a consideration and declines to advise further about such ships. . . . Why have they closed Mr. Collier's mouth, instead of employing him as they should do, to obtain evidence and bring the guilty to punishment?"[1]

Adams was still smarting from the escape of the *Alabama*, and frequent press reports of her conquests and those of the *Florida* kept the fire of his indignation burning. In a dispatch to Russell, while not intending to imply that the government had actually *countenanced* the violation of the laws, he pointed out that the *Alabama* had been built, armed, and manned by Englishmen. Nothing less than redress for the injuries she had caused and protection for the future would satisfy the American minister.

Russell declined to entertain claims for compensation but did intimate that certain amendments might be introduced to the Foreign Enlistment Act. Behind the scenes, he put that very suggestion to the cabinet, only to meet with fierce opposition. It was hard to see, his colleagues advised him, how the law could be improved.

While the government was appearing as enigmatic as ever to Adams, Russell was about to put an end to Confederate shipbuilding activities, even if it meant doing so without the immediate support of his fellow ministers. The customs surveyor at Liverpool confirmed that the *Alexandra* was well adapted to be a small gunboat, and subsequently even Collector of Customs Samuel Price Edwards acknowledged his impression that the vessel was indeed intended for the Confederate service. The home secretary, Sir George Grey, instigated further inquiries to ascertain whether the ship was being equipped for that purpose, and on April 4 the law officers of the Crown (Sir John Harding had been replaced as Queen's advocate by Sir Robert Phillimore) recommended that the *Alexandra* be seized under the Foreign Enlistment Act. The following day, Russell sent to Liverpool the official order empowering the surveyor of customs to board the vessel and make the king's broad arrow mark on one of her masts, signifying government property.

The *Alexandra* was "seized and arrested, to the use of Her Majesty, as forfeited . . . together with the furniture, tackle and apparel belonging to and on board the said ship." There followed some ninety-eight offenses under the Foreign Enlistment Act with which the ship's owners were to be charged (two of them were later dropped) in which it was asserted that the defendants did "equip, furnish, fit out, attempt or endeavour to equip"—all words vital to a testing of the law.[2] Fawcett, Preston naturally protested the firm's innocence, but in London Adams was regarding the foreign secretary in a new light. "I think we may infer from this act," he wrote immediately to Seward, "that the government is really disposed to maintain its neutrality."[3] The government may have been so disposed, but when the *Alexandra* trial opened at Westminster on June 22 (it was decided the case should be heard in London rather than Liverpool), there were perceptions that the presiding judge, Lord Chief Baron of the Exchequer Sir Jonathon Frederick Pollock, harbored a bias toward the South.

The case seemed doomed from the start, with Dudley's paid informants being quickly discredited. Clarence Yonge, who had been Bulloch's own private secretary and had joined the *Alabama* as paymaster, only to be dismissed by Semmes for dishonesty and drunkenness, was a crucial witness for the Union camp, but he too was soon dispatched, the words of the defense counsel, Sir Hugh Cairns, ringing in his ears: "How am I to describe this specimen of humanity?"[4]

In his summing up three days later, Pollock addressed the jury with a rather leading conclusion: "If you think the object was to build a ship in obedience to an order, and in compliance with a contract, leaving it to those who bought it to make what use they felt of it, then it appears that the Foreign Enlistment Act has not in any degree been broken."[5]

It took the jury just a few minutes to reach a decision, finding against the Crown. Fawcett, Preston immediately applied for the release of the ship, but the Crown had lodged an appeal with the House of Lords. That lengthy legal process would result in a similar verdict a year later, and in time Fawcett, Preston would settle for damages of £3,700. By then, however, the deterioration of both the vessel and the Confederacy's fortunes would curtail the *Alexandra*'s career. Sold and fitted out as a blockade-runner and renamed the *Mary,* she was eventually detained in Nassau after revenue officers found a gun recently taken on board stamped "Fawcett Preston & Co. 1862." In December 1864 she was again the subject of a court hearing, but her eventual release came too late. The war was over.

Adams was deeply angered by the result of the *Alexandra* case, and Moran noted bitterly in his journal: "The verdict was received with wild applause."[6] While the *Alexandra* had been caught up in her own troubles, the lady after whom she was named had become the Princess of Wales, and the American minister was invited to a ball honoring the newly wedded royal couple. Moran recorded that Adams described it as a "vulgar and crowded medley. . . . The mob were almost servile enough to go on their knees at the Prince and Princess."[7] Earlier that year Moran himself had written, with his customary wit, "Today I bought the best photograph of the Queen I have ever seen. It is a full length and shows her in all her washerwoman frowsiness . . . the price is one guinea."[8]

As the *Alexandra* drama played out, Bulloch made significant progress toward fulfilling his navy secretary's dreams of warfare waged by ironclad vessels. Nothing struck more fear into the heart of the U.S. Navy than the word "ram," and Bulloch had two of these beasts nearing completion at Lairds' shipyard. Each ironclad vessel had an iron piercer, or "ram," at its bow that was dangerously concealed below the waterline when the ship was in motion, ready to crash through the protective plating of wooden warships. The rams were comparatively small vessels at 230 feet, but they were designed for maximum maneuverability, with turret batteries and a shallow draft that would allow them to operate in Southern rivers and harbors. Bulloch had placed the order with Laird Brothers in 1862, and the first of the two ships was launched in early June 1863. "A steam vessel of war," Adams described it to Russell, "of the most formidable kind now known."[9] The skillful design and engineering of the ships was a testament to their builders' craft and the source of many sleepless nights for Dudley and Adams. "The Laird rams," as they had become known, represented a deadly form of naval warfare with their power to break Lincoln's blockading fleet, and once again Adams was prepared to exert every energy to stop them leaving England.

Dudley and Adams again amassed witness depositions and evidence. A visiting New Yorker, George Temple Chapman, claimed to have met Bulloch at the offices of Fraser, Trenholm, and Company and heard him boast of having fitted out the *Florida* and *Alabama*. Bulloch had further claimed "that he was fitting out more, but that he managed matters so that he could defy anyone to prove that he was fitting them out for the use of the Confederate government."[10]

Russell was finding his hands tied now by the decision in the *Alexandra* trial, and in any event, Bulloch had preempted Adams' case against the rams by transferring ownership of them to a French firm, Bravay and Company. The firm's two principals, François and Adrien Bravay, had something of a shady past that included a failed lawsuit for slander after an accusation of having kept a house of ill fame in Paris. Bulloch might not have wished to keep such company, but beggars could not be choosers, and the Bravay brothers were prepared to state that they had already made inquiries regarding the possible purchase of armored frigates on behalf of the Egyptian government. That had the ring of truth and gave Bulloch a straw at which to clutch as he set about constructing another elaborate smoke screen. This time, however, he knew he could not afford to be so confident.

Bulloch had long since known that he was operating on borrowed time. At the beginning of the year he had written to Mallory regarding the impending opening of Parliament on February 3, "I am reliably informed that the question of furnishing supplies to the belligerents will come up. I am consulting the best legal authority, but confess that the hope of getting the ships out seems more doubtful—indeed hopeless, unless there be a change in the political character of the Ministry."[11] Several months earlier he had told Mallory, "I have reason to be sure that if I had not sent the *Alabama* and her armament away before the arrival of Captain Semmes and his officers, she would have been stopped."[12]

The mechanics of Bulloch's latest foil ran smoothly at first. With the legal work handled by Frederick Hull and his firm in Liverpool, Bravay and

Company purchased the rams from Laird Brothers for a nominal sum, the terms of the transaction providing for them to resell the ships beyond British jurisdiction for an amount that would give them a generous commission. Bulloch covered his tracks and protected Lairds' integrity in formal correspondence with the builders, who, on the face of it, would be selling the rams to Bravay and Company as agents for the pasha of Egypt.

By July, when the anticipated inquiries instigated by the Foreign Office were made at Liverpool, the Lairds were able to assure the collector of customs that the rams were not being built for the Confederates but for the Frenchmen who had contracted for them. The British consul general at Cairo had advised Russell in February that Bravay and Company had been claiming to have a verbal order in England for two steel-clad frigates, but that after visiting the docks in England and France, the late viceroy of Egypt had decided against that type of ship.

With Lairds' assertion looking increasingly suspicious, Russell referred the correspondence to the law officers of the Crown. Their response to the Foreign Office on July 24, however, was that Her Majesty's government ought not to detain or in any way interfere with the vessels.

By now, Adams had received further confirmation from the French embassy that the rams were not intended for the French government either, and the tenor of his communications to Russell became increasingly fraught. His earlier delight at finding the government prepared to demonstrate its neutrality by seizing the *Alexandra* had given way to annoyance and exasperation—first at the verdict in the trial and now at the apparent inertia in the present crisis.

Russell, finding himself in an invidious position, must have almost hoped that the Bravays *were* buying the rams for the French government, but a telegraph to his man in Paris produced the not unexpected negative response. Now Russell could only await a reply to his latest inquiry. That, too, was soon forthcoming from Cairo. The viceroy of Egypt absolutely repudiated all connection with the rams. Such information would not have surprised Dudley in Liverpool. Writing to Washington on September 3, the American consul declared, "There is scarcely a man, woman or child in the place but knows these rams are intended for the Confederates."[13]

The judgment of the law officers, however, was colored by the result of the *Alexandra* trial, and still they advised noninterference. While Russell hesitated to deliver notice of this final blow to Adams, tempers at the American legation had been sufficiently aroused to allow veiled threats to be made. Lincoln's government had directed him, Adams pointed out, "to describe the grave nature of the situation in which both countries must be placed in the event of an act of aggression committed against the Government and the people of the United States by either of these formidable vessels."[14] When Adams did at last receive a note from Russell declining to seize the rams, the rhetoric escalated from implied ultimatums to a specific threat. "It would be superfluous in me," Adams wrote in reply, "to point out to your Lordship that this is war." Relations between Britain and the United States had hit their lowest point since the *Trent* affair. Russell responded immediately. The matter, he told the American minister, was receiving "the serious and anxious consideration of Her Majesty's Government."[15]

A bitter exchange of letters followed between Adams and Russell, culminating on September 25 with a note from the foreign secretary robustly defending Britain's neutrality. In response to what he considered "intimation of hostile proceeding towards Great Britain on the part of the United States" and the Americans' expectation that the law should be altered to suit them, he advised Adams that Her Majesty's government "would not be induced by any such consideration, either to overstep the limits of the law or to propose to Parliament any new law." With a final thrust, Russell warned that Great Britain would not "shrink from any consequence of such a decision."[16] Palmerston read and approved his foreign secretary's note. So too did Queen Victoria.

Behind the public arena of their acrimonious correspondence, Russell and Adams had been plying their diplomatic skills with the utmost caution, each hoping to avoid what neither of them wanted—a total breakdown in the already strained Anglo-American relations. Now, Russell wrote to Palmerston confidentially, "The conduct of the gentlemen who have contracted for the two iron-clads at Birkenhead is so very suspicious that I have thought it necessary to direct that they should be detained. The solicitor general has been consulted, and concurs in the measure as one of policy though not strict of law."[17]

It was indeed policy versus law. The law officers were extremely wary of a seizure, which might, when tested in the courts, result in punitive damages being awarded against the Treasury. Although doubts might be cast on the intent involved in the sale of the rams, that and the now familiar avalanche of "hearsay" depositions from the American legation did not, in the opinion of the legal minds, constitute sufficient grounds to arrest the ships. However, contrary public opinion was pressing Russell to do something; insurance companies and London underwriters were suffering heavy financial losses as a result of the depredations of the *Alabama* and *Florida*, and the City was not happy with the situation.

The middle-class public at large had shifted much of its indifference to favor the North following Lincoln's long overdue proclamation of emancipation; for the first time, the image of slavery could be clearly identified with the cause of the Southern states. The British middle classes, if not the aristocracy, could at last give voice to the nation's distaste for that abhorrent institution.

Characteristically, Palmerston worried that seizure of the rams would appear to be "humble submission to Yankee bullying," a galling thought for the man who had once told Russell that the proper tone for answers to Adams' more bellicose notes was to say in civil terms, "You be damned."[18] Nevertheless, Palmerston gave his foreign secretary his full support, and on October 8 an order was sent to Liverpool for customs officers to seize the vessels. Simultaneously, the Admiralty dispatched an order to the captain of HMS *Majestic* to assist port officials, and thereafter the rams lay helpless under the guns of Her Majesty's navy.

At the American legation, a suspicion had taken root that the government had "private information" of the Confederates' intention to run the vessels out, and hence the watchfulness. It was an intriguing idea, given the "private and most reliable source" to which Bulloch would later attribute his own intelligence.

Although work was allowed to continue on the rams at Lairds' yard in order to mitigate the economic impact on Birkenhead, in the coming months the government rebutted all requests to free the ships. Bulloch hoped for French intervention based on the Bravays' interest in the matter, but in the event, that lifeline was not forthcoming. Instead, the future of the Laird rams was to be determined by Palmerston, who had long since considered that Britain was failing to keep up with France in the development of ironclad ships.

By the spring of 1864 Admiralty officials had inspected and appraised the vessels, and "with the law-suit in one hand and the valuation in the other," an offer was made that the Bravays could not refuse.[19] Of the £220,000 the British government paid for the ships, £188,000 reverted to the empty coffers of the Confederates—a drop in the ocean since Bulloch estimated the current deficit to be £700,000. The Laird rams were now renamed *Scorpion* and *Wyvern* and, having been deprived of a "glorious" war, were commissioned into the Royal Navy.

The year 1863 was not totally without success for Confederate shipping activities in Britain, however; nor did it close without another Foreign Office intrigue. The renowned oceanographer Matthew Fontaine Maury, a passionate Southerner who had arrived in England the previous year on a purchasing and political propaganda mission, had succeeded in buying, and getting to sea, the *Japan*, a type of iron steamship vessel built on the Clyde. She was to become the CSS *Georgia*.

Union spies had quickly targeted Maury and his ship while it was being partially fitted out in Liverpool (where Commander North's daughter officiated at the launch). Dudley was finding no shortage of evidence with which to bombard officials, and the *Japan* was already achieving notoriety in the press as a case "as mortifying to the Federals as the escape of the *Alabama*."[20]

A crew for the vessel had been trawled from the Seamen's Home, but having drunk away their advance wages, the men reported to Dudley instead. They had been shipped for service on board the *Japan*, they said, which was fitted out to "burn, sink and destroy all Federal vessels she came up with."[21] The American consul immediately contacted Adams, whose urgent protest to the Foreign Office elicited prompt action by Russell.

In the meantime, the *Japan* had cleared for Singapore and other Far Eastern ports and had left Liverpool for Greenock, where she would continue shipping a crew. It was a detail the flustered American consul had inadvertently forgotten to mention to Adams, according to a report in a north of England newspaper, which was relishing the story.[22] When Russell sent orders to Liverpool to detain the vessel, customs officials there reported back that no ship answering Dudley's description could be found.

The mistake at last realized (Moran complained that the consul in Scotland should have been more vigilant), telegrams were sent to Greenock, but by then the *Japan* had hastily departed for an unknown destination. The 150-ton steamer *Alar*, owned by Henry Pearson Maples and registered from Southwark, was to rendezvous with the *Japan* in a mission distinctly similar to that of the *Agrippina*, which Archibald Hamilton had supplied for the *Alabama*. The possible involvement of the gun merchant on this occasion is suggested by Maury's proud boast to his cousin Lt. Lewis Maury, who was to command the raider: "Say what small arms and big guns you want and you shall have them."[23]

A little after midnight on April 5, the Confederate officers assigned to the ship made their way to New Haven in Sussex, where a large crowd had been assembled. About sixty of the seamen present climbed on board the waiting *Alar*, and as the lines were cast off, someone on shore called for three cheers for the *Alabama*. The *Alar* sailed for France, and off the coast of Brest transferred the armaments it had brought to the *Japan*. After a large and rather obstinate Blakely gun had at last been hoisted onto the deck, the steamer stood out to sea, the Confederate flag was hoisted, and the CSS *Georgia* was formally commissioned.

Some of the men who had shipped at Liverpool chose not to throw their lot in with the Confederacy and returned to England on the *Alar*. The reports of two of them to Dudley and Adams resulted in protests to Russell that the law had been flouted, and subsequently two of the shipping agents, Messrs. Jones and Highatt, were prosecuted for violation of the Foreign Enlistment Act. At the Liverpool assizes, before Lord Chief Justice Coburn, both men were found guilty, although the severity with which the court regarded their offense was perhaps reflected in the penalty imposed—a fine of fifty pounds each.

While orders to detain the *Japan* had been arriving too late at Greenock, a curious chain of events was facilitating the *Alar*'s departure ahead of a detention order. The Board of Customs at New Haven had reported there was no evidence "to call for any interference on the part of the Crown," but in what was later described as an "unaccountable mistake," the letter of instruction to the port authorities issued by the Foreign Office had mysteriously gone astray and was then delayed for five more hours because the commercial telegraph had closed for the day.[24]

Such a deliberately contrived, or fortuitous, incident might have favored the Confederates, but in general their luck was running out. Although the subsequent opinion of the law officers was that the *Japan*'s departure was not preventable, the ship itself, originally a merchantman that was never really suited for warfare, was to have a comparatively short career. The *Georgia* captured only nine Union vessels before returning to Liverpool for repairs, arriving there on May 2, 1864. In order to change her character (and thus legal status) from that of a warship, her ownership was transferred to the shipowner Edward Bates—the man who had, in the early days of the war, purchased the steamers *Anglia* and *Scotia* from the railway company in which Mary Stirling's uncle, Ross Donnelly Mangles, was a director. Fearing that there was no intention of converting her to a merchant vessel, Adams protested to Russell, the result of which was a change to the law prohibiting ships of either of the belligerent American powers from entering Her Majesty's ports for the purpose of being dismantled or sold.

Bates, his bill of sale signed by Bulloch, did indeed send the *Georgia* forth, as a merchantman, to Portugal. Cdr. Thomas Tinsley Craven, brother of Cdr. Tunis A. Craven of the USS *Tuscarora*, happened to be patrolling there with the USS *Niagara* and considered the former commerce raider to be fair game; he promptly put a prize crew on board and she was taken back to America. A dismayed Bates protested to the Foreign Office, but Russell washed his hands of the affair. The ship's title, he informed Bates, was a matter that must be decided by a court in the United States.

CHAPTER 12

War-Torn Waters

The autumn of 1863 was dismal, wet, and foggy, its grimness reflecting the mood of the Confederate naval agents in Britain. Bulloch's efforts to create a British-built navy for the South were at an end, yet he plowed on relentlessly, turning to French shipyards with his audacious plans. Britain's Foreign Enlistment Act continued to plague him and the other agents attempting to acquire ships in the United Kingdom. While Commander North was still a constant thorn in his side, the activities of Matthew Fontaine Maury and Lt. George T. Sinclair now garnered much of Bulloch's attention.

Sinclair, who belonged to a respected seafaring family, seven of whom served in the Confederate navy, had arrived in England in 1862 to acquire another cruiser for the Confederate navy. On finding that Bulloch did not have sufficient monies or credit to fund the building of a cruiser, Sinclair became party to a skillfully engineered financial plan formulated by a representative of the London firm William S. Lindsay and Company, which also had business dealings with Sinclair, Hamilton, and Company.

William Schaw Lindsay, MP, a close friend of most of the influential figures and leading aristocrats who supported the South, and so well connected that he could claim to be a confidant of Emperor Louis Napoleon, devised a scheme whereby money was raised from cotton manufacturers against cotton certificates, the resulting £62,000 being used to finance the building of a screw steamer of similar size to the *Alabama*. Ownership of the vessel would be vested in a consortium of seven British subjects. The transaction's veil of secrecy worked well at first. The shipbuilding contract was given to the Clyde firm of James and George Thomson, who were also constructing an ironclad for Commander North. Bulloch and Sinclair supplied the plans for the new vessel, but in the autumn of 1863 the *Pampero* (also known as the *Canton*) ran afoul of the Foreign Enlistment Act after the discovery of a careless letter written by Sinclair that finally vindicated the government's intense scrutiny of the ship's complicated ownership.

The British consortium quickly reached a compromise with the government (whose correspondence in the matter was handled by Victor Buckley's uncle, Edward Pleydell Bouverie, in the Lord Advocate's department) whereby legal proceedings would be stayed and the owners would agree not to transfer the vessel to any other party without the Crown's consent. Accordingly, the *Pampero* remained in the hands of customs officials until some months after the war ended.

Throughout the war, the Confederates had wooed Napoleon in the hope of gaining France's support, their position strengthened, they considered, by the possible danger the Union posed to France's Mexican empire. Bulloch had begun to transfer his shipbuilding operations to France in the spring of 1863 after initial negotiations with the Bordeaux yard of Lucien Arman had resulted in an order for the construction of four ships. Arman's position as a member of the French legislative body and his closeness to Napoleon seemed to imply top-level approval for the venture, and in time the order was extended to include two ironclad rams.

Problems arose, however, when Arman, under pressure in his own yard, farmed out some of the work. Information on the scheme soon leaked to the U.S. minister in Paris, and the usual labyrinth of insufficient funds and punitive commissions compounded Bulloch's difficulties. Emile Erlanger stepped in with a magnanimous offer of financial assistance—which was, in fact, nothing more than a clever sleight of hand in which he guaranteed Arman the first two payments for the ships, for a commission of 5 percent, in the event that Bulloch's funds should not be forthcoming. Since those monies stemmed from the sale of the Erlanger loan bonds and were already in his hands, the commission ensured him a handsome windfall for doing nothing. But for Bulloch, the situation was much as it had been for Huse at the beginning of the war. It was still a seller's market. "We are in the condition of all purchasers on credit," he reflected to Mallory. "We must pay the creditor for the risk he runs in trusting us."[1]

While Bulloch was pinning what was left of his faith on the assurances of his French associates, Archibald Hamilton was orchestrating his own activities from his room at the luxurious Grand Hotel in Paris. The Grand was built to satisfy Louis Napoleon's wish for a hotel unique in the world, its construction financed by wealthy banker brothers Emile and Isaac Pereira. The Pereiras competed with the Rothschilds, had links to the Saint-Simonians, and were actively involved in the Scottish shipbuilding industry. Occupying a commanding triangular position that would soon overlook the magnificent Opéra Garnier, the opulent hotel was a favorite haunt of prominent Confederates and their associates.[2] Hamilton was in Paris to take advantage of a deficiency in Lincoln's blockading strategy. He was planning to run arms to the Confederacy via Mexico, having "made arrangements with certain gunmakers" as a result of which seven thousand rifles were sent on board the schooner *Caroline Goodyear*, loaded at London.[3]

Adams deplored the exploitation of the neutral waters of Mexico, complaining to Seward, "The plan has been entered into by wealthy and influential merchants and capitalists in this city, and it has an intimate connection with the base of the Confederate loan."[4] Adams was right. Hamilton was liaising closely with Slidell in Paris and with Edward P. Stringer of W. S. Lindsay and Company. Stringer earned himself a 5 percent commission by introducing Nelson Clements, purchaser of the arms on behalf of the Confederacy, with delivery to be made to the Gulf of Mexico port of Matamoras.

Ever mindful of the precariousness of Confederate fortunes, Hamilton prudently obtained a guarantee from Huse that he would pay the amount of Sinclair, Hamilton, and Company's invoice should the actual payment, which was to be in cotton shipped back to England, not materialize. Describing Clements' contract as "monstrous," the Confederate agent C. J. McRae complained, "He is to be paid 100% of his invoice, consequently his ingenuity has been greatly exercised in devising means to increase the amount of his invoices." McRae claimed to know of many other contracts "of various shades and hues floating about the London markets, all . . . having one object, namely to enrich contractors at the expense of the government."[5]

Hamilton's operation did not run altogether smoothly. Mexico was a fragmented country still beset by military and political upheaval, and the *Caroline Goodyear* sailed into war-torn waters. She was seized by French cruisers as she approached the mouth of the Rio Grande and, on the grounds that her cargo of arms was destined for Matamoras (which had earlier been under siege), was taken to Veracruz, which French forces had occupied "temporarily" on the premise of protecting free trade.

Mexico was a hotbed of revolution and countercoups during the mid-nineteenth century. The liberal chief justice of Mexico, Benito Juárez, took over the government in 1858 and then faced a bloody counterrevolution. Many foreign residents suffered loss or damage to their properties during the violence; some even lost their lives. Russell and Palmerston demanded compensation on behalf of injured British citizens but were met by stubborn refusal from Juárez. Further, Juárez stopped interest payments to Mexico's foreign creditors, of whom the most important were Britain, France, and Spain. In 1861 the Spanish government put forth a proposal that the three injured parties should send a joint military force to occupy the port of Veracruz and appropriate customs revenues until the debt had been satisfied.

Louis Napoleon, however, had a private agenda. It soon became apparent that the occupation of Veracruz was a prelude to French troops marching on Mexico City, intent on overthrowing Juárez's government and installing Archduke Maximilian of Austria as a puppet ruler for France with the title emperor of Mexico. Russell was inclined to protest the deception, but Palmerston's own preference seemed to be to keep Napoleon occupied with events in Mexico, thus distracting him from European affairs. Against the judgment of his foreign secretary, Palmerston gave his cautious approval to France's aggression. By the time Hamilton's ship arrived off Matamoras, a guerrilla war was taking place in which Juárez's men were fighting the French. Fearing that the arms on board the *Caroline Goodyear* were destined for the wrong hands, the French seized the ship.

Hamilton turned to the Foreign Office, which ascertained on his behalf that the ship had been released by the French authorities at Veracruz to go where she pleased, "always, however, excepting to a Mexican port."[6] The news must have filled Hamilton with dismay, as indeed it did Judah P. Benjamin. Matamoras, in northeastern Mexico, was geographically well placed for the Confederates' purpose, although the shallow coastal waters necessitated vessels anchoring some thirty miles away at the mouth of the Rio Grande. Supplies brought to Matamoras had to be ferried across the river to Brownsville, Texas, a potentially lucrative route into the Confederacy for speculators such as Hamilton were it not for the difficult logistics. Once supplies had been landed, transporters had to run the gauntlet of Indians and bandits and outwit the increased vigilance of Union gunboats; consequently, the fortunes promised by arms running through Mexico were short-lived.

Although Slidell was working tirelessly, and not without personal profit, on behalf of the Confederacy in France, Benjamin harbored doubts about the support the French were providing. "It is impossible to refrain from the remark," he wrote to Slidell, "that by some fatality every movement made by the French government, however amicable its intentions, has been disastrous to us." Having not yet received news from Slidell of the *Caroline Goodyear*'s release, Benjamin wrote to him that "the blow struck at us by this act was much more severe than you or the [French admiral's] government can well appreciate. Every musket then seized was equivalent to capturing a soldier from our ranks."[7] Such was the Confederacy's desperate need for arms.

As the Foreign Office was addressing Hamilton's concerns about the *Caroline Goodyear*, the American legation in London was toying with the possibility of seeking retribution for the activities of the *Agrippina*. "This vessel has been a source of great injury to us," Moran wrote in his diary, relishing an offer of betrayal from a French sea captain who said he was to sail shortly as a passenger on the tender carrying a letter from Huse to Maj. Norman S. Walker, the Confederate agent at Bermuda. Consul Morse subsequently engaged the spy in the hope that he would signal Union warships to enable them to capture the *Agrippina* at sea, but the rogue vessel ultimately slipped through their fingers.[8]

Like the British public at large, the legation was also enjoying a scandal involving Palmerston. The Irish radical journalist Timothy O'Kane publicly alleged that his wife had committed adultery with the prime minister on a number of occasions at his London residence and claimed from Palmerston damages of £20,000. Confronted by a robust denial of the allegation, O'Kane then petitioned for divorce, citing Palmerston as co-respondent. It was the type of high-profile case that appealed to every level of society, with the public delighting in the salacious gossip accompanying it. When Palmerston was at last exonerated (Margaret O'Kane denied committing adultery and claimed she had never been legally married to O'Kane), he emerged from the fray with his reputation not only unsullied but greatly enhanced. The scandal gained Palmerston some public sympathy for the forthcoming election, and many seemed pleased to see the "human" side of their aristocratic prime minister. Timothy O'Kane changed his first name to Thadeus and left for a new life in Australia, where he became a successful newspaper editor.

Palmerston's private trials, however, were overshadowed by the concerns of foreign affairs. Not only did the British government have to hold its invidious position in the American Civil War, it had also to keep a wary eye on Napoleon; maintain its stance on the uprising taking place in Poland; and address the ominous Schleswig-Holstein situation between Denmark, Austria, and Prussia, which portended a European war and was, in the closing months of 1863, hurtling toward a crisis. Small wonder that Palmerston remained content to let the American war take its fateful course without British intervention.

To complicate matters for Palmerston, the Polish revolution had created the possibility of hostilities between Britain and Russia, and, in naval maneuvers designed to remove Russia's ships from ice-ridden waters, the Russian Baltic fleet had entered the harbor of New York while the Pacific fleet made for San Francisco. Some of the American public, and many in Europe, interpreted the move as signaling Russia's support for the Union. The incident gave rise to an interesting legend—that the price eventually paid for Alaska represented, in part, recompense for expenses incurred by Russia in sending its fleet to America. In fact, Russia's only potential impact in the war came as rumors reached San Francisco of the *Alabama*'s approach. Rear Admiral Papov, whose six vessels were in the harbor, gave orders to protect the city, an action for which he was later reprimanded by his superiors.[9]

As 1863 drew to a close, the Confederates might well have conceded that it had not been a good year. General Thomas "Stonewall" Jackson had died after the battle of Chancellorsville; the battles at Gettysburg and Vicksburg had foretold the death knell for the Confederacy; and Union forces had effectively seized the offensive, relentlessly bombarding the symbolic and emotive target of Fort Sumter in Charleston Harbor. The Union blockade now held its tightest ever grip on the Southern coastline, and hopes of foreign intervention were fading fast. The strident Confederate commissioner in London, James Mason, who had failed to persuade the British government to warm to his cause, was being recalled to Richmond. By December, as news of another Union victory reached London, the Erlanger loan bonds had plunged to an all-time low.

By the spring of the following year the situation had hardly improved. Bulloch's shipbuilding activities in France were curtailed when the American minister in Paris presented the French government with damning evidence that France's neutrality was being breached. For some months Bulloch had been apprehensive. The assurances of top-level support had begun to sound shallow, and in February 1864 he wrote to Mallory with the worst of news: "The Emperor, through his Ministers of Foreign Affairs and of the Marine, has formally notified the builders that the ironclads cannot be permitted to sail, and that the corvettes must not be armed in France, but must be nominally sold to some foreign merchant and despatched as ordinary trading vessels."[10]

Bulloch was both deeply disappointed and embittered by the sudden change of policy, describing the French government's turnaround as "crooked diplomacy"; but the coming months held in store even more devastating news. On June 11 Raphael Semmes, ill and exhausted after covering 75,000 miles during almost two years at sea with the *Alabama*, entered the harbor of Cherbourg on the Normandy coast of France and dropped anchor. The ship was in urgent need of repairs. "We are like a crippled hunter, limping home from a long chase," Semmes had written in the log less than three weeks earlier.[11] The decks were leaking, and she was taking on water and in urgent need of coal. Prophetically, as a channel pilot guided the *Alabama* safely up the English Channel, Semmes wrote, "We have brought our cruise of the *Alabama* to a successful termination."[12]

The port admiral would not sanction the repairs until he communicated with Napoleon, who was presently taking the sun at Biarritz and would not be back in Paris for several days. The absence of formal protection for the *Alabama* opened a window of opportunity for a formidable U.S. warship. News of the *Alabama*'s arrival was telegraphed to Paris, and the American minister there quickly relayed the information to Capt. John Winslow of the USS *Kearsarge*. Three days after the *Alabama*'s arrival, her nemesis steamed into the harbor at Cherbourg, sent a boat to confer with the authorities, then steamed out again and took up a position off the breakwater.

Semmes had been anticipating as much and knew that the *Kearsarge* could soon be joined by a flotilla of Union warships. Faced with the realization that his cruise was effectively at an end, all he had left now was pride—Confederate and personal. There was something of the cocksure about Semmes; he and his ship were weary, but the prospect of a glorious finale may well have seemed appealing as he set about making the necessary preparations. The collection of valuable chronometers he had confiscated from the fifty-five prizes he had burned would be transported to Liverpool to be sold off—an English yacht, the *Hornet*, would perform that duty—and it remained only for him to formally challenge Captain Winslow.

Semmes' cavalier attitude manifested itself in the note he passed to the Confederate agent at Cherbourg, Monsieur Bonfils: "I desire you to say to the United States consul that my intention is to fight the *Kearsarge* as soon as I can make the necessary arrangements. . . . I beg she will not depart before I am ready to go out."[13] He needed only to take on coal before confronting his adversary.

Cherbourg was a favored coastal retreat, and visitors multiplied its population in the summer months, but the town was particularly popular the weekend of June 18 and 19 as celebrations to mark the opening of a new casino and bathing facilities were taking place. It was also the strawberry season, and a festive mood prevailed. A few days earlier officials of Manche (that region of Normandy) had held a banquet that was attended by representatives of all the major Paris newspapers, so the news quickly spread of the duel about to take place between the two formidable warships.

It is thus not surprising that Henry Hotze was among those present in Cherbourg that weekend. He may even have been one of the visitors whom Semmes noted had come on board the *Alabama*. In recent months the trilingual Hotze had been successfully exporting his propaganda techniques to Paris following the recall of the Confederate agent Edwin de Leon. Through Slidell and

Erlanger he had raised funds to support his work, and with his usual adroitness he tailored his approach to suit the French system and its audience. Hotze identified the part played by the Havas Agency, which held a monopoly in supplying news to French papers, and he assiduously courted the friendship and services of its head, Auguste de Havas. By June he could boast that he was "seeing the columns of the French papers filled with correspondence from New York, New Orleans and Richmond."[14] He would undoubtedly have been a prominent figure at the grand banquet of the Paris newspaper chiefs in Cherbourg.

On Saturday, June 18, the mood in Cherbourg was one of anticipation. Those watching the *Alabama* would have noted that a rather elegant steam yacht had appeared in the harbor—the *Deerhound*, owned by John Lancaster, a wealthy industrialist from Wigan, Lancashire, who was acquainted with Gladstone. By coincidence, the *Deerhound* had also been built (in 1858) by the Lairds, and during a refitting she stood in the dock adjacent to the one that cradled the 290.

Earlier in the month Lancaster and his family had been enjoying a cruise of the Channel Islands before the yacht's Welsh master, Captain Evan Parry Jones, had landed them at Saint-Malo. Jones anchored the *Deerhound* close to the *Alabama* and witnessed the *Kearsarge* steaming in and out of the harbor, evidently surveying the enemy.

John Lancaster was a member of the Royal Yacht Squadron at Cowes and the Royal Mersey Yacht Club, and he and his captain were Confederate sympathizers. On Saturday, Jones collected Lancaster and his family from the railway station. That evening their boat went across to the *Alabama*, pulled alongside, and asked permission to visit, but they were apparently refused because the ship's company was busy preparing for the following morning. Semmes was anticipating victory by boarding the enemy vessel, and his men were practicing boarding drill.[15] The request and refusal would later be confirmed in a statement by Lt. Arthur Sinclair: "Little did we imagine at the time that we were treating these English people with such scant courtesy, when they were to be the means of saving the lives of so many officers and men."[16]

Later that evening, according to Jones, the Lancasters held "a consultation" as to whether they should take the yacht out the following day to watch the fight or go to church. Lancaster's twelve-year-old daughter, Louisa, cast the deciding vote.[17] The Union side would view the involvement of the *Deerhound* rather differently, believing she was actually a prearranged consort standing by to rescue officers and crew from the *Alabama*.

The pro-South British writer George Meredith wrote later that his friend and employer, Charles Warren Adams (whose pseudonym was Charles Felix) of the publishing house Saunders and Otley, hastened to Cherbourg on learning that the *Alabama* had put in there. On the eve of the battle, Semmes gave Adams his journals, the ship's log, and other papers, with permission to do as he wished with them. The subsequent publication, rapidly produced but insightful (Meredith wrote the first and last chapters), was a disappointment to Semmes, who later described it as a "meagre and barren result."[18]

Many years later a suggestion would be considered that Hotze might have gone on board the *Deerhound* after the battle and that his subsequent report was consistent with his having been on the yacht, though neither Jones nor Lancaster mentioned his presence.[19] Nonetheless, the important engagement about to take place off Cherbourg would be particularly poignant for Hotze, and more than just a newsworthy spectacle. The famous Confederate cruiser had been named for his home state of Alabama; time would show that he had been privy to the secrets of her construction and escape; and now her audacious captain was taking a dramatic gamble—the outcome of which would become a notable event in the annals of history.

CHAPTER 13

The War Is a Thing of the Past

On the bright, sunny morning of Sunday, June 19, crowds were still flocking to Cherbourg. A special excursion train brought many more from Paris to join the spectators who were already finding every favorable position from which to view the coming battle. The upper floors of houses overlooking the sea were filled, people clambered onto the walls of the harbor and the forts, and telescopes were in great demand.

The son of the American minister to France, William L. Dayton Jr., refused an invitation to join the *Kearsarge*, instead finding a vantage point in the nearby village of Querqueville. Within a month the artist Édouard Manet would be exhibiting his own vision of the spectacle (painted retrospectively) in a Paris gallery. Prominent Confederates are likely to have been among those who traveled from Paris—the Slidells; Emile and Mathilde Erlanger; Mary Louise Senac with her daughter Ruby; and Judah P. Benjamin's wife, Natalie, who for some years had lived apart from her husband in Paris with their young daughter, Ninette.

Just after 9 a.m. observers saw the *Deerhound* sail a wide counterclockwise loop around the *Alabama,* as if in some form of communication. Then, flying the pennant of the Royal Yacht Club at her masthead, she followed the *Alabama*, which was cheered by Southern supporters as she steamed out of the harbor to meet her destiny.[1] A French ironclad frigate, the *Couronne*, escorted the *Alabama* to ensure that the neutrality of French waters was not violated, while her opponent waited some six or seven miles offshore.

As the *Alabama* neared her enemy, Semmes mounted a gun carriage and addressed his officers and seamen with a rousing speech: "You have destroyed and driven for protection under neutral flags one half of the enemy's commerce which, at the beginning of the war, covered every sea. The name of your ship has become a household word wherever civilization extends."[2] Semmes knew that the guns of the *Kearsarge* had the advantage of the *Alabama*, but he did not know, he later claimed, that Winslow had armored his midship with a coat of chain cable covered over by planking, affording her engines a shield of protection.

The watching crowds were not disappointed by the battle that followed. The two ships began circling each other, and the *Alabama* opened by firing her entire starboard battery. Early in the engagement, a 100-pound percussion shell fired by the *Alabama* landed in the sternpost of the *Kearsarge*—a potentially lethal strike—but failed to explode, at which dawned the realization that the *Alabama*'s powder was damp. The ship was hardly in fighting form after her long time at sea; soon the pounding of the *Kearsarge*'s guns began to take a toll. The *Alabama* acquitted herself well, firing at least two shots for every one of the *Kearsarge*'s, but as Semmes' first lieutenant, John McIntosh Kell, who was standing near an 8-inch pivot gun, later recalled, when an 11-inch shell exploded through the gun port, it wiped out "like a sponge from a blackboard one-half of the gun's crew."[3]

The battle raged for an hour before Semmes conceded. With the *Alabama* unable to run in to shore, the colors were struck and the final order given: "All hands save yourselves!" The *Alabama* settled stern first into her watery grave, her final death throes described as "a remarkable freak . . . making a whirlpool of considerable size and strength."[4]

Throughout, while the French *Couronne* kept a respectful distance, the *Deerhound* had stayed faithfully within reach of the *Alabama*. She was now able to lower a boat to rescue Semmes and Kell. Semmes crouched down in the boat to conceal himself, and it was said later that Winslow had looked the other way, not wishing to see his old shipmate executed.[5] The *Deerhound* rescued other officers and seamen as well—a total of forty-one—but others were obliged to surrender to the *Kearsarge* or to be rescued by a French pilot boat and brought back to Cherbourg. Many of those who escaped drowning were badly injured, and there was later an acrimonious debate on whether the *Kearsarge* had fired on her adversary after she had surrendered, the point at which she struck her colors being unclear. At 1 p.m. Captain Evan Parry Jones turned the *Deerhound* with her rescued passengers toward England.

On receiving news of the battle, Bulloch and Rev. Tremlett traveled down to Southampton. When the *Deerhound* put in, the "Confederate Parson" quickly spirited Semmes away to his Belsize Park vicarage in north London for a period of rest and recuperation before sending him forth on a leisurely tour of Switzerland. The two men shared a mutual dislike of Yankees and everything the North stood for. Tremlett's attitude had been shaped during his time in Boston, and Semmes certainly harbored a strong dislike for what he regarded as Puritan hypocrisy. Among the anecdotes he included in his memoirs was the *Alabama*'s capture of a Lisbon-bound brig whose cargo included religious tracts. "These tracts had been issued by that pious corporation, The American Tract Society of New York," Semmes reflected, "whose fine, fat offices are filled with sleek, well-fed parsons of the Boynton stripe." (It was the Massachusetts-born abolitionist Rev. Charles Brandon Boynton, founder of the Western Tract Society and participant in the Underground Railroad for fleeing slaves, who gave credence to the erroneous belief that 290 Englishmen sympathetic to the rebel cause had financed the building of the *Alabama*.) Referring to an accompanying note on which a warning that it was against Portuguese law to take any tracts ashore had been crossed out, Semmes observed that it was "as though the protagonists of 'grand moral ideas' had become a little bolder since the war and were determined to thrust their piety down the throats of the Portuguese." Semmes was particularly delighted to come across a further instruction in the notes: "As may be convenient, please report (by letter if necessary) anything of interest which may occur in connection with the distribution." Without hesitation, he made a bonfire of the ship and her cargo.[6]

Semmes, who was certainly far from puritanical himself (he subsequently embarked on a questionable relationship with Tremlett's sister, Louisa), was fêted as a hero in England. Gladstone's sister Helen, for whom support of the Confederacy had been a cause célèbre, wrote with an offer of financial assistance, and the press lamented the loss of the *Alabama* with the sentiment, "She was a good ship, well handled and well fought, and to a nation of sailors that means a great deal."[7]

Henry Hotze wrote his own narrative of the battle, which appeared in the *Index* of June 23. His report confirmed that as the *Alabama* steamed out, "a small English yacht, the *Deerhound*, followed close in her wake. . . . It was noticed on board the *Deerhound* that the *Alabama* fired far more rapidly and with greater accuracy but that the shells of the *Kearsarge* did the more damage."[8]

The role of the *Deerhound* continued to be viewed with suspicion. Captain Winslow wrote to Secretary of the Navy Gideon Wells on July 30 that some of the Confederate prisoners said there had been activity between the *Alabama* and the *Deerhound* the night before and on the morning of the battle, and "strange men who were supposed to be naval reserves were brought in on the *Deerhound* to captain guns."[9] In his reply the Navy secretary agreed, setting the foundation for America's postwar claim for reparation: "The *Alabama* was an English built vessel, armed and manned by English men; has never had any other than an English register; has never sailed under any recognized national flag since she left the shores of England."[10]

The *Alabama* had taken her place in history with a record of sixty-five ships captured and either destroyed or released on ransom bond, a career for which the U.S. government might well bear a grudge. The *Florida* could also boast a respectable tally. She and the satellite cruisers she spawned by converting captured prizes into Confederate corsairs accounted for $4,051,000 of destruction to Union shipping, with a total of sixty prizes among them. The *Alabama*'s reckoning amounted to $4,792,000.

The cruise of the *Florida* came to an end in October when she put into the neutral port of Bahia. Thinking himself safe in South American waters, her commander, Lt. Charles Manigault Morris, went ashore for the night. In his absence the ship was taken under force by the USS *Wachusett* and, with only a feeble attempt at protest by the Brazilian authorities, was taken by her captors to Newport News, Virginia. Although the actions of the *Wachusett*'s captain, Cdr. Napoleon Collins, were manifestly a violation of international law, the *Florida* was sunk at Hampton Roads on November 28. A court of inquiry concluded that the accident was occasioned by a leak and failure of her pumps. It was later claimed that Adm. David D. Porter (under whom Bulloch had once served in the U.S. Navy) had given orders to the engineer in charge of the ship: "Before midnight open the sea cock . . . at sunrise that Rebel Craft must be a thing of the past." Accident or not, the controversial nature of the *Florida*'s capture rendered her an embarrassment to the U.S. government. When the sinking was reported, Admiral Porter remarked that it was "better so."[11]

During the autumn of 1863 Matthew Fontaine Maury had managed to get to sea the *Rappahannock*, originally HMS *Victor*, which he had purchased and outfitted as a cruiser. Repairs to the ship were carried out at the government's dockyard at Sheerness. On receipt of information that Confederate agents had bought the vessel, the American legation lodged its customary protest with the Foreign Office. A subsequent inspection by a member of the customs authorities failed to condemn the ship, but amid Union claims that the vessel was being prepared as a warship with the collusion of Royal Navy employees, Maury worried that a detention order might be forthcoming from Russell and slipped her out of Sheerness in the dead of night.

The hasty departure of the *Scylla*, as she was temporarily known, was so premature that twenty British workmen were still on board when she sailed. In mid-channel, a Confederate officer commissioned the *Rappahannock* into the

Confederate navy, but her career ended almost immediately when faulty boilers rendered her unseaworthy. She was obliged to put into Calais, destined never to go to war for the South, while the Foreign Office was left to deal with the connivance at Sheerness that had permitted the flagrant breach of neutrality.

Toward the end of 1864, while the *Rappahannock* was blockaded in the port of Calais and Bulloch was still dealing with the embarrassment she had become, one of the French-built rams was at last made available to him. Arman had ostensibly negotiated the sale of the *Sphinx* to Denmark, but that nation's war with Germany was coming to an end, and the warship was "surplus" to the Danes' needs. Renamed the *Stonewall*, the ironclad's initial promise of naval prowess soon turned to disappointment. She performed badly in heavy weather and was obliged to put into a Spanish port just days after fleeing French waters, her only claim to Confederate dominance of the waves coming as she steamed out of her refuge at the end of March 1865, fully repaired and prepared to battle the two U.S. warships that were awaiting her departure. To her captain's surprise, neither gunboat came forth to engage her. The *Stonewall*'s hyped reputation as an invincible man-of-war ensured her a smooth passage past the enemy, but such fighting capabilities, real or not, came too late for her to save the South. When she reached Nassau, her captain learned that the war was over. The *Stonewall* then put into Havana, where she was sold for just enough money to pay off her crew.

Of greater success for Bulloch was a vessel he had first noticed in the summer of 1863 as she prepared for her maiden voyage from the Clyde. The *Sea King* became available for purchase in the autumn of the following year, and Bulloch moved swiftly, enlisting the help of Prioleau's father-in-law, Richard Wright, whom he knew from the yard of Miller and Company. Wright moved the *Sea King* to London, carefully covering his tracks so that she would continue to exhibit all the characteristics of a merchantman. In the meantime Bulloch acquired a recently built steamer, the *Laurel*, which he began loading at Liverpool with a formidable battery for the future cruiser.

Dudley's spies were suspicious of the *Laurel*, and Adams knew that something was afoot in London, although his detectives had failed to identify which ship belonged to Bulloch.

As a precaution, he ordered two Union warships to patrol the mouth of the Thames. There was much subterfuge in getting the *Sea King* and her tender away—the shipping agent for the *Laurel* advertising for freight and passengers for a voyage to Havana, then diplomatically turning people away. The *Laurel*'s freight was the arms for the cruiser, and the real passengers were Confederate officers whose tickets were issued under assumed names. In a further "cloak-and-dagger" drama, Bulloch instructed one of her senior officers to sit in the coffee room at Wood's Hotel in High Holborn with a white pocket-handkerchief through the buttonhole of his coat and a newspaper in his hand to await the appearance of an agent who would identify himself with a series of signals. Bulloch was taking no chances in slipping his men on the ship without attracting the attention of Union spies.[12]

The ploy worked. On October 8, 1864, the *Sea King* slipped down the Thames while a telegraph to Liverpool sent the *Laurel* out into the Mersey. The tender went to sea that evening, the last of Bulloch's "Confederate navy" to leave Britain. The ships rendezvoused at Madeira, where, on October 19, the Confederate flag was hoisted and the CSS *Shenandoah* was formally commissioned to embark on her mission to harass and destroy the New England whaling fleet. Again, though, the *Shenandoah*, magnificent cruiser though she was, and a worthy successor to the *Alabama*, came too late into the war to make a difference. After leaving Melbourne, Australia, in February 1865, she continued making captures for some months, out of range of communication from Europe or America and oblivious to the fall of the Confederacy. There seemed to Bulloch only one way of relaying that information to her captain. He arranged for James Mason, who was still in England, to contact the Foreign Office, which in turn forwarded a copy of Bulloch's letter addressed to the *Shenandoah*'s commander to Her Majesty's representatives and consuls at the Sandwich Islands, Nagasaki, and Shanghai.

In the event, it was not until August 2 that the *Shenandoah* sighted a British bark, the *Barracouta*, fourteen days out of San Francisco, and hove to in order to address her. A boat was sent across from the *Shenandoah*, and her British officers learned the devastating news—or rather, as Bulloch later wrote, "the definite information"—that the Confederate armies had surrendered. One of the officers who received the painful tidings was Bulloch's own half-brother, who had also served, as the youngest officer, on the *Alabama*. "The war," Irvine Bulloch remarked, "is a thing of the past."[13]

The *Shenandoah* accounted for $2,041,000 worth of damage to the maritime commerce of the United States. Beyond the quantifiable figures, she and the other Confederate cruisers caused less measurable damage as marine insurance premiums rocketed; the cost of essential goods spiraled; and American shipowners registered their ships in other countries, sometimes never to return, in what a twentieth-century author would describe as "the flight from the flag."[14]

CHAPTER 14

Black Friday

Lady Margaret Beaumont looked musingly into her teacup at the breakfast table and said to herself in a languid voice that was quite audible to her guests, "I don't think I care for foreigners." To the son of the American foreign minister seated next to her, the remark was not only offensive but seemed to encapsulate the indifference with which he had been treated by the aristocracy during his tenure as his father's secretary in London. Even here, in the lovely and unusually pro-Union country estate in the heart of Yorkshire, with its charming hostess, Henry Adams was reminded of the coolness with which British society had received him. His presence had been tolerated, but he was never quite accepted into the social clique of the English aristocracy. "Every young diplomat," he later observed, "felt awkward in an English house from a certainty that they were not absolutely wanted there, and a possibility that they might be told so."[1]

Bewildering though English society may have been to Henry Adams, he and his father could at least draw some comfort from the fact that the power of the aristocracy had failed to persuade its own aristocratic prime minister that the Confederacy should be recognized. In the closing months of the war they may well have looked back on the previous year with some satisfaction because those who still believed in such a reversal of policy had fallen victim to the experienced cunning of the aged Palmerston and his equally weathered foreign secretary.

In the spring of 1864 prominent supporters of the Confederacy, led by William Schaw Lindsay, had made concerted efforts to secure Britain's intervention in the war. Lindsay was a prominent member of the Southern

Independence Association, the movement spawned by the London Confederate States Aid Association, which boasted on its committee such notable names as Lord Robert Cecil and his brother, Lord Eustace Cecil; the ubiquitous Alexander Beresford Hope; the financial agent James Spence; and Layard's friend William Gregory. The list of committee members was peppered with titles apart from those of the Cecils: the Marquis of Lothian, the Marquis of Bath, Lord Wharncliffe, and Lord Campbell, whose brother married Beresford Hope's eldest daughter. But it was William Lindsay, wealthy shipowner, financier of Matthew Fontaine Maury's *Georgia*, and a member of Parliament with heavy personal investments in cotton certificates, who came forward to spearhead the structured attempt to secure British intervention.

Maury had joined forces with Rev. Tremlett in London to create the Society for Promoting the Cessation of Hostilities in America, and this organization was the vehicle for Lindsay's discussions with Palmerston. The prime minister, still guarding his slender majority in the Commons, was anxious to secure every wavering vote in a forthcoming showdown on the government's policy in the Schleswig-Holstein situation, and to this end was prepared to entertain Lindsay and those other supporters of the cause that had ignited the political passions of so many. Lindsay was proposing a further parliamentary motion for mediation and intervention in conjunction with other European powers, and Palmerston and Russell saw this meeting as an opportunity to dangle a carrot of hope while delaying Lindsay's motion until after the crucial division over the Danish question.

Ironically, James Mason, who as Confederate commissioner in London had failed to ingratiate himself with Palmerston and Russell, returned to England unofficially to accompany Lindsay, Maury, and Tremlett in the audience with Palmerston. Unfortunately for the Confederates, the wily prime minister suddenly postponed the meeting so that it did not take place until *after* the crucial vote for which the government needed the support of some dissenting Tories. The delaying tactic worked, with the pro-South members giving the government their vote. "Palmerston and Her Majesty's Government," Maury wrote to his wife, "is in entire sympathy with the South but the time is now not auspicious to interfere."[2] Palmerston won his vote in the Commons by a majority of eighteen. His government was safe and, having outfoxed the Confederate supporters, he could revert to his usual pragmatism.

Alarming though the suggestion of a U-turn in government policy might have been to the Union diplomats, their emotions were soon stirred by attempts on the other side of the Atlantic to settle the war. In the early weeks of 1865, as Sherman and Grant were laying waste to the South, the Hampton Roads

Conference, as it became known, was taking place in Virginia. Southern commissioners were attempting to find common ground for settlement with representatives of Lincoln's administration in the prospect of a war with a foreign power. Seward was still stridently criticizing the British and Canadians for allowing the Confederates to use their shores, and that seemed to bode ill for Great Britain, although France's activities in Mexico could provide a more accessible and less challenging target.

Lincoln's characteristic calming influence ultimately prevailed. No moves could be made, he insisted, until the South had laid down its arms. When the Confederate commissioners cited a precedent in the form of an agreement in advance of cessation of hostilities made between Charles I and Oliver Cromwell at the time of the English Civil War, Lincoln responded with his customary adroitness, "I do not profess to be posted in history. On all such matters I turn you over to Seward. All I distinctly recollect about the case of Charles I is that he lost his head in the end."[3]

Although it had been apparent in Britain for some time that the Confederacy was in its death throes, news of the Hampton Roads Conference, with its implication of a sudden end to the war, created panic on the London Stock Exchange and in the banking fraternity. Suddenly the commercial future looked decidedly uncertain.

At the American legation, Adams was quick to gauge the rising temperature of fear and speculation. "The impression is now very general," he wrote to Seward, "that peace and restoration at home are synonymous with war with this country."[4] As a skilled and perceptive diplomat, Adams believed the best interests of the United States would be served by Palmerston's government retaining its power at the forthcoming general election, and he urged some form of reassurance from Seward that would help secure that electoral victory. With resentment over the *Alabama* and the other Confederate raiders still simmering beneath the surface, those words of comfort were not forthcoming.

The sudden turmoil in the money markets was compounding the troubles of the British gun-making industry, which had been struggling to pull itself out of the economic downturn. The former premises of the London Armoury Company had indeed become a financial burden to Robert Adams, who had been slow to rein in his prosperous lifestyle as the recession hit and had become the target of adverse publicity, accused of "making a better profit than a gun."[5] In fact, Adams was making no profit at all by the end of 1864 and was obliged to surrender in bankruptcy on January 13 of the following year, with debts amounting to more than £21,000 and a net indebtedness of £6,045. Although he satisfied his creditors within a few months and was granted a discharge, he never quite recovered from his insolvency, perhaps, it has been suggested, because he was speculating with his personal fortune. That was certainly the temptation to which other businessmen had succumbed, and as the year wore on, a universal financial disaster threatened.

While the London stock market was shivering on the news of the Hampton Roads Conference, the South itself was suffering defeat. Judah P. Benjamin made one last attempt to establish the Confederacy's credibility by offering the South's own emancipation declaration (dependent on slaves' enlistment in the Confederate army), but by now the war was lost. Jefferson Davis and his cabinet evacuated Richmond on April 22, and just hours later both the Confederate capital and Petersburg fell to Union forces.

On Palm Sunday, April 9, Lee surrendered the Army of Northern Virginia to Ulysses S. Grant at the historic meeting in the courthouse at Appomattox. Confederate sympathizers were "staggered" when the news reached England, Moran noted. Fears that the end would come suddenly had been justified and did nothing to stem the panic in financial circles. Cotton certificates lost all value, and businesses overexposed to Southern interests faced ruin.

On the morning of Wednesday, April 26, the telegraph buzzed with even more dramatic news: Lincoln had been assassinated. In the already brittle economic climate, the latest tidings rocked the nation. The Bank of England immediately sent a secretary to the American legation to ascertain whether it was true, and *The Times* extended its print run, with extra copies changing hands at five shillings each. Union stocks fell heavily, and Moran consoled himself with the information that at least one broker who had dealt heavily in Confederate bonds was now ruined.

Recent events had signaled the end of the road too for the London Armoury Company. Bond's prudent management had kept the business active, and it had assets in the form of a manufactory, machinery, expertise, and a reputation for having supplied the largest number of revolvers to the Confederacy. The directors themselves may have been grappling with their own financial problems, or even fears of involvement in litigation, and it is possible that personal motives lay behind the next move. A winding-up petition was presented to the court on November 2 by Benjamin Bloomfield Baker, a contractor, and Frederick Edward Blackett Beaumont, a British army officer who had patented an improvement to Robert Adams' revolver in 1856.

Some of the shareholders were furious at what, on the face of it, seemed to be a curious voluntary liquidation, and Robert Adams himself may have been one of those whose protests delayed the planned disposal of the company's assets. On April 12, 1866, at a special general meeting of the company held at its offices at 36 King William Street, the resolution for winding up was finally confirmed after it had been rejected at an earlier stormy meeting in March. Six liquidators were appointed, but any two of them could exercise the group's powers. Although he had never been a director of the company, Frederick Bond emerged from the shadows as one of those liquidators.[6]

On May 10, 1866, the respected finance house of Overend, Gurney, and Company, whose clients included speculators in blockade-running, closed its doors, facing an insolvency of £5 million. The announcement precipitated a panic in the financial district of London, where crowds gathered. The following day, dubbed "Black Friday," saw Gladstone step in to grant the Bank of England emergency measures.

The catastrophe did not dampen the ingenuity of Archibald Hamilton and Frederick Bond. At the same time the London Armoury Company was closing, a new enterprise was conveniently forming—the London Small Arms Company, which could compete with the government's Royal Small Arms Factory at Enfield and further unite the Bond and Barnett gun-making families.[7] John Barnett became chairman of the company, Bond's brother Edward Philip was appointed managing director, and the list of subscribers included Edward Barnett and Bond's other brother, Eyton, who, having long since put his bankruptcy behind him, was now firmly ensconced in the Midlands as a director of the counterpart Birmingham Small Arms Company, which had been formed in 1861.

The London Armoury Company was able to make a substantial contribution toward the new business: its rifle factory premises at Old Ford Road, Bow, passed to the London Small Arms Company, which had begun manufacturing operations there even before the final winding-up meeting of the London Armoury Company took place in April 1866. The shareholders evidently smelled a rat, because the directors of the London Armoury Company were called upon to give an account of themselves. On July 9, 1867, the following notice appeared in the *London Gazette*:

> The London Armoury Company (Limited)
>
> NOTICE is hereby given, that a General Meeting of the London Armoury Company (Limited), will be held on Saturday the 10th day of August, 1867, at one o'clock in the afternoon precisely, at No. 17, St. Helen's-Place, in the city of London, and that at such meeting the account showing the manner in which the winding up of the said London Armoury Company (Limited), has been conducted and the property of the Company disposed of, will be laid before and read to the meeting; and at such meeting He (Liquidator of

the said Company) will be prepared to give any explanation that may be required of them respecting the matters aforesaid.

Dated this 2nd day of July 1867.

A. Hamilton, for Self and Co-Liquidators.[8]

Such was the standing of Frederick William Bond in the arms industry that he had enjoyed the freedom of the prestigious Gunmakers' Company in London since 1858. Now, with the American Civil War episode behind him, he would devote time to the Livery's activities, becoming rector warden in 1869, upper warden the following year, and in 1870, the year of Robert Adams' death, achieving the coveted title of master. But it was his connection with the African Steam Ship Company that would ultimately determine Bond's future, and his Machiavellian personality would become instrumental in that company's success.

Although Hamilton and Bond had successfully steered the London Armoury Company through the economic storm to its eventual winding up, the months following the end of the war saw many cases of financial difficulties, not only in the City but also in the devastated cotton districts of the North. The end of the war and the reinstated flow of cotton had come too late for many of the mills. The enviable Lancashire model of capitalist industrialization, dubbed "Manchesterism" by German economists, would soon grind back into action, but not for the Stirling family's mill. In November 1865 its steam engines were removed and the mill was put up for sale.[9]

Hard times hit many people who had prospered during the war. James Mason, the former Confederate commissioner who had so often enjoyed the opulence of Beresford Hope's hospitality, even spending Christmas of 1864 at his country estate, was reduced to penury, and friends rallied to raise funds for him. Fraser, Trenholm, and Company was vigorously pursued by the U.S. government in the courts, and even the best efforts of lawyer Frederick Hull could not prevent the resulting bankruptcy that cost Prioleau his personal fortune and his luxurious homes. The duplicity of Isaac, Campbell, and Company might have gained short-term profit, but the firm had greedily accepted payments in cotton bonds from Huse before the market collapsed and was now left holding worthless certificates. For a time, the economic woes showed no sign of abating.

Elsewhere, however, the effect of the South's defeat was having less of an immediate impact. Alexander Beresford Hope had earlier formed an association with the object of erecting a statue to the memory of General Stonewall Jackson. Thanks to the generosity of his wealthy associates a sum was raised far in excess of that required, and when the sculpture was eventually unveiled in Virginia in 1875 (the delicate situation prevailing between Britain and the

United States after the war caused a delay, as did some remodeling), the remaining money was given to the Virginia Military Institute so that a yearly income could be used to produce two gold medals, annual prizes that would bear the inscription "The Jackson Hope Medal—The Gift of English Gentlemen."[10] There had been no shortage of money either when officers of the Royal Navy had contributed to a new dress sword to be presented to Semmes to replace the one he had lost when the *Alabama* went down.

Beresford Hope's brother-in-law Robert Cecil had acquired a print of Stonewall Jackson that hangs today in Hatfield House, Hertfordshire. No doubt the image tormented the already troubled future prime minister, who was a passionate supporter of the South. Never in her knowledge of him, his wife later told her daughter, did he suffer such extremes of depression and nervous misery as at that time.[11]

The news of Lincoln's assassination jerked the British public into a swell of sympathy for the North. Condolences and tributes flooded into the American legation, and in the House of Lords what Moran had dubbed "the haughtiest aristocracy in the world" paid its respects to the late president. Moran noted, though, that when Russell was speaking for an address to the throne on the assassination, one of the "young lordlings . . . said he was sticking the Address into the American Eagle's beak."[12]

Lincoln's successor was Vice President Andrew Johnson, who had also been an intended victim on the night of the assassination, his life spared because his would-be assassin lost his nerve and fled from Washington. On May 6, 1865, there was a brief drama in London when it was thought, erroneously, that a man recently arrived in the country was Lincoln's assassin, John Wilkes Booth. The flurry of activity at the American legation did, however, result in a visit from Edmund Hammond of the Foreign Office. During the course of Hammond's meeting with Adams, Moran noted some verbal sparring in which Hammond said, "They kept their secrets well in the F.O. by allowing everybody to know them, and by trusting to *honour*." It was a remark Adams and his secretary might well recall in the near future.[13]

Aside from the effusions of praise for Lincoln, which filled the chambers of the Houses of Parliament, the fall of the South had left a question mark over future Anglo-American relations. In the dying days of the *Index*, Hotze had capitalized on the uncertainty by suggesting that a preemptive war against the United States would spare Britain possible reprisals by the victorious North, a notion that was nothing more than clutching at straws. The accord of belligerent rights to the Confederate States was partly withdrawn on May 11 and terminated on June 2.

Nevertheless, Anglo-American diplomacy was still strained. Adams was tenaciously maintaining his demands for compensation for the *Alabama*'s depredations, but the suggestion of referring the matter to arbitration vexed the foreign secretary. Quoting diplomat Sir Andrew Buchanan's words to Lord Clarendon, Russell wrote to Gladstone, "We have no arbitrator to whom we can refer. We always used to refer to the Emperor of Russia because he always decided in our favour. But now you have gone to war with Russia we must refuse arbitration."[14]

The government had to undertake some deep soul searching. At stake was its honor and integrity, and as Russell pointed out, "Her Majesty's Government are the sole guardians of their own honour."[15] It seemed inconceivable to him that a foreign power should sit in judgment of Great Britain. However, Russell's order to seize the *Alabama* had, by its very nature, confirmed the illegality of the ship, and he had since admitted, to Adams' gratification, that she had "escaped" from Liverpool.

How the *Alabama* had been permitted to escape remained a mystery, and the critical delay of three days in placing the papers before those law officers of the Crown able to consider them was a key factor in the intrigue. That delay, in the words of Charles Adams' historian son, Brooks, "has never been well accounted for, but . . . was momentous." The words are as true today as they were when the American minister's son wrote them in 1911.

CHAPTER 15

"Little Hudson"

In 1865, as some form of arbitration was becoming inevitable, Adams was standing by his conviction that the *Alabama*'s escape had been facilitated by a tip-off. But if Palmerston and Russell knew or believed as much, they did not betray the fact. In the absence of any revelations, during the early months of the year, diplomacy between Britain and the United States plodded on while at the American legation Adams and Moran were confiding daily in their diaries, the former rather more prosaically, although his opening line in the new journal he started on July 1 reveals his state of weariness with his position: "I commence another volume, still in England, contrary to my hope and expectations."[1]

The end of the war had provided Adams' secretary with a new impetus for his own diary. In the coming months Moran would pick over the debris of the Confederacy's operations in Britain and relish each nugget of information he could glean that vindicated the suspicions he had harbored during the war. His incisive mind eagerly sought out anything relevant to the events, and when Arthur and George Sinclair, who had served on the *Alabama* and *Florida*, respectively, called at the legation to swear the amnesty oath of allegiance, Moran seized the opportunity to quiz them. He was delighted when they corroborated all Dudley's reports about the *Agrippina*, the *Alabama*'s tender, as well as confirming Dudley's information on other suspect vessels. But most important to Moran was the desire to solve the mystery surrounding the *Alabama*'s escape. That would be a coup beyond the wildest dreams of a legation secretary with his grim basement life and constant malcontent, craving compliments from his superior. Yet Moran's dreams were about to come true.

At three o'clock on the afternoon of Saturday, July 22, "a little dark haired fellow with a long bullet head" arrived at the legation with information to sell. Moran lodged at the home of Joshua and Martha Nunn, who had become close personal friends, and it was Nunn, the vice consul at the legation, who had given the visitor a card of introduction. He introduced himself as Henry Hudson of Bridge Street, Hammersmith. Hudson's credentials, if true, were interesting. He told Moran he had been a subeditor of the *Index* and could supply a list of the people, apart from Henry Hotze himself, who worked on the paper. Hudson claimed to have been badly treated by the rebels and was now disposed to turn against them. His principal reason for calling at the legation was to sell information regarding a disputed cargo of cotton that presently lay on board the *Almie*, a vessel in port at Liverpool, and he went on to volunteer the fact that, according to the cotton's shipper, there was £2 million worth of rebel property in England.

Moran might have hesitated, but Hudson's inference that he could supply much more information of value to the legation appealed irresistibly to the secretary. "The fellow may be useful," he wrote in his diary, "but he is clearly a rogue and a needy one at that. Still, I think we should keep him and pay for his evidence if need be."[2] Henceforth, "Little Hudson," as Moran referred to his informant, became a regular visitor and increasingly gained Moran's confidence.

The suggestion that there was £2 million worth of rebel property in England was a niggling issue for those who believed that astute Confederates had made provision for themselves in the event of losing the war. It was a suspicion further fueled by the arrival in England of Judah P. Benjamin, well known for his shrewdness and guile. Having been a successful lawyer before the war, he now expressed a wish to practice in England. "Nothing is more independent, nor offers a more promising future," he wrote to a friend, "than admission as a barrister to the bar of London." The prospect of the Northern Circuit, which included Liverpool with its lucrative cases of mercantile and maritime law, was also appealing to him.[3]

Benjamin had fled Richmond just hours before the city fell, fearing personal reprisals by anti-Semitic Unionists. By using various disguises, which included that of a French peddler who spoke no English, he was able to make his way to the southwest coast of Florida, where he had friends who had been actively involved in blockade-running and supplying Confederate troops. For a short time he took refuge at the Gamble Mansion at Ellenton in Manatee County, the home of Capt. Archibald McNeill. Narrowly escaping federal troops, he made his way to Key West and thence to Havana, Cuba, from where he was able to take passage to Europe, landing at Southampton on August 30.[4]

Benjamin had made some judicious provision for his new life by purchasing six hundred bales of cotton, and although just one hundred "escaped Yankee vigilance," their sale enabled him to start his new life in England with $20,000. To this amount he added a further $10,000, which, he later explained, was the result of "information furnished by a kind friend in relation to the affairs of a financial institution in which I invested my little fortune."[5] He was settled in London when Moran noted in his diary that Dr. Robert J. Black had called upon him there to inquire when the Confederate bonds would be paid. "Never," replied Benjamin, raising his hands. "They are not worth a cent."[6]

Benjamin did indeed qualify as a barrister and went on to become a Queen's Counsel, taking time along the way to write his *Treatise on the Law of Sale of Personal Property*, which became a valuable textbook for generations of British law students. During his time as a "student" in London (his intellect and legal expertise were such that he had only to familiarize himself with the English system), Benjamin lived frugally, apparently giving lie to the belief that he had a pot of gold awaiting him in Liverpool, although he spurned the offer of financial assistance from Beresford Hope. Before long, he was so successful as a barrister that he was able to earn his own very comfortable living. That, however, did nothing to dispel Moran's belief that "Confederate treasure" had found its way to England.

Hudson was keen to show Moran he was keeping abreast of events. He revealed that Huse had left London and was now at Dieppe, and that Henry O. Brewer, who had helped Hotze finance his start-up of the *Index*, "went off" to Paris. A period of resolution that seemed to be following the South's defeat was now gathering momentum. Within the next few days, Moran would have the satisfaction of watching Charles Prioleau come to the legation with his solicitor, Frederick Hull, to provide his deposition for pending litigation.

While "Little Hudson" was whetting Moran's appetite for retribution, the country had been going to the polls in a summer election. Palmerston was now showing his age, occasionally falling asleep in the House, his hat pulled over his face so that members would not notice, and his memory was said to be unreliable. The great man was failing, and those politicians who sought electoral reform knew they had only to wait for him to die before their progressive ideas could move forward. It might have been an interesting prospect for Victor Buckley's father, politics standing on the brink of change, but the aftermath of the Civil War had brought opportunities to delve deep into its mysteries. General Edward Pery Buckley made a decision. He was sixty-nine and perhaps ready for retirement from politics, and whether or not he was persuaded by the possibility of forthcoming inquiries and revelations, before the general election that July he stood down as a member of Parliament.

For Henry Hotze, the months following the end of the American Civil War would have provided ample pause for reflection on his time spent in England. On a personal level, in January 1863 he had joined with Dr. James Hunt and the well-known explorer Richard Francis Burton, breaking from the Ethnological Society (of which Archibald Hamilton became a member) to help form the Anthropological Society of London, for which he sat as a council member.[7] The society held some racist views that Hunt believed lent legitimacy to the Confederacy's refusal to commit itself to emancipation.[8]

During the summer of 1864 Hotze welcomed a heroine of the Confederacy to his home. A Union vessel had captured the fearless spy Belle Boyd in May as she attempted to sail for England on board the steamer *Greyhound* carrying dispatches for Hotze. A romance developed between Belle and one of her captors, Prize Master Lt. Samuel Hardinge, who helped her escape to Canada. After a brief exile there she traveled to England and stayed with Hotze until August 25, when she and her fiancé were married. Hotze was no doubt one of the high-ranking Confederates who joined with British sympathizers to attend the wedding at St. James' Church, Piccadilly. Moran would later derive some pleasure from turning the penniless Harding away when he called at the legation begging for financial assistance.[9]

At the close of 1864 Hotze compiled his expense accounts for his secret service and sent them to Benjamin. They told their own story. In 1862, for example, "Entertainments, Presents and Miscellaneous Expenses" had accounted for more than £114. There was the cost of Havana cigars and American whiskey, which had warmed their recipients to his cause, and contributions to the library of the Anthropological Society. About other expenses he was more circumspect: "The delicate nature of such expenditures, some of which are not susceptible of vouchers, and others involve the names of persons and the expositions of motives not easily made in writing."[10]

Hotze was one of the last to leave the proverbial sinking ship. Perhaps buoyed by advertising revenue and subscriptions still in hand, he kept the *Index* alive. He reported the assassination of Lincoln and the succession to the presidency of Andrew Johnson; he announced the arrest of Jefferson Davis; and on June 1 he offered an emotional lament: "The South has fallen, the triumph of brute force and popular fury over national spirit and chivalrous devotion is complete."[11] He continued publishing until August 12, when the *Index* announced its own demise—*Our Last Number.* Then Hotze left for Paris, where Bulloch's paymaster, Felix Senac, with his wife and daughter Ruby, had already arrived, although they had moved on for the summer to Wiesbaden.

At the beginning of October a great many prominent people were feeling distinctly uncomfortable. Already, the war was a subject many of them wished to consign to the past, but now they suffered the embarrassment of having their names revealed as bondholders, subscribers to the Erlanger cotton loan. In purchasing bonds they had nailed their colors irrevocably to the mast, and they must now bear the scrutiny of the press and, at the American legation, of Adams and Moran. That revelation was a preliminary to a far worse one, but it was nonetheless startling. The names included Gladstone, several members of Parliament and peers of the realm, John Delane and Marmaduke Sampson of *The Times* (which had been considered pro-Confederate), and G. Seymour, principal proprietor of the *Daily News*, a listing that Adams found awkward because the paper's affiliation was with the North.[12]

Other events, however, soon eclipsed the bondholder news. Moran had decided to pose the inevitable question to Henry Hudson: "I asked him to find out for me the name of the person who furnished the rebels with information of the intention of the British government to stop the '290' and thus enabled them to get that ship away from Liverpool and avoid her seizure."[13] On October 21 Hudson returned to the legation with a "curious narrative." It turned out to be something of a red herring, but the story did contain some truth. Hudson claimed that a James or Joseph Buckley, who worked with someone by the name of Davidson at 57 Cannon Street in the City, was involved in recruiting for the *Oreto* and the *Rappahannock* and had a relative, Victor Buckley, working as a clerk in the Foreign Office. Mr. Buckley, he stated, furnished the information of the intended arrest of the ship to his relative, who at once communicated it to Fraser, Trenholm; Bulloch; and others. There was also, Hudson claimed, a Rev. Dr. Buckley implicated, as was a Liverpool firm, Beach, Root, and Company.

Between 1864 and 1866 a firm by the name of Joseph *Davison* and Company, merchants, had offices at the address Hudson gave Moran and, with two other Davison businesses, was on a list published by the *New York Times* of companies that were rebel agents.[14] A James Buckley ran a chandler's shop at 18 Dean Street, Holborn, between 1862 and 1863, but it is most unlikely that either trade establishment would have had a connection to the aristocratic Buckleys. Archibald Hamilton had a cousin, Robert Elias *Davidson*, who was staying at his home in Kent at the time of the 1861 Census. Like Hamilton, the twenty-seven-year-old Davidson described himself as a merchant in the colonial trade (the Tenerife connection) and could well have been present at business and social meetings with Hamilton and Bond.

Victor Buckley's elder brother, Felix, had come down from Merton College, Oxford, in 1861, having attained an MA. He had been curate of the church of Buckland-Monachorum in Devon from 1858 to 1861, and a year later he was in London officiating at a wedding at St. George's Hanover Square. The family had a connection to the Clapham Park Estate, which was becoming fashionably developed in the mid-century, and there is certainly the possibility that in London Felix had financial interests outside his clerical life.

The firm of Beach, Root, and Company had been established in Liverpool in 1861 by partners John Newton Beach and Sidney Dwight Root of Atlanta, Georgia. Both were originally from the North, but in 1858 the two had founded a rapidly prosperous business together in Atlanta. Sidney Root had been unable to join the Confederate army because of an injury sustained in a railroad accident (as a result of which damages were reputedly obtained for him by Abraham Lincoln's law firm, Lincoln and Herndon, which handled many railroad suits), and he was therefore available to be on the committee that accompanied Jefferson Davis to his inauguration as president of the Confederate States. John Newton Beach set up a Liverpool office in 1861 and from there operated the firm's successful blockade-running ships while Sidney Root concentrated on the American side of the business.[15]

Undoubtedly Beach made concerted efforts to cultivate contacts in high places. The store he and his partner had set up in Atlanta had not only grown from relatively humble beginnings into a highly successful enterprise, but both men had invested in property and quickly accumulated wealth. Beach appears to have been one of those confident and affluent Americans whose passion for the South had such a persuasive effect on so many members of Parliament and the aristocracy.

When his partner Sidney Root visited England in 1864, it was to promote the confidential idea of gradual emancipation being considered by the Confederate government. He later wrote in his memoirs that although Beach had previously introduced him in London "in order to enable me to meet prominent government officials in Europe," he was now a private gentleman with no commission. Confederate commissioner James Mason took him to visit the Marquis of Bath at his country seat, Longleat in Wiltshire, and he had been invited to the home of Lord Derby and "an intense Confederate Englishman by the name of Campbell, who seemed to know everybody" and who arranged for him to meet several members of Parliament at a house on Baker Street on a Sunday afternoon. The meeting consisted of "about a dozen men, including Lord Derby, all in the Opposition. . . . Lord Derby said that if he had had charge of the Government, he believed the Confederacy would have been recognized soon after the Seven Days' battles around Richmond." Root continued, "I had the satisfaction of hearing much of the information I had furnished quoted by Lord Derby in his address on the Queen's speech in the House of Lords," and he was convinced that with few exceptions, the aristocracy were sympathetic to the South.[16]

Mason then accompanied Root to Paris for exploratory meetings with Louis Napoleon on the gradual emancipation proposal. Apart from his memoir, Root subsequently produced a short book for his wife in which his descriptions of Liverpool, Manchester, and London—as well the Grand Hotel in Paris—provide a revealing American perspective on Europe at that time.[17] His partner, John Beach, was one of those bankrupted after the South's defeat.

Beach and Root had a link to the arms trade inasmuch as they shipped large quantities of Enfield rifles to the South, but there is no evidence to suggest that at the time of the *Alabama*'s escape, the standing of John Beach was such in society that a clerk in the Foreign Office would have risked compromising his reputation and career by making him privy to high-level confidences; a far stronger and more intimate acquaintance was required for such a consideration. But Moran was excited by Henry Hudson's claims and the fact that he had now had an actual name.

Moran immediately referred to the Foreign Office list, where he found confirmation that Victor Buckley was a clerk in the department in charge of state correspondence with the United States. "Much color is given to Mr. Hudson's statement," he remarked in his diary; on considering the implications he added, "If I can prove this charge, Britain will be obliged to yield at once their *Alabama* claim."[18]

Two days later Hudson was again forthcoming with information. He brought a list of sixty-four individuals and firms who were either agents for or suppliers to the Confederates, and he went on to suggest that Victor Buckley had been in communication with Henry Hotze, "through Joseph Buckley of the firm of Davidson, City, London."

One piece of news infuriated Moran: someone had listed a "Mr. B. Moran" as one of the subscribers to Beresford Hope's Stonewall Jackson Statue Fund, putting him down for one pound. "These rogues are up to all kinds of tricks," he complained in his diary that night. However, he was also ebullient about Hudson's revelations. "From what the little fellow tells me, it seems I am on the track of the person who gave the notice about the decision to stop the 290."[19]

So far, Moran had not thought fit to tell Adams of Hudson's revelations. Even at this early stage he must have realized that the information trickling through to him had the potential to be momentous, and he needed more time to set out his findings. In the meantime, Adams' attention, and indeed that of the whole country, had been diverted by some startling news: Palmerston was dead. The charismatic statesman who had dominated politics and held the hearts of the British public for so long died on October 18, and with the passing of this great champion of Waterloo men that era of unassailable pride was pushed a little further back into history. "This is another link with the past that is broken," Queen Victoria wrote sadly to Russell as she offered him the "arduous duties of Prime Minister."[20]

The official account of Palmerston's death indicated that he had caught a chill earlier in the month while out riding in his carriage on Lady Palmerston's country estate, Brocket Hall in Hertfordshire, but an alternative and more colorful version, which would have endeared his memory no less to the British public, was that the spry eighty-year-old actually died of a heart attack while making love to a parlor maid on a billiard table. The rumor was appealing to those who delighted in his rakish reputation, and to this day it is offered as a serving of relish to some histories of Brocket Hall and to the life of Viscount Palmerston.

The night before the funeral, Moran received a visit at home (the house of Joshua and Martha Nunn) from Henry Hudson, who now told him that the proceeds of sale from more than 2 million bales of cotton run out through the blockade during the war was on deposit at Gilliats in London. He also claimed that the Queen's own printers, Spottiswoode and Company, had printed the greater part of the *Index* as well as the handbills posted about London as propaganda to "cry down" the Reverend Henry Ward Beecher, brother of Harriet Beecher Stowe. Huse and Hotze had both now decamped to Paris, and Moran was persuaded to give his informant ten pounds to cross the Channel himself and further his investigations. "Hudson is after Buckley," he wrote in his journal.

While Moran awaited further revelations, changes were afoot at the Foreign Office. On becoming prime minister, Russell passed the seal to the Earl of Clarendon (Victor Buckley's relative by marriage), and with it the ongoing American claims, which were for the moment just a little less thorny. Sir Frederick Bruce, the British minister in Washington, had recently ascertained to everyone's relief that Britain's refusal to entertain the claims would not result in war—just a taste of its own medicine when Britain next found itself in the position of being a belligerent. The Foreign Office could now address the issue of whether or not Britain had preserved a faithful and diligent neutrality, a point on which Russell felt, publicly at least, confident.

The following month, on 6 November 1865, the last of the Confederate cruisers, the *Shenandoah*, sailed up the Mersey and struck her colors, having made the long, final journey home after learning of the South's defeat. Her arrival opened old wounds for Adams, and he vented his wrath in correspondence to the Foreign Office:

> This proceeding seems to have been the last of the series conceived, planned and executed exclusively within the limits of this kingdom. It emanated from persons established here since the beginning of the war as agents of the rebel authorities, who have been more effectively employed in the direction and superintendence of hostile operations than if they had been situated in Richmond itself. In other words, so far as the naval branch of warfare is concerned, the real bureau was fixed at Liverpool, and not in the United States . . . all the war made on the ocean has been made from England as the starting point.[21]

Adams was particularly incensed that none of the principal Confederate operators had been brought to justice, and he was pointedly referring to Bulloch when he railed, "It cannot, therefore, be at all a matter of surprise when the mainspring of the various enterprises, namely the director of the *Alabamas*, *Floridas*, *Georgias*, and *Shenandoahs*, was left wholly undisturbed."[22]

Clarendon's reply was couched in terms quite familiar to the American minister: "No information supported by evidence on which a prosecution could be judiciously instituted or successfully maintained had been laid before Her Majesty's Government for the purpose of showing that the laws of this country have been violated by any of those persons." On the subject of the principal naval agent, Clarendon wrote, "The agency of Capt. Bulloch for the Confederate Government was, indeed, to some extent disclosed by parts of the evidence relating to ships which were the subject of actual or contemplated proceedings by Her Majesty's Government, but not in such a manner, not to such an extent as to make it probable, in the judgment of Her Majesty's advisers, that if proceedings had been instituted against him personally, they would have been attended by a successful result."[23]

Clarendon did concede, however, that at least in one instance—the message to the captain of the *Shenandoah* to cease operations—the government had considered itself in possession of sufficient evidence of Bulloch's authority to control or prevent hostilities. But Bulloch had carefully distanced himself from the issue by using the former Confederate commissioner James Mason to relay the message via the Foreign Office.

While the past was being aired in London, an event was taking place on the other side of the country that no doubt provided some degree of comfort for one of the leading figures in the *Alabama* drama. On November 15 a service was held in the Church of Saint Mary Redcliffe in Bristol to mark the anniversary of the founding of the Canynges Society, a group of affluent benefactors dedicated to maintaining the fabric of the magnificent medieval building. With its tall spire overlooking the harbor, the church, dating to 1292, had witnessed the growth of Bristol through the centuries, its prosperity founded on the slave trade. It was from Bristol's harbor that John Cabot set sail in 1497 on the *Matthew* and reached the mainland of America, and there is a monument in the church to Admiral Sir William Penn, whose son founded Pennsylvania.

After the service, about one hundred people—the great and good of Bristol—attended a luncheon at which it was announced that restoration of the twelve pillars in the north and south transepts of the church would shortly be commenced, and the cost of six had already been provided. The benefactor of one of them was Sir John Dorney Harding, still incarcerated but nevertheless making a significant contribution to the city with which his family had a long and close association. That same month, a sixteen-foot-high stone cross was erected in his name on the south side of the church at Rockfield, Monmouthshire, bearing the inscription *In honorem Dei et memoriam avorum, J.D.H. 1865* (in the glory of God and in memory of ancestors).[24] By this time Harding's mental state had deteriorated further and these timely gifts, no doubt arranged by his wife, Isabella, lend themselves to be regarded as acts of contrition.

Predictably, John Bright spoke out in support of damages being awarded to the United States. In preparing his arguments for Parliament, he used a pamphlet written in 1863 by an American, Grosvenor Porter Lowrey (later famous as Thomas Edison's lawyer), titled *English Neutrality, Is the* Alabama *a British Pirate?*—an examination of international maritime law. Some time later Bright fell into conversation with a fellow traveler in a railway carriage whom, by coincidence, he discovered to be Porter Lowrey on a visit to England.

By the latter part of December the British press was reporting the stance of the new American president, Andrew Johnson, whose annual message seemed to bode well for Britain. "It is conceded," noted *The Times*' editorial, ". . . that no new differences can arise with England, and the President's high flown language on the subject of the *Alabama* Claims, as it is nothing but glittering generalities and expressly refuses to recommend any legislative measures for redress, is scarcely worth the paper upon which it is written." The same editor referred later to a dispatch by Lord Clarendon and remarked: "After the untoward escape of the *Alabama* no evasion of our law took place which could by any constitutional means have been prevented."[25]

There was no such mood of complacency at the American legation, where Moran had once again been receiving visits from Henry Hudson.

CHAPTER 16

Britain Is Condemned out of Her Own Mouth

Henry Hudson had not yet gone to Paris, being but newly returned from Liverpool, but Moran could hardly contain his excitement. "He got but little information about Buckley," he wrote in his diary, "but what he did get was good." Unfortunately for Moran, Hudson's report was not accurate. He claimed that Captain Butcher had left London on July 26, 1862, with the notice that the 290 was to be stopped, and that he arrived at the Angel Hotel on Duke Street in Liverpool at three o'clock in the morning of the 27th, a train of events that did not square with the facts. On other claims too Hudson had been only partially reliable; Eyre and Spottiswoode had indeed printed parts of the *Index*, but not the bulk of it, because the main printing house was that of Henry F. Mackintosh. Hudson's earlier linking of Victor Buckley to a modest commercial enterprise was extremely unlikely as well, and Moran may have thought as much, for when he reflected on the situation, he declared, "The next thing is to connect Victor Buckley in this matter." Hudson had produced one small piece of interesting and verifiable evidence: Buckley's name had been, and still was, on the list of subscribers to the *Index*. This and the other revelations with which Hudson was forthcoming prompted Moran to keep him on the payroll with regular payments of ten pounds to cover his expenses. As Hudson departed for Paris, the secretary's eager pen began a lengthy summary of what he knew. The report, sent to Seward in Washington, outlined Hudson's investigations and repeated the charge against Victor Buckley of "his having told the rebels that the government had decided to seize the 290."[1]

The ink was hardly dry when Hudson returned from France with the most damning evidence yet against Victor Buckley. In Paris, where Henry Hotze was now living, he had seen a note, "in H. O. Brewer's hands," a copy of which he now produced and handed to Moran:

> July 26th 1862
>
> The order will be issued "immediately" for Liverpool staying your protégé. Excuse haste,
>
> Ever truly,
> Vr. Buckley
> H. Hotze
> 17 Savile Row[2]

Moran quickly found a few notes the legation had received from the Foreign Office and showed them to Hudson, who was able to recognize some as being in the same handwriting; the style of signature on the copy note was also almost identical with that on the photograph taken of the Foreign Office clerks in August 1861. With another ten pounds in his pocket, Moran's informant was again dispatched to Paris.[3]

The note seemed to have more than a whiff of authenticity about it. The young, erudite Henry Hotze was a credible friend and confidant for Victor Buckley. His background and easy social graces had ingratiated him into London society, and the tenor of the note suggests a friendship that was more than a passing acquaintance. There was also a viable connection between Hotze and Frederick Bond at the London Armoury Company. Hotze, with his expert knowledge of arms, having been introduced to the company during his visit to England in the autumn of 1861, would undoubtedly have been informed by Anderson that Bond had claimed to have a near relative holding a confidential position in the Foreign Office. The reliability or accuracy of that statement aside, the "friend in the Foreign Office" mentioned in Anderson's diary had apparently since proven his worth to the Confederate agents. Henry O. Brewer, who had exported a vast number of arms to the Confederacy from Britain, was Hotze's friend and financier, and indeed, was in Paris at that time as Hudson claimed.

Adams had recently met with Clarendon to discuss the American claims, and the two men were thinking about ways forward toward reviving the negotiations. When Moran revealed his discoveries to his superior, Adams was shocked. He had met Victor Buckley several times in society, and Buckley had occasionally been "quite cordial" to Mrs. Adams and their daughters. But there was worse. He looked at the list of Confederate bondholders and found

Buckley's name there, for an apparent two hundred pounds. "This is not of itself conclusive evidence," Adams wrote in his journal, "because I find several other names in it which it is not possible to suppose have stood with the consent of their owners. They are all placed in one category by the fact that the interest due on the term is marked as not paid whereas the genuine subscribers are noted as having received it." Adams' interpretation may not have been entirely correct, although it is certainly possible that some influential names had been included to bolster interest from potential purchasers of the bonds. But he went on to concede, "Nevertheless, the fact is significant of a possible contingent interest had the rebellion succeeded."[4]

Adams was feeling particularly bruised. The mysterious publication of his correspondence with the Foreign Office regarding the cruisers in the *London Gazette* had prompted him to remark, "I am very much mistaken if Great Britain is not condemned out of her own mouth."[5] He was trying to deal with problems concerning his own personal property at home in the United States, and now he had learned that his secretary was writing reports to Seward behind his back containing highly sensitive information to which he was not privy. He assured Moran that he had done the right thing in alerting Seward, and agreed that Buckley's letter would go very far to settle the U.S. claims, but he must have been nettled by Moran's connivance.

Moran had even sent Seward a copy of the list of bondholders, and the secretary of state wasted no time in passing it on to the press. Soon it was being analyzed and printed in the *New York Times*. The occupation and standing of all the people whose names were on it had been studied and recorded—and their publication that must have devastated the investors. Apart from Gladstone and those members of the press already noted by Adams, the list included the predictable names of Beresford Hope (whose investment totaled £40,000), Sir Henry de Houghton (£180,000), the pro-Confederate London shipowner Thomas Sterling Begbie (£140,000), Lord Wharncliffe, Robert Cecil, James Spence, Charles Prioleau, John Laird Jr., and Sinclair, Hamilton, and Company. Also listed was G. A. Spottiswoode, "the Queen's printer" (the *New York Times* alleged Beresford Hope had introduced Spottiswoode to Hotze for the purpose of printing the *Index*, although his firm had never put its name to the paper), and a host of other names that would certainly create a stir.[6] Sir Frederick Pollock, who had presided over the *Alexandra* case and who had been a subscriber to the *Index*, was also among the bondholders, as were Rev. Francis Tremlett—once a curate at the Church of the Advent in Boston—and, most tellingly, perhaps, Victor Buckley, who was noted as having purchased 250 bonds totaling as much as £2,500. Buckley's name was also included in some "personal sketches" that accompanied the list: "This man is a clerk in that department of the Foreign Office through which passed all correspondence with and about the United States."[7]

It was there for the world to see, Victor Buckley's name under the provocative headline "The Rebel Loan" with a subheading, "Who Got Their Interest and Who Did Not." Buckley, it appeared, along with many other unfortunates, did not. The list had been compiled in 1864 at the payment of the last interest, showing which individuals had received their money, and its publication was met with fierce denials from some of those whose names were on it. By the very nature of the bondholding, the people concerned were condemned for their support of the Confederate cause, and when copies of the newspaper were received at the Foreign Office, with Buckley's position severely compromised, it is reasonable to suppose that the esprit de corps would have sprung into action to support a vulnerable colleague.

Yet this was no newspaper libel. The editors had chosen their words carefully to imply Buckley's special interest in Anglo-American affairs; they had made no specific allegation. It was just as well—the young man conceivably at the center of an international dispute with the potential to damage Britain's honor was a godson of Her Majesty Queen Victoria, and his father had been one of her valued equerries. No breath of scandal was allowed to taint the monarch. Even Adams, as aristocratic in his own way as any American could be in the republican system, would have appreciated that.

Buckley himself might have been feeling the pressure of the circumstances in which he found himself, but there was perhaps some consolation in the steadfastness of his engagement to be married. Since 1863 he had been officially affianced to Mary Stirling. A letter dated December 10 that year, written by Charles to Walter Stirling and apparently responding to the news received, confirmed the match: "I was very glad, as we all were, to hear of Mary's intended marriage, for many reasons. It is a great comfort and particularly as it seems to afford James and Ellen so much pleasure. All the accounts you have of the gentleman seem to be much in his favour, affording a prospect of happiness to Mary and satisfaction to all."[8] The death of Admiral Sir James Stirling on April 22, 1865, may have protracted the engagement further.

The New Year dawned, and on January 19, 1866, Adams had a meeting with Clarendon, although afterward he was not disposed to reveal the reason to Moran. As spring approached, the tenacious secretary was still paying Hudson and clinging to the hope that Buckley's exposure would dramatically affect the impasse over the American claims. These days, however, Hudson seemed to be procrastinating. He had been ill, he claimed, and had been robbed in Paris;

and when he had gone to collect all the papers relating to Hotze's involvement with Buckley they were gone—Hotze himself had removed them. Moran declared the story too theatrical but relented at last. "His health is broken and he looks bad. And as ugly as his course has been, I am disposed to have faith in him and try him again."[9]

Hudson was in fact becoming a drain on Moran's purse, providing only titbits of information to keep his paymaster biting at the bait. He had acquired the entire box of correspondence, he claimed at one point, and it included the original of Victor Buckley's note to Hotze. But then he said he was being watched and could not pass on the letters; he thought he should go to Le Havre and embark for America. Moran had his doubts but telegraphed John Bigelow, the American minister to France, to let him have the cash. "The affair looks shady," Moran conceded, "but I can do no better than go on now."[10] In the event, Hudson failed to follow through, and the papers were not forthcoming. On May 12 Moran wrote a full account of Hudson's reports from Paris and sent it to Seward. But the weeks were passing and now there was no further communication from the man.

The first day of August was Moran's forty-sixth birthday and an opportunity to indulge in a little self-pity. "What have I done?" he asked himself. "I am comparatively poor and my prospects are far from good." His mood of despondency was destined to last a little longer. Hudson came a few weeks later to announce that he had been obliged to hand the papers back but was offering to get them again. In the meantime, Adams had annoyed his secretary by revealing that he had written "privately" to Seward a full report of his last meeting with Clarendon, and he did not think it worthwhile to record it. "The result some day," Moran complained in his journal, "will be great confusion because these private reports cannot be found."[11]

That summer, for the first time in five years, Queen Victoria set aside her mourning for Prince Albert and attended the official opening of Parliament. Moran, whose bile was inclined to rise on grand state occasions, was annoyed to hear her proclaim the close of the American Civil War as a triumph of freedom over slavery. It smacked of hypocrisy to him in view of her announcement at the outbreak of the war and her expressed doubt about its result.

The diplomatic maneuvering over the American claims had now entered a quiet time. As a prime minister having to concern himself with the long-awaited Reform Bill, Russell was presiding over a slim majority in the House. Clarendon at the Foreign Office had taken only one initiative, to suggest that both countries should revise their neutrality laws and disclaim national liability in any case of future *Alabamas*—a suggestion promptly dismissed by Seward, who insisted that no negotiations could begin until the British government acknowledged the validity of America's claims.

Adams, his own reception in society being somewhat more cordial these days, sensed conciliation toward America among the new order in the Houses of Parliament, but the political pendulum was about to swing again. The defeat of Russell's government in the summer of 1866 put into place a new Conservative administration under the Earl of Derby, with his son, Lord Stanley, taking the Foreign Office. The change of government provided a new opportunity for Washington and provoked Seward to suggest that Adams should sound out the British about a settlement. The irascible secretary of state was worried by the inertia of the past months. It seemed to him that the political fervor surrounding the claims had subsided, and with Derby's new government now finding its feet, the moment was ripe to apply pressure.

In fact, the new foreign secretary was setting up a royal commission to review the neutrality laws and, for the moment, was quite content with the status quo. The perennial problem of Ireland was more worthy of his attention. Indeed, at the American legation, Adams was also dealing with fallout from the war related to Ireland. Revolutionary Fenians arrested for plotting an uprising against the British government had claimed to be American citizens, and whenever their status as Irish Americans could be proven, Adams worked to secure their release from British jails on condition that they leave the country.

During the war Ireland had been a ripe recruiting ground for the Union, much to the annoyance of the British government and the embarrassment of Adams. The Catholic Church, perversely, had leaned in favor of the Confederacy, not wishing to see the youngest and fittest of Ireland's men forsake their country for the United States. Confederate recruiters had likewise sought enlistments in Europe, prompting the Confederate commissioner Ambrose Dudley Mann (who had served as a diplomat in Europe before the war and arranged treaties with German principalities) to remark that the Germans "trained to war by the military system of their own little kingdoms and duchies, seem to sniff the carnage from afar."[12]

On the grander chessboard of the world, Seward was also keeping a wary eye on the Irish revolutionaries. Expansionist Americans had long viewed Canada as a tantalizing neighbor, and when the Fenians planned incursions and raids into that territory, the United States was quick to step in to suppress them, a move for which the British government was not entirely ungrateful.

As a dreary autumn descended on London, Moran was still clinging to the faint hope that Hudson would produce the ultimate evidence of Victor Buckley's treachery. At the end of October he endeavored to interest Dudley in the quest by sending Hudson to Liverpool. Matters looked hopeful when the "little man" returned with news that the U.S. consul was to accompany him to Paris, yet disappointment once again lay in store. Hudson returned alone from Paris a few weeks later with nothing to show for the trip, and Moran's patience was finally exhausted. "This, I think, will end our dealings," he wrote decisively in his journal.[13] Hudson made a final attempt to keep Moran on the hook, but this time his paymaster declined. The original of Buckley's note, the conclusive evidence that Moran so desperately craved, had eluded him, and the legation's secretary had to resign himself to that fact.

Across the Atlantic, Seward remained bullish. The Duke of Argyll described the U.S. secretary of state as "the very impersonation of all that is most violent and arrogant in the American character," and the bellicose Seward, once bridled by the calming hand of Lincoln and the influence of Secretary of War Edwin Stanton, was unfettered to dream wildly of retribution against Great Britain and ways of furthering his grand expansionist ideas.[14] His earlier nudging of Derby's new government had done him no good, for Parliament's summer recess provided a delay before the matter would again be considered. Russell's stance of self-righteousness had rather set the standard by which the government must proceed, and in his official response at the end of November, Lord Stanley predictably issued a robust defense against Seward's claims.

Behind the scenes, however, the Foreign Office was keen to reach some sort of settlement, and Stanley was tactfully inquiring whether America had any plan for resolution at hand. Crucially, he was also prepared to compromise and submit to arbitration, although Britain's refusal to bow to Seward's contention that premature recognition of the South as a belligerent had encouraged the dissident Southerners and led directly to the launching of the commerce raiders was to prove a major stumbling block. Thus another year ended with Moran no closer to conclusively proving Victor Buckley's guilt; Britain and America still deadlocked in their mutual desire to reach a settlement; and Adams still hoping his tenure of office would draw to a close so that he could return to the United States.

Victor Buckley's life, however, had changed dramatically in the past year. After their long engagement, he and Mary Stirling finally married on March 15, 1866, at St. George's Church, Hanover Square. Victor's salary from the Foreign Office was now about £450 per annum, and the couple's first home was no doubt modest in comparison with his father's town house in South Audley Street, where a butler, housekeeper, footmen, ladies' maids, and other residential staff made up the household.[15]

As to Frederick William Bond's connection to Victor Buckley, the claim was to remain unresolved. Bond's early years in the City had been lived in an incongruous world of guns, gold, and precarious finance where the line between the aristocracy and trade might at times be a little less well defined. The inquest into his father's suicide had touched on the precariousness of that life, memories of which became more opaque with the passing years.

The Foreign Office continued about its business as usual. With the exception of a brief move to the librarian's department (intriguingly, in 1862) Buckley had remained in the American department. He was there still, with a few years to go before significant promotion, but seemingly untouched by the scandalous inference the *New York Times* had placed on his position. With every passing month the momentous events surrounding the *Alabama*'s escape slipped a little further back in time.

In October 1867, over dinner in Baden Baden with the American politician, writer, and artist John Pendleton Kennedy, Lord Houghton, once a close associate of Palmerston, seemed at pains to reveal "a secret of the time." Lord John Russell, Houghton explained, who was "so much blamed for allowing the *Alabama* to escape the vigilance of the government, really could not help it, being prevented by a most inopportune accident." Russell had referred the question of the right and duty of the government to interfere with the sailing of the *Alabama* to the solicitor general. "This officer, just at this time became insane and, of course, gave no opinion. The government could not make known the real state of the case and was obliged to defend itself, as well as it could, without displaying the real cause. Mr. Adams knew the fact and made a generous allowance for it." It was this untoward event, Kennedy recorded in his journal, "that brought about all the trouble."[16] Sir John Harding's insanity was legally confirmed in May 1868 when his wife petitioned for a ruling by Her Majesty's Masters in Lunacy. The subsequent inquisition found him to be "a person of unsound mind" and unfit to manage his estates.[17]

Harding's disabilities aside, there were still grave questions about the *Alabama*'s escape. Had someone in the Foreign Office, or indeed the government itself, known of Buckley's alleged betrayal, or perhaps even condoned it? Had the young man's connection to Queen Victoria facilitated a cover-up? If so, was giving no credence to the allegations the most effective way to stem a potential scandal? Such a policy certainly echoed of Earl Russell's pride and Edmund Hammond's sense of honor.

The American claims would soon require a response, but the Foreign Office could draw on some powerful resources. To assist in addressing the legal issues of the claims against Great Britain the government turned to Mountague

Bernard, a distinguished international lawyer and professor of international law and diplomacy at Oxford who was highly respected for his powerful intellect. Bernard's intellectual stature would indeed prove invaluable, but first he was to access the secret archives of the Foreign Office.

In international diplomacy, common interests sometimes prevail to temper disagreements. In the highly charged and provocative situation involving the American claims, some type of Anglo-American fraternity or brotherhood would clearly be a useful tool. Such a brethren existed. Prince Edward, the Prince of Wales (and future King Edward VII), was formally initiated into the fraternity in 1868 and became its titular figurehead; Earl de Grey, who had joined Palmerston's cabinet as secretary of war in 1861, was an influential and highly respected member; and at the American legation, Joshua Nunn was a prominent "brother."[18] The brethren were the Freemasons. In the not very distant future, they would claim that the efforts of their Anglo-American fraternity in the *Alabama* claims had averted war between the two nations.

The Foreign Office had among its staff a rising star who was also a Freemason. The cool-headedness of Buckley's fellow clerk in the American department—the other old Etonian, Charles Abbott—was about to prove its worth.

CHAPTER 17

Prospects for a Solution

Charles Stuart Aubrey Abbott epitomized the perfect Foreign Office clerk—aristocratic yet personable, studious yet well respected, and in every way the type of gentleman on whose honor that department of government depended. Some four years older than Buckley, and with a dense beard lending an air of gravity to his features, he possessed no special credentials to advance through the Foreign Office ranks with any greater rapidity than might be expected, yet as Britain and the United States continued on their path toward settling the *Alabama* claims, an opportunity would present itself for his promotion. In fact, he would ultimately be promoted above the heads of all the senior clerks.[1]

Abbott's grandfather, as lord chief justice, had written the important *Treatise of the Law Relative to Merchant Ships and Seamen*, and maritime events had certainly played a part in his own career as the Foreign Office grappled with the problems of the Confederate cruisers. Now, in the early spring of 1867, Abbott could watch the continuing ebb and flow of prospects for a solution to the impasse, suspecting, perhaps, that he would soon play a major role.

Seward's response to Lord Stanley's bold rebuttal of the previous year was penned on January 12. He wrote that Great Britain should acknowledge and pay the claims outright, although he had no objection to arbitration. In that case, however, he would expect to refer the whole quarrel, just as it was found in the diplomatic correspondence, *together with whatever other evidence either party wanted to present*, allowing no conditions, restrictions, or limitations.

Adams felt Seward's stance was "scarcely conciliatory" and feared the negotiations for settlement might founder, but Seward was in fact keeping a weather eye on public opinion in the United States and protecting his own position at the same time. His expansionist policies had so far proven successful, with plans for the purchase of Alaska coming to fruition. By the summer he would express ebulliently to Adams' son Charles Francis Jr. the belief that "the *Alabama* Claims would soon be settled, but *now* they could only be settled in one way, by such acquisition from England as would enable us to round off our North-Western territory."[2] Seward had long since coveted Canada, but it was a notion Adams felt obliged, albeit tactfully, to dismiss.

Queen Victoria's proclamation of neutrality at the outbreak of the Civil War was a sticking point for Seward. For some weeks he appeared to be procrastinating, refusing to give up the sensitive debate about the proclamation, but the British government was adamant that Her Majesty's proclamation of neutrality should not form part of any arbitration, and would accordingly not concede on the point. Nor, Seward advised Adams, would the American people. The proclamation, he asserted, was "unnecessary, ungracious, unfriendly, irritating and injurious."[3]

In December Seward played his trump card, putting forward his proposal that America might purchase the Bahama Islands from Great Britain to settle the *Alabama* claims. "Mr. Seward's thirst for more land seems insatiable," Adams confided in his diary.[4] Privately, he despaired of the intransigence of both parties to the dispute and must have welcomed the spring of 1868 with profound relief. Seward had at last accepted his resignation, and he could return home.[5]

While negotiations moved from one stalemate to another, "Little Hudson" was still trying his luck with the American legation, going so far as to send Adams a bill. "He is," Moran concluded, "a double distilled rascal."[6] The Buckley revelations, it seemed, would be allowed to rest, but sooner or later someone would have to take the blame for the *Alabama*'s escape; a sacrificial lamb must be found for the altar. Russell was sensitive to any aspersions being cast on his conduct during the period in question and was still deeply protective of the country's honor, but John Forster, editor of the *Examiner*, made a suggestion that Russell found quite appealing: "Neither the Secretary of State nor the law officers were at fault, but that the official persons employed at Liverpool were wanting in due diligence, and that this country might, in reparation of that neglect, grant compensation for the losses incurred by merchants in consequences of captures made by the *Alabama*."[7]

Three years later, rather more at peace with himself over the events, Russell would state, "I assent entirely to the opinion of the Lord Chief Justice of England that the '*Alabama*' ought to have been detained during the four days

I was waiting for the opinion of the law officers. But I think that the fault was not that of the commissioners of customs; it was my fault as Secretary of State for Foreign Affairs."[8]

On March 6, 1868, Adams presented himself at court for the last time, dressed in full diplomatic uniform for his audience with Queen Victoria. Afterward he annoyed the legation secretary by maintaining a tantalizing silence. "Mr. Adams subsequently said nothing of what occurred at Buckingham Palace," Moran observed.

Less taciturn was John Laird in the House of Commons. On the day that saw Disraeli deliver his first speech as the Conservative prime minister, Laird was loudly cheered for declaring he was proud to have built the *Alabama.* But such uncomfortable reminders of his tenure in office were no longer of any importance to Adams; nor were the offers of a banquet in his honor, which he declined, as he prepared to leave London.[9] He sailed for America in May, unaware that feelings were running high against him in his own country because angry Irish Americans felt he had let them down over the naturalization issue stemming from the troubles in Ireland.

Moran became chargé d'affaires after Adams departed and enjoyed wielding the responsibilities of the post until Adams' replacement, former Maryland senator Reverdy Johnson, arrived in London in August during the long parliamentary summer recess. Another autumn would come before Johnson was able to seriously start his mission.

If Moran had found Adams occasionally irritating, he was shocked by the new minister's seeming indifference to old grudges. By December Johnson was receiving, of all people, "that rogue [Emile] Erlanger, the negotiator of the rebel loan." The French banker had brought a letter from his mother-in-law, Mrs. Slidell, for Reverdy Johnson, but Moran did not consider that a sufficient excuse for the minister to receive him cordially. "Indeed," Moran growled to his diary, "that gentleman is always gurling with rebels and their friends. The fellow sat here for half an hour telling Mr. Johnson what to say for him at the banquet tonight of the Franco American Cable Co. and got complete possession of the old man." Betraying anti-Semitic sentiments, Moran went on, "And this Jew is come here at 5 to take Mr. Johnson to dinner. I know not what will be said at home about these proceedings but if there be not a storm, I mistake my fellow countrymen."[10] With his customary eye for portrait detail, Moran noted Erlanger's features—"Erlanger is a young German with dark brown hair and large dark blue eyes . . . altogether a rather handsome man."[11]

In spite of his tendency to fraternize with the associates of former rebels, Johnson was committed to the task ahead of him. Seward had suddenly, almost inexplicably, abandoned his expansionist plan (public opinion, it has been suggested, was no longer in favor of it), and he was urging Johnson to settle the naturalization issue, which had been heightened by the refusal of the British government to release two imprisoned Fenians whose origins as Irish citizens bound them, in accordance with British law, to their mother country. Assured that a naturalization law would be passed in Britain the following spring, Johnson was instructed by Seward to pursue the other outstanding issues, which included, apart from the *Alabama* claims, a quarrel over fisheries and the San Juan dispute, a disagreement that predated the American Civil War and involved a difference of opinion as to the exact position of the middle of the channel between Vancouver Island and the mainland. The festering dispute had escalated to a more serious situation when an American on the island of San Juan shot a pig belonging to the Hudson's Bay Company. Both countries had agreed to submit to the arbitration of the Swiss Confederation on the matter, but the outbreak of the Civil War interrupted the process.

Johnson was well aware that Disraeli's days as prime minister might well be numbered because the power of the Tories hung on a slender majority, and accordingly he pressed for an early protocol before the government changed again. By November (the month that saw the death of Sir John Harding at the lunatic asylum in Gloucestershire) Johnson thought he had fared well.[12] Lord Stanley had been quite accommodating to most of the Americans' demands, but Johnson's efforts were seriously undermined by blustering telegrams from Seward that threw impossible obstacles in his path: a sudden demand that the commission formed to settle the other claims should sit in Washington, despite Johnson having agreed to London, and then orders to drop the claims convention entirely because Seward thought it discriminated against the *Alabama* claims.

Johnson experienced something of his predecessor's frustration when his superiors in Washington appeared to find his diplomatic efforts wanting. Moreover, his sense of urgency had been well founded, for on December 10 Gladstone, who had once so famously declared that Jefferson Davis had built a navy and made a nation, became prime minister. Returning to the post of foreign secretary in the new Liberal government was Lord Clarendon, who balked at Seward's demands and, like many others in the country, was irritated by the recent appointment of a known Fenian to the office of the U.S. consul at Leeds.

In the middle of January 1869, however, Johnson was empowered by Washington to proceed in accordance with his most recent negotiations with Clarendon, and three treaties were quickly signed, dealing with the naturalization issue, the San Juan dispute, and the other claims. The claims, which included some by British citizens who had suffered losses as a result of the Civil War, were to be referred to a commission in Washington, where two commissioners from each country would agree to decisions made by an arbitrator. While not openly acknowledging the inclusion of the neutrality dispute, Clarendon accepted that it would be introduced into the arbitration by the United States—a face-saving tactic whereby Britain was not admitting that a previous government had been prejudiced.

In Washington, the convention was scrutinized by Seward, the Congress, and, it seemed, every newspaper in the land before this latest, earnest attempt at reaching a settlement was defeated. By the spring, a more alarming tone was emerging from America. Charles Sumner, former chairman of the Foreign Relations Committee in Lincoln's government, made a bold and impassioned speech that captured the imagination of the American public. The British neutrality proclamation, he stated, was indefensible because it relied on the interpretation of Lincoln's choice of the word "blockade" instead of "closing ports," and British blockade-runners had used its protection to feed the South with munitions. The British government, while committed to abolition, had hastened to help the Confederacy and had fed it to the end with British supplies. The true cost of suppressing the rebellion, Sumner asserted, was more than $4 billion, a large proportion of which remained as a national debt for which Great Britain, having prolonged the war by this pro-Confederacy intervention, should be liable. Astutely, Sumner had also recognized the enormous ongoing losses that American mercantile shipping had suffered. Insurance costs had risen, tonnage had diminished, and imports and exports had fallen off. Sumner calculated the cost of the ships lost in the war and the destruction of American mercantile marine prospects to total $110 million.[13]

That was fighting talk. "The *Alabama* and her depredations and burnings, making the ocean blaze," were words uppermost in everyone's mind as they applauded the barrage of accusations against the British government. Expansionists resurrected Seward's desire to annex Canada, and in London, Consul Morse, who had watched relations between the two countries degenerate to alarming levels on more than one occasion, was moved to remark that the British thought war was next to certainty.

The press in Britain was quick to respond with indignation, and the debate was further inflamed when, on May 27, *The Times* printed a letter from the Lairds that defended their building of the *Alabama* and damned the government's defense. It had been a normal business transaction, they said, and there had been no haste or secrecy in the construction; the government, the public, and the American minister all knew that the ship was intended for the Confederates, and Lord Russell had had ample opportunity to seize her. The attacks on them, the Laird brothers concluded, were simply unjustified.[14]

And so the argument raged on, and the hopes for settlement entertained by Reverdy Johnson and Clarendon seemed a distant memory. With a few passionate words, Sumner had galvanized Britain and America into new heights of enmity. If any explanation was to be offered for his vitriolic eloquence, it would come from none other than Charles Abbott, who, in his later role in the proceedings, wrote that Sumner was "fool enough some year or so ago to marry a young and pretty widow. She found that he was not gifted with 'full powers' and has left him and I was told that there is a suit proceeding for dissolution *a vinculo*. He therefore makes up by vigour of tongue for his want of capacity in other organs."[15]

Abbott, like Buckley, had entered the Foreign Office under the patronage of Clarendon. He was destined for rapid advancement, but the reason why he was promoted above the heads of all the other clerks was destined to remain a mystery, with Foreign Office records containing only one indirect reference to his promotion.[16] Nevertheless, promotion did come easily and quickly. He had already written papers for Clarendon answering the American charges, and he had been appointed précis writer to Lord Stanley in 1866. But his eventual elevation to a very senior position came about through a series of fateful events that began in 1869 with the retirement of the assistant under-secretary, James Murray. Murray's successor, the Hon. Thomas Spring-Rice, died unexpectedly, and the post was then given to Odo Russell, who, in turn, was soon sent to the British embassy in Berlin.

The path that would shortly take Abbott to the prestigious position of assistant under-secretary was already opening in 1869 as events in America moved on. Former Union general Ulysses S. Grant had taken office as president in March and had appointed as his secretary of state Senator Hamilton Fish of New York. Along with the post, which Fish was reluctant to accept, came the legacy of the *Alabama* claims. But the new secretary of state was a capable, moderate, and patient negotiator who saw a flaw in Sumner's inflammatory words: Britain possessed the right, as did every sovereign power, to issue a proclamation of neutrality whenever it might choose to do so.

Between them, Grant and Fish decided to let tempers cool. Reverdy Johnson was returning to the United States, and his replacement, John Lothrop Motley, had not yet taken up his post, so a period of inactivity seemed judicious. Despite receiving instructions to that effect, however, Motley, to everyone's dismay, upon his arrival in London sought a confrontational meeting with Clarendon. A furious President Grant was in favor of demanding his immediate recall, but Fish thought the best way of averting a crisis was to allow Motley to remain in his post for the time being while ensuring that all negotiations were conducted in Washington. Fish established a cordial relationship with the British minister in Washington, Sir Edward Thornton, and by 1870 had brought the desired calming of tempers.

Charles Abbott was now about to undergo the metamorphosis that would ensure his name a place in the pages of history. On the death of his uncle, the second Baron Tenterden, he came into the family title and was henceforth known as Lord Tenterden. As a colleague of Buckley, Tenterden had been privy to the entire history of the *Alabama* problem, and his rectitude and strong sense of protectionism made him the perfect choice for an enhanced role in the *Alabama* claims. Moreover, he seemed to have a sharp grasp of the situation, identified grounds for compromise where such existed, and recognized the importance of arbitration. In 1871 Tenterden would be appointed assistant under-secretary, a post which, in 1873, would lead him to fill the vacancy left by the retirement of Sir Edmund Hammond himself, that of permanent under-secretary of state for foreign affairs.

If intrigues abounded in the Foreign Office, at the American legation Moran was unwittingly creating a mystery too. Charles Dickens, arguably the most popular writer of his time, had instigated an acrimonious separation from his wife, Catherine, in 1858. The total estrangement gave him the freedom to pursue his relationship with the young actress Ellen Ternan, and it has been said that communications between Charles and Catherine Dickens ceased. In 1870 Dickens was renting a house at 5 Hyde Park Place in London from which he could continue the public readings of his works, which were in great demand. The house belonged to Thomas Milner Gibson, MP, and Dickens was occupying it until the end of May. On April 26, 1870, Moran made a curious entry in his diary: "Dined with Mr. Charles Dickens and Mrs. Dickens at 5 Hyde Park Place, the house of Mr. Milner Gibson." There were several other guests present (including John Delane, editor of *The Times*), and Moran clearly enjoyed the evening. It is unusual for Moran, who was so precise in his diary, to be wrong about the company he was keeping, and yet none of Dickens' biographers have suggested that Catherine Dickens was present with her husband at any event following their bitter separation. Just six weeks later Moran would be visiting Dickens' grave in Westminster Abbey.

On May 11, at about one o'clock, Lord Tenterden called at the American legation to discuss the draft of the naturalization treaty that Clarendon and Motley had been authorized to sign.[17] Moran and Tenterden were to review and sign the draft document, and they adjourned to a private room for that purpose. Moran, of course, knew that Tenterden had been formerly Mr. Abbott in that sensitive department of the Foreign Office, and his association with Victor Buckley must have been on the secretary's mind. It is unlikely that Moran breached etiquette by mentioning Buckley, and he made no record of doing so in his journal. And yet, three days later something occurred that precipitated a significant change in his life. A note arrived for Moran from Tenterden. It was a small gesture of courtesy, perhaps typical of Tenterden's amiability, but Moran must have read and reread it, and thought it worthy of copying in the pages of that closest of friends, his journal: "Thanks to your care and attention, the treaty signing yesterday went off with a smoothness which I trust is of happy augment for future negotiations."[18]

At last, the recognition, the praise that Moran had so often craved had been bestowed on him—and by a member of the British aristocracy, an associate of Victor Buckley, no less. They were but a few words, yet Moran swelled with pride at their significance. From that point on his diary entries exhibited a newfound confidence as London society seemed increasingly to be opening its doors to him.

The effect was not immediate—in his annual complaint to his diary on August 1 he was bemoaning a milestone: his fiftieth birthday: "It is a mark in any man's life and I must say I have reached it somewhat a disappointed man." Yet now he seemed to accept Emile Erlanger's presence at dinners with a degree of equanimity. Before long, Disraeli himself would talk to Moran and introduce his wife, Lady Beaconsfield, with whom Moran had an interesting conversation about his favorite subject, art. Suddenly Moran was no longer a misfit in England. He attended grand banquets at Stafford House and Northumberland House, inspecting their internal architecture with the eye of a practiced dilettante, and visited Buckingham Palace without suffering the ignominy of standing in the minister's shadow. Tenterden's few words, if they had not been intended to buy Moran's discretion, had certainly imbued him with a rather different perspective on his situation.

Motley was recalled to Washington on December 6, 1870, and Moran prepared for the arrival of yet another minister under whom he would serve, this time Gen. Robert C. Schenck, whose military rank stemmed from the Civil War.

In the meantime, changes were taking place at the Foreign Office. The sudden death of Clarendon (while working at his desk in the office) had brought Lord Granville to the post of foreign secretary, and with him came a renewed impetus to settle the *Alabama* claims. The long period of inactivity had set the scene for fresh overtures to be made to the United States, and to this end an appropriate representative was appointed.

Granville turned to Scottish-born Sir John Rose, who had immigrated with his family to Canada while in his teens, studied law, and built up a successful commercial law practice. Rose had held important positions in Canada's legislative bodies and government and was a director of several major banks. In 1860 Rose had managed the arrangements for the visit of the Prince of Wales to North America. The future Edward VII had stayed at Rose's palatial residence in Montreal before continuing to the United States, and during that stay the two established a strong rapport. Eventually Rose became financial adviser to the prince. Rose came to prominence in Washington in 1863, applying his skills to the settlement of the dispute between the United States and Britain over the boundary between Oregon and Canada. The following year he was appointed to represent the British government on a joint commission established to settle the claims of the Hudson's Bay Company and the Puget Sound Companies. The American counsel to the commission was Caleb Cushing, a statesman and diplomat with whom Rose struck up a friendship (both were Freemasons), and who was also to play a part in the *Alabama* claims.

In 1869 Rose became a partner with the American tycoon Levi Parsons Morton (fiscal agent to the U.S. government) in Morton, Rose, and Company, a bank in London that would be the counterpart of Morton, Bliss, and Company in New York and deal with fiscal matters relating to the Joint High Commission that would be established to settle the *Alabama* claims.

The British government made a prudent decision in choosing Rose to lay the foundations for a satisfactory resolution to the *Alabama* claims. When he set off for Washington it was on the pretext of establishing commercial arrangements between the United States and Canada, but in fact his mission was to meet Cushing (whose expertise was currently being employed in the Department of State) and negotiate an accord. "We are taking several bites at that big cherry—reconciliation with the States," Granville wrote to John Bright, concluding after explaining the role Rose was playing, "We of course wish Rose's mission to be a *perfect secret*."[19]

Behind the spotlight of the political stage, Rose and Cushing worked quietly to lay the necessary groundwork. The English mediator returned to Washington in early January 1871 in a confidential capacity as the officially accredited agent of the British government. That same month the representatives of both governments agreed to form a Joint High Commission that would meet in Washington and consider all the subjects in dispute. With the prospect of a settlement now looking decidedly tangible, Britain and America moved swiftly. Even before the Republican-controlled Senate had rid the Committee on Foreign Relations of the extremist Sumner, the commission was being established.

The joint high commissioners representing the United States were Secretary of State Hamilton Fish; Gen. Robert Schenck, the newly appointed minister to Britain; Samuel Nelson, a revered associate justice of the U.S. Supreme Court; Ebenezer Rockwood Hoar, former attorney general; and George Henry Williams, who was soon to be appointed attorney general. The secretary of the commission was Assistant Secretary of State John Chandler Bancroft Davis.

The British government chose for the commission eminent and well-respected men: Earl de Grey and Ripon, president of the council and a member of Gladstone's cabinet; Sir Stafford Northcote (later Lord Iddesleigh); Sir Edward Thornton, the British minister to the United States, who had worked tirelessly to bring about the commission; Mountague Bernard, the legal expert; and Sir John Alexander Macdonald, the premier of Canada. In a twist of irony, Sir Stafford Northcote had traveled on the *Deerhound* to Egypt in November 1869 to be present at the opening of the Suez Canal. Sold by her much-maligned owner John Lancaster in 1868, her fame was enhanced by claiming the distinction of being the first British steam vessel to enter the Suez Canal.[20]

Britain's secretary to the Joint High Commission was a man long since poised to take up the position whose inside knowledge of the Foreign Office during the crucial time qualified him for that role: the assistant secretary for foreign affairs and an obvious choice for the post—Lord Tenterden.

CHAPTER 18

The Massive Grievance

It was ironic that behind the British government's eagerness to settle the *Alabama* claims lay the awareness that if the opportunity were not seized, problems might be stored up for the future. Yet that indeed was to be the case, and it was due largely to the commissioners' eagerness to come to terms when the British met with their American counterparts in Washington toward the end of February 1871. Both parties to the Joint High Commission were irritated by the interference of their respective governments as they worked out the principles for the desired arbitration—sitting in some thirty-seven sessions between February 27 and May 8. But they built on the good works of Sir John Rose and Hamilton Fish, who at the beginning of the year had discussed in a conciliatory and gentlemanly manner the possibility of Britain stating that the *Alabama* had been allowed to escape from Liverpool as the result of the incompetence or treachery of a local official, and the government had therefore become liable for the escape, a statement that could be combined with an expression of regret for the consequences.

The brethren of Freemasons played an important part in mollifying tensions between the two sides. The distinguished members of the Grand Lodge and the Masons of the District of Columbia gave a reception and banquet for Earl de Grey, grand master of the Masons of England, and his fellow diplomats, with guests arriving from all over the country; among them were thirty senators and representatives.

There were other social events too. Sir Stafford Northcote wrote in his diary of "dinner parties, dances, receptions, and a queer kind of fox hunt, with picnics and expeditions in the beautiful Virginia country, [that] alternated with serious business and grave discussion."[1]

The discussions certainly embraced a great deal more than America's "massive grievance," Sumner's label for the *Alabama* claims. Also on the agenda were the outstanding fisheries issue, the San Juan dispute, and the ever-present problem of the hostile Fenian raids and incursions across the Canadian border. When Fish hinted to Lord de Grey that the cession of Canada might end the quarrel, the earl "contented himself with the dry remark that he did not find such a suggestion in his instructions."[2]

The telegraph lines between Washington and London buzzed. Britain did not want to be judged on the rules for neutrality that would be set down for the forthcoming arbitration but which had not been in place during the American Civil War. Gladstone also objected to the Americans' use of the word "rebellion" because it undermined Britain's stance in acknowledging the South as a belligerent.

By Friday, May 6, the wording of the Treaty of Washington had been agreed, both parties had read the documents, and ribbons were placed ready for the final ceremony and sealing. "Confirmed the protocol and then made flattering speeches to one another," wrote Northcote in his diary. In such good spirits the commissioners exchanged signed photographs and kept bits of the ribbon as mementos.[3]

The actual signing of the Treaty of Washington on Monday, May 8, 1871, was a turning point in Anglo-American diplomacy. A room was decked out with flowers sent in by the ladies for the occasion, and the signatories to the document assembled. The brightly shining sun seemed a good omen, and Tenterden and his American counterpart, John Chandler Bancroft Davis, jovially tossed a coin to determine who should sign first. The British won the toss, and thus was sealed the case and countercase, the arguments and the responses, that were to be placed before the arbitrators.

Northcote had been especially ebullient, not to say arrogant, when the wording of the treaty had been agreed, writing in his diary, "Latterly, I think we have had the whip hand of them, and de Grey has managed Fish most skilfully."[4] America's eminent Masons were less haughty but nonetheless self-satisfied. They had deplored "the general tone of the English press" but asserted that "Freemasonry has its press as well as its influence and we are very proud as Masons to acknowledge that this 'cousinly spite' has never found its way into the English Masonic press." The American Masons stressed that Masons and non-Masons alike would "have to learn" that two treaties had been signed:

one by the Joint Commission of the Department of State, and a separate one at the Masonic temple between the American and English Masons. "The first may or may not be successful in settling the political differences which have existed between the two countries. On this issue politicians differ . . . but we are sure that the second is already producing the happiest results, in securing a warmer and kindlier feeling between the peoples of the two countries."[5]

The *London Freemason*, the leading organ of Freemasonry in England, reciprocated: "That our ancient science of Freemasonry can contribute to so blissful a result none but the veriest skeptic can doubt, and that it *will* may be fairly predicted from the cordial relations which are now established between British and American Craftsmen."[6] Britain's *Masonic Mirror* crowed about the success rather more pointedly:

> The visit of our M.W. Grand Master to the United States of America, on an important mission, which though of a political nature, was, as stated by him, of a truly Masonic character, the chief object—that of establishing and cementing friendly relations between the two great branches of the Anglo-Saxon race. It would not be too much to say that the enthusiastic reception of our Grand Master, as a Mason, lent additional weight to his well-known character as an able statesman and diplomatist, and that Masonry thus may claim a share in the happy work of settling differences, which in other and less judicious hands, might have lead [*sic*] to a serious rupture between the nations concerned. It is gratifying to record that in recognition of his services on this occasion, Her Majesty has graciously raised our M.W. Grand Master to the rank of Marquis, under the title of Marquis of Ripon.[7]

For his services Tenterden was rewarded with a Companion of the Most Honourable Order of the Bath (CB), an acknowledgment of conspicuous service to the Crown.

On July 4 the U.S. flag was hoisted on one of England's most impressive country houses, Alton Towers in Staffordshire, home of the 19th Earl of Shrewsbury, a Freemason who had just been appointed by Earl de Grey, provincial grand master of the county. A lavish reception and banquet then followed for a party of visitors from the United States—representatives of the Knights Templar. "The Star Spangled Banner" and "God Save the Queen" were sung, and complimentary speeches were made by brethren from both countries. A banquet was also held in Blackfriars, in the City of London, to reciprocate the hospitality the British Masons had received in the United States.

On the face of it, the treaty signed in Washington appeared most satisfactory. The first article contained a statement "in friendly spirit" expressing "regret felt by Her Majesty's Government for the escape, under whatever circumstances, of the *Alabama* and other vessels from British ports and for the depredations committed by those vessels."[8] The treaty contained forty-three articles in all, the first eleven of which dealt with the *Alabama* claims, the generic name for *all* the claims stemming from acts committed by the Confederate vessels, and provided for their referral to a tribunal of arbitration that would sit at Geneva and be composed of five arbitrators (to be chosen by Great Britain, the United States, Switzerland, Italy, and Brazil) who would decide all the issues laid before them on the part of both governments. The hand of Mountague Bernard was evident: three rules were also agreed upon governing the duties of a neutral government in respect of vessels intended to carry on war against a power with which it is at peace, although the British government did not accept them as a statement of principles of international law that were in force at the time the claims arose. In order to strengthen the friendly relations between the two countries, however, the arbitrators could assume that Great Britain would act on the principles set out in those rules in the future.

An honorable basis for settlement had thus been reached. But in the heat of their fervor to seal an agreement the commissioners had allowed an ambiguity to creep in involving *indirect* claims—grievances involving the very considerable damage to the United States itself, such as the prolific plunder and burning of vessels by the *Alabama* and the other cruisers and tenders of the Confederate navy that had prompted shipowners to register under foreign flags. One commentator went as far as to say that "the commerce of the United States had been almost totally wiped out of existence."[9] Further, the treaty did not properly address the cost to the U.S. Navy of pursuing the cruisers.

For the moment, however, a sense of achievement still prevailed, and the signing of the treaty in Washington had been a moment to be captured for posterity. And so it was, by the well-known American artist Francis Bicknell Carpenter, who had painted the famous *First Reading of the Emancipation Declaration by President Lincoln*, to which this work would be a companion. Although not actually present at the signing itself, Carpenter was invited to a banquet and reception given for the British commissioners on the eve of their departure, and there he was able to study their personal characteristics. Interviews with the American commissioners enabled him to reconstruct an image of the seating, familiar poses of the individuals, and other minor details that enabled him to create a retrospective yet important work of art.

Carpenter discarded three canvases before he was satisfied. The final image measured five feet by eight feet and was presented to Queen Victoria in 1891 (twenty years after the historic event) by Abraham Lincoln's son, Robert Todd

Lincoln, then American ambassador. The painting was at Windsor Castle for a time but then disappeared. The only image remaining of it is a photograph of the artist himself seated before the canvas, which is still on its easel. In a later published explanation of the work and the poses of his subjects, Carpenter wrote, "It should be remembered that these sessions were secret, neither photographers nor reporters were admitted, and the two secretaries' reports were therefore the only record of those very weighty proceedings. Lord Tenterden is regarding his manuscript."[10]

The actual presentation of the painting to Queen Victoria was marked by a dinner in New York on December 1, 1891, in Carpenter's honor. Among the eminent people invited who sent their regrets was Frederick Seward, son of the recently deceased William Seward, who wrote of the Treaty of Washington, "A sense of relief was experienced throughout the civilized world. The threatened conflict was averted. International good feeling gradually began to grow again between the two branches of the English speaking race, separated by the Atlantic."[11]

Carpenter himself was well acquainted with prominent figures on both sides of the ocean, many from the press and literary world, and was a friend of the American newspaper editor Horace Greeley. In 1868 he was present at a dinner given for Charles Dickens' second visit to America, and he received visiting cards from Arthur Conan Doyle and Malcolm Doyle.

In order that the Treaty of Washington might take effect, the designated governments soon chose their arbitrators for the Geneva Tribunal. The United States appointed Charles Francis Adams, and Great Britain put forward Sir Alexander Cockburn, Lord Chief Justice of England. Italy fulfilled its obligation by appointing Count Frederic Sclopis of Turin, a distinguished lawyer and judge; and the president of the Swiss Republic chose Jacques Staempfli of Berne, a prominent figure in business and political circles. The fifth arbitrator, appointed by the emperor of Brazil, was Baron d'Itajuba, who was then in a diplomatic post in Paris. The Treaty of Washington had also provided that each party should name one person to attend the tribunal as its agent, to represent it generally in all matters connected with the arbitration, and America and Britain availed themselves of their two secretaries who had struck up a rapport in Washington—John Chandler Bancroft Davis for the United States and Tenterden for Great Britain.

To assist him in the demanding role ahead, Charles Francis Adams took as his personal secretary his son Brooks, who had been at school in England during his father's tenure as minister there. Brooks was destined to become a respected historian, and when he set off for Geneva with his father in November 1871 he was embarking on an experience that would provide excellent material for his future work.

Each country appointed counsel to represent its case. Britain chose Sir Roundell Palmer, assisted by Mountague Bernard and Thomas Sanderson; the United States called on the distinguished Washington lawyer Caleb Cushing, William Maxwell Evarts of New York, and Morrison Remick Waite from Ohio, with Frank Warren Hackett assisting.

The arbitrators had their first meeting in December 1871 in the room set aside for the tribunal in the Hotel de Ville in Geneva, and Tenterden was given a copy of the American case. In London the new American minister, Robert C. Schenck, left copies at the Foreign Office. No one, it seems, allowed the reading of the papers to interfere with the festive season, and it was not until after Christmas that scrutiny of the American case revealed the inclusion of the indirect claims that Sumner had so vehemently advocated and for which the United States was demanding reparation of $2 billion.

For a time, the arbitration stood in danger of collapse. In their eagerness to reach agreement in Washington, the commissioners had overlooked a serious flaw in the treaty, which at best could be described as a misunderstanding, and at worst as a deliberate ploy on the part of the Americans to adhere to Sumner's extravagant demands in spite of the amicable rhetoric. The impasse created considerable annoyance in Great Britain, with the mood of the press and Parliament once again furious. The tribunal was temporarily adjourned. Adams returned to the United States, and Moran cynically noted in his journal that the six-month delay that followed was nothing more than a chance for the Americans to see Europe with their families.

The Foreign Office, during the hiatus, benefited from a chance mishap. Soon after his appointment the previous year, one of the American counsellors, on leaving the offices of the Department of State in Washington where he had been in consultation with Secretary Fish, had the misfortune to drop the secret papers of the case of the United States. The person who found the package, aware of its potential value, promptly took it to the British legation and disposed of it for a price. From there, it found its way to London.[12]

Britain had been hoping that the dispute with the United States could be settled quickly and amicably because problems were potentially looming with Russia over the Black Sea. It may therefore have been a subtle bluff when Tenterden requested a further eight-month adjournment as soon as the tribunal reconvened on June 15, 1872, a move that demanded of Adams his most finely honed diplomatic skills. Consulting his colleagues one by one, he brought them round to a face-saving proposal whereby the arbitrators should make a spontaneous declaration that on the principles of international law, the indirect claims ought to be excluded from their consideration. It was a successful move that kick-started the tribunal and earned Adams the lasting respect of Tenterden, who considered that "the dignity, tact, self-command and moderation with which Mr. Adams discharged his functions as arbitrator, did honour to his country."[13]

And so the American case was heard—the accusations that Britain had pursued an unfriendly course toward the United States; the duties that, as a neutral, it should have observed; its failure to perform those duties; and, of course, the activities of the blockade-runners and the cruisers. One by one, the names were wheeled out—the *Florida* (with the claim that *before* the ship left Liverpool the British government had received information from the king of Italy that the vessel was not being constructed for the Italian government), the *Rappahannock*, the *Georgia*, the *Shenandoah*, et alia, but none more notorious than the *Alabama*.[14]

Through the seemingly endless accusations, Adams had to relive the torment of his frustrated efforts to stop the cruisers. The most damning indictment of the British defense, perhaps vindicating his suspicions, would appear in print later that year when a noteworthy American lawyer, Charles Cotesworth Beaman, in his treatise on the *Alabama* claims, stated, "When Earl Russell admitted to Adams that the cases of the Alabama and Oreto were a scandal, and in some degree a reproach to English laws, he knew of some reasons for the delay to seize the '290' which he had never given to Mr. Adams, and of some scandalous act of English officials which has never been made public."[15] Beaman's treatise also quoted a statement made by Semmes describing the *Alabama*'s departure as "just in time": "That morning the seizure was to have been made. At the very moment that 'No. 290' was heaving up her anchor, a huge dispatch 'On Her Majesty's Service,' was travelling down to Liverpool at the top speed of the north western mail, commanding the Customs authorities to lay an embargo on the ship."[16]

The British government might plead the mental breakdown of its chief law officer in mitigation, but on the subject of the *Alabama*'s escape the American case stated, "The departure of the 290 from Birkenhead was probably, it may be said certainly, hastened by the illicit receipt of the intelligence of the decision of the Government to detain her."[17] That the government must have inevitably reached that decision, and her guilty status was established, was implied (firstly) "by the opinion of Mr. Collier who, soon after giving it, became a member of Her Majesty's Government, under the lead of Lord Palmerston, and with Earl Russell as a colleague. They must, therefore, be held to have adopted his views on one of the most important questions, half legal and half political, that came before Lord Palmerston's Government for determination."[18]

It was not an unreasonable assumption, and if true, condemnation of the *Alabama* may well have preceded the law officers' supposed first sight of the final papers intended for Sir John Harding. Adams recalled the copy of the warning note from Victor Buckley that Moran had shown him and confided in his son Brooks, showing him the diary entry he had made at the time. Oddly, either Brooks' memory was later at fault or he had misread his father's writing, for one day he would state that the note had been addressed to Caleb Huse. Brooks made the error in his paper titled "The Seizure of the Laird Rams," which he presented in 1911 to the Massachusetts Historical Society. He referred to his father's diary entry of December 22, 1865, which, he asserted, contained the following: "Incidentally he (Mr. Moran, secretary of legation) told me that he had also been able to trace the source of the betrayal of the decision of the Government which prompted the sudden escape of the *Alabama*. He showed me what purported to be a copy of a short note signed by V. Buckley and addressed to Mr. (Caleb) Huse, the rebel agent, warning him that what he called his 'protégé' was in danger. This Victor Buckley is a clerk in the Foreign Office."[19]

Moran's journal clearly shows the name Hotze, as does the diary of Charles Francis Adams, but Brooks Adams' error was to be picked up and repeated, in good faith, by subsequent historians. It was a mistake that the historian E. D. Adams, author of the definitive *Great Britain and the American Civil War* (1925), would repeat in a quote, and it would be taken up in 1940 by George W. Dalzell in his book *The Flight from the Flag.* Thus was laid a false trail that obscured the path to the truth and enabled the facts and the motivations of the protagonists to be buried in the sands of time. The legacy Brooks Adams inadvertently left became an example of what the historian Frank J. Merli (author of the classic *Great Britain and the Confederate Navy, 1861–1865)* would have aptly described as "the baleful influence of error."[20]

Victor Buckley's name, however, did not appear in the official case of the United States. His close friend and fellow Foreign Office clerk, Thomas Sanderson (later dubbed the "super-clerk" for his skill and service), had supported him throughout the difficult times and assisted in the preparations for the arbitration, which he then attended. Whether through lack of evidence or tactful diplomacy, Buckley's role in the affair had been buried before Adams left his ministerial position in London. Queen Victoria, it has been said, was very keen to see the *Alabama* claims settled. Perhaps, behind the desire for good Anglo-American relations and a preference to restore British equilibrium (republicanism favoring the American system had reached a new height in England in 1871) lay a personal wish that the potential scandal involving the son of her former equerry should not gain credence. Whatever the intrigues behind the public face of the Queen and her government, some words in the U.S. case hold a certain truth: "Flagrant as was the violation of neutrality in the case of the *Alabama*, it was but a part of the great scheme which was set on foot when Huse, Bullock [*sic*] and Fraser Trenholm & Co. combined together in Liverpool."[21]

Far from Liverpool now, in a large hall within the ancient Hotel de Ville in Geneva, counsel for both governments aired the "massive grievance." Great Britain, its counsel asserted, *had* observed due diligence in performing its duties as a neutral; and in the case of the *Alabama* the British government had taken a little more time in satisfying itself that there were sufficient grounds to warrant seizure than the United States thought necessary. At times the arguments became heated, and after one particular exchange of words, Sir Alexander Cockburn and the usually placid Charles Francis Adams both rose to their feet as if to leave the table in protest. Yet no one could doubt the momentous significance of settling the *Alabama* claims—and settled they were. The arbitrators found for the United States; Great Britain would not bear responsibility for the activities of the *Georgia*, which Matthew Fontaine Maury had built, but it was culpable for the depredations of the *Florida* and the *Alabama*, as well as for the *Shenandoah* once she had left Melbourne, Australia, where she had put in for repairs.

The British arbitrator, Sir Alexander Cockburn, was furious at the decision and gave vent to his anger, but by now all that was left to decide was the amount of damages to be awarded. Cockburn considered his country liable for the *Alabama* alone and suggested $4 million, but the other arbitrators unanimously settled on $15.5 million (£3.2 million) in gold. Cockburn refused to sign the public statement, but his sourness failed to affect the other parties to the arbitration, who had been socializing amicably when away from the hearings. Frank Warren Hackett, secretary to the American counsel, Caleb Cushing, reflected later, "We were not unmindful of the fact that the United States aimed not only to settle the *Alabama* Claims by gaining an award, with the proceeds of which to make reparation to those who had suffered losses, but what was of greater moment, to sow the seeds of a new and lasting friendship with England. . . . We began to look upon the two parties as one family—trying to make up a family quarrel and start anew."[22]

That sense of goodwill would endure. Hackett's sentiments were later reciprocated in London by Henry Markheim, the amiable secretary to the less conciliatory Sir Alexander Cockburn: "I think the results of the Geneva Arbitration are more and more appreciated, and will continue to be so, by the two countries, now that our family quarrel is settled."[23]

The final paper detailing the tribunal's decision and the award of damages was to be signed on Saturday, September 14, in the room that would thereafter always be known as the Salle de l'Alabama at the Hotel de Ville. Geneva had been in a festive mood for some time, with a musical fête and fireworks display held toward the end of August, and representatives of the British and American press had swelled the town's population. On September 11 the federal government arranged for the arbitrators and others concerned in the tribunal to be taken by special train to Berne, where the president of the Swiss Confederation received them in the chamber of the Council of State. Cockburn declined the invitation, but Tenterden did attend, the only prominent Englishman to do so. The party was treated to a trip to Interlaken and, on their return to the capital, attended a state dinner.[24]

At 2:30 on the afternoon of September 14, the doors of the Hôtel de Ville were thrown open to allow people other than those involved in the arbitration to attend the conclusion. Apart from members of the press, the crowd included British and American visitors who would afterward hear a twenty-two-gun salute fired in celebration of the historic event. History is silent regarding whether any of the protagonists in the *Alabama* story were present, yet it is with little sense of surprise that we find at least one of them in Switzerland at about that time. Just five weeks later, on October 24, 1872, Frederick William Bond married Marion Turner, younger daughter of the late George James Turner of Cheltenham, Gloucestershire. The wedding took place at the British embassy in Berne.

CHAPTER 19

The Foreign Office Thief

Charles Francis Adams could at last close the chapter of his life that would forever ensure the association of his name with the *Alabama* and the acutely fragile nature of Anglo-American diplomacy. En route back to the United States, he stopped off in London and paid a visit to Earl Russell, whom he found quite deaf but little changed otherwise. It was a poignant meeting for both men as they looked back on a troubled period in their lives, and Russell took the opportunity to confide in his old adversary that at the crucial time when the Laird rams were built and Adams had made his "this means war" threat, he had personally ordered the seizure of the vessels without consulting the law officer Sir Roundell Palmer, who, he thought, might dissuade him. Palmerston had approved the decision, and Palmer later defended it in Parliament. After the escape of the *Alabama*, it seemed, the British government had indeed decided to close the stable door.

In this exchange of conciliatory words Adams, for his part, pointed out that the nature of the decisions that had been made bore "much less in the government itself than in the laxity of the officers whom they trusted."[1] And so the two wise statesmen made peace with each other.

By December 1872 the San Juan dispute had been settled—in favor of the United States. For many years, however, and perhaps into the next century, the *Alabama* claims lingered as a ghost in the background, an ancient grudge to which complainants on both sides of the Atlantic might refer in default.

The man responsible for building the *Alabama*, James D. Bulloch, remained in Liverpool and became a naturalized British subject, a supporter of the Conservative Party, and something of a bête noire to Gladstone. He settled into the gentility of Liverpool's middle-class society and adapted to the life and commerce of the city, embarking on various business ventures, with varying degrees of success. When visiting America for a time he was obliged to travel under an assumed name because his own was on a proscribed list that his unforgiving mother country maintained. Tragedy struck in February 1871 when his young son, Henry Dunwoody, died at the age of nine. He was buried in Anfield Cemetery, but his remains were later disinterred and laid to rest in the cemetery at Toxteth where Bulloch's wife, Harriott, was buried in 1897. The headstone also bears the name of his son James Dunwoody Jr., who died in 1888 and was buried in Lynchburg, Virginia, where he had been engaged in the tobacco trade. This piece of ground in Toxteth is Bulloch's own resting place as well and an enduring reminder of Liverpool's link to the Confederate States of America.[2]

Bulloch remained stubbornly reticent about the identity of the informant whose warning enabled the *Alabama* to escape. His memoirs, written in 1883, contain statements that were clearly intended to be evasive but sometimes also simply distorted the truth. He referred to the arbitration at Geneva and to the British countercase, rebutting allegations in those documents that the departure of the *Alabama* from the Mersey was "hastened by the illicit receipt of intelligence of the decision of the British Government to stop her" and pointing out that the report of the law officers was not made until July 29. No decision had been reached when the vessel left, his defense continuing, "if it had been so, the British Government could never be held responsible for the treachery of some unknown subordinate, who may have become informed of their decision or may have anticipated that it would be made." That statement, Bulloch contended, was rather an insinuation than a charge, and he went on to a categorical denial that "any officer, high or low, in any department of the Government, did ever convey to me, or to anyone who afterwards repeated it to me, a word or a hint which led me to anticipate what the action of the Government would be, or was likely to be in any pending case."[3]

That robust denial must, however, be considered in the context of Bulloch's life in England at the time he wrote his sensitive memoirs and set against his own proud boast in the same recollections of a "private but most reliable source" from whom he received his information and who gave him "the means of knowing with well nigh absolute certainty the state of the negotiations between the United States minister and Her Majesty's government."[4] The *Alabama*'s captain, Raphael Semmes, who resolutely defended the legality of the vessel for the rest of his life, admitted that she had come "within an ace" of being seized. A letter written by Bulloch just five days after her departure and to be carried by his brother-in-law Seth Grosvenor Porter to Navy

Secretary Mallory included the message, "He [Mr. Porter] can tell you why I was forced to send the *Alabama* away before the arrival of Captain Semmes and can inform you of the difficulty I have experienced."[5]

In the face of so much pressure to reveal the truth, Bulloch carefully gave himself a caveat:

> Although the Confederate Commissioners were not officially recognised, and therefore could have no diplomatic intercourse with the Government, it is well known that outside official circles they were received with very marked and gratifying cordiality, and it is probable that through private friends, Mr. Mason could and did have very favourable opportunities of learning the general, and in some instances the specific, purposes of the government. Whatever he learned that had any bearing upon our naval operations was always repeated to me without delay, and the information thus received often proved to be correct, although it was gathered merely from conversation with those who were accustomed to observe the conduct of ministers and to draw their own conclusions, and not from statements of any persons who were in a position to know the actual purposes of the Government.

Read from the distance of the twenty-first century, Bulloch's words have a tone of prevarication.

So anxious was Bulloch to protect his associates that he stretched the truth in the case of his dealings with the Lairds and rather discredited his own recollections by stating that after the *Alabama*'s departure, Mathew Butcher did not enter the Confederate service and the two did not meet again for many years. In truth, Mathew Butcher's connection to Liverpool remained strong. He was actively involved in the fitting out of blockade-runners and captained the steamers *Southerner*, *Julia*, and *Owl*. In the autumn of 1864 a Liverpool newspaper reported Butcher's death in Bermuda, where yellow fever was raging, describing him as "perhaps one of the greatest Confederate navigators afloat, second only to Semmes . . . indeed he has always played an important part in Confederate business in English waters."[6] The newspaper had been misinformed of his death, however, and subsequently published a retraction. Butcher was proud of his association with the South and used a portrait photograph of himself in Confederate naval uniform taken by the respected photographer Marcus Guttenberg as his *carte de visite*. After the Civil War, financially comfortable, he married his Liverpool sweetheart, Louisa Jane Wells, and captained vessels for Jardine Matheson in the Far Eastern trade before becoming a shipowner himself. It was on his forty-eighth birthday, in his cabin on the SS *Moray* in the harbor of Hong Kong, that he penned his memoir of the *Alabama*'s escape. Butcher died in Edinburgh in 1904.

Bulloch's memoirs fail to answer many of the questions posed by the legendary escape of the *Alabama*, but then he was, as his associate John George Witt, lawyer and assistant to Henry Hotze, later recalled, "gifted beyond all men with the power of holding his tongue and guarding his secrets."[7] The Confederate commissioner James Mason, whom Bulloch brought conveniently into his smoke screen of explanations, had in fact been the most prominent figure smoothing Henry Hotze's path into society and into the sphere of those most sympathetic to the Confederate cause. Since Moran showed that Hotze was the recipient of the note from Victor Buckley, Bulloch's implication of Mason does his rebuttal no favors.

In looking to the future, passionate Confederates such as Matthew Fontaine Maury had envisaged Mexico as a utopian new world for their ideals, but that dream was not to be. The withdrawal of French troops had left the puppet emperor Maximilian exposed, and the army of Benito Juárez executed him by firing squad on June 19, 1867. When the news reached France on July 1, it fell to Louis Napoleon's wife, Eugenie, to break the tidings to his widow in her room at the Grand Hotel in Paris.

There was to be a rather novel happenstance in the summer of 1878 when Jefferson Davis visited England, to be greeted, not unsurprisingly, by Beresford Hope. Before moving on for stays with the Earl of Shrewsbury at Alton Towers and friends in Glasgow, and a visit to Great Yarmouth, Davis was reunited in London with Judah P. Benjamin, by then a successful barrister. John George Witt took his American guests to his old school, Eton College, where they had lunch with Provost Goodford—who had been headmaster when Victor Buckley was at the school. While there, Davis and Benjamin added their signatures to the visitors' book in the Eton College Library.[8]

As to the other players in the drama, Maj. Caleb Huse and his family lived in France for a while, in a house owned by Emile Erlanger, before returning to the United States. After several failed business ventures, he eventually set up a successful school preparing students for entry to the Military Academy at West Point. In his old age he was prevailed upon to write his memoirs, but the resulting pamphlet contained no revelations. Huse had consigned the American Civil War to the past, and his readers had to be content with a few anecdotes. He died in New York State in 1905 leaving a rather ironic legacy—one of his sons became an admiral in the U.S. Navy.

The Confederate paymaster, Felix Senac, and his family moved from Paris to Wiesbaden, Germany, where they stayed while a cholera epidemic gripped the French capital. Following Senac's death in 1866, his widow and daughter Ruby returned to Paris, where Henry Hotze was living. On December 9, 1867,

Hotze married Ruby Senac at the American legation. The couple enjoyed reunions with other Confederates in exile, but Hotze's life took another turn as he became embroiled in Romanian politics. In the arms industry he was a partner in the business of Friedrich von Martini (whom he may well have known in his youth and who was noted for the Martini-Henry rifle) trading as Martini, Hotze, and Company at 24 Rue de Lisbonne in Paris. He did not lose contact with his British friends, and Eyton Bond was no doubt one of them as he corresponded on arms matters with the factory of the Birmingham Small Arms Company.

Around 1870, with Prussia threatening the peace, Hotze left for England, but he returned even before the siege of Paris had ended, and he and his wife were soon traveling again, this time visiting Constantinople. As the years passed, disillusioned with French politics and with failing eyesight and deteriorating health, he relied increasingly on his wife for help. He died on April 29, 1887, in Zug, Switzerland; a death notice appeared in the *Mobile Register.* Ruby Hotze returned to America and spent the rest of her life in Washington, working for the newly organized U.S. Weather Bureau.[9]

John Laird would never shake off his controversial association with the *Alabama*. The whole affair, with the resultant damage to British pride, may well have left a bitter taste in the mouth of Queen Victoria, for legend has it that he believed she personally blocked the knighthood to which he felt entitled. Another object of her prejudice was Austen Henry Layard, who had hardly concealed his scorn at the elitism of the aristocracy. Such views may well have persuaded the Queen to deny him a peerage (Robert Cecil, by then Lord Salisbury, also opposed it), but Layard did receive recognition for his work on the British Museum, for which a bust of him was commissioned. In later years he abandoned his radical ideology and became a Conservative. He died in London in 1894 having bequeathed eighty works of art from his collection to the National Gallery.

Benjamin Moran was elevated in 1875 from his disenchanted existence in England as the legation's secretary to U.S. minister to Portugal, a temporary rank before relegation again, this time to chargé d'affaires at Lisbon. In 1882 he tendered his resignation and, in failing health, chose to live out his days in England rather than America. He died at Bocking Hall, the home of Joshua and Martha Nunn, at Braintree, Essex, on June 20, 1886. That same year saw the Freemasons' founding of the Joshua Nunn Lodge at Halstead in the same county. After Moran's death, Nunn fulfilled a promise to his friend. He sent a crayon portrait of Moran to Moran's sister, Mrs. Mary Moran Mcmanus, in Philadelphia and presented to the city of Philadelphia a painting of George

Washington along with the diaries Moran had so assiduously kept.[10] With those came the stipulation that they should not be published until five years after his death.

Victor Buckley was at last given promotion at the Foreign Office. In February 1872 he was made assistant clerk. The following year he attended a commission of inquiry into consular establishment in ports north of Germany and the Baltic. In December 1875 he served as secretary on (Sir) Stephen Cave's special mission to Egypt with a commission as acting secretary of the legation, a position in which he was the senior Foreign Office representative.[11] Victor and Mary, with their four children, had set up home at 28 Stanhope Gardens, Kensington, and lived to a high standard with a household staffed by nine servants. Mary Buckley's name appeared in the correspondence of the eminent artist James McNeill Whistler, who had painted her sister's portrait.[12] If Buckley had overzealously embraced the Southern cause in his youth, he had by now consigned that episode to the past. His father, General Edward Pery Buckley, died on May 18, 1873, after spending his final years as colonel-in-chief of the 83rd Foot Regiment in Ireland.

In the meantime, Frederick Bond's life and career had been progressing most satisfactorily. He and his wife, who was fourteen years his junior, lived for a time at his home in Victoria Street, Westminster. Through her family's Gloucestershire connections he became a director of the Banbury and Cheltenham Direct Railway Company and, in London, of the less successful Latimer Road and Acton Railway Company. He was still highly respected in the arms fraternity, though holding no company directorships in the industry. But of greater importance was his position with the African Steam Ship Company, which in time would place his name once again in the same arena of mysteries as that of Victor Buckley.

For some years the directors of the African Steam Ship Company had not been capitalizing on the firm's potential. Their flagship, the *Macgregor Laird*, was wrecked in December 1871, and two years later there were only nine vessels in the fleet. The company was also facing competition from a group of Glasgow businessmen who had formed the British and African Steam Navigation Company, appointing as their agent Elder, Dempster, and Company. The firm sailed further into stormy waters when it was discovered that the company secretary had embezzled about £20,000 and invested it in jewels. The subsequent loss of an important mail contract compounded the problems.

Matters reached a head in 1875 when an urgent meeting of the directors (who included Edward Barnett) was convened at 79 Great Tower Street, the company's City office. The need for drastic action provided an opportunity for

Frederick Bond to join the board, placing him just one step away from heading the company. That year the African Steam Ship Company turned in losses and moved to cheaper premises at Great St. Helen's, also in London. The directors instigated a ruthless plan, dispensing with the services of the company's Liverpool agency, Fletcher, Parr, and Company, whose owners then canvassed the shareholders for support. By now, though, the company was passing into shrewder hands. A year later, the chairman resigned and Frederick William Bond was unanimously elected to replace him.[13]

Bond was now in a very powerful position, although in the days ahead the African Steam Ship Company would have to claw its way out of its difficulties. Trade with Africa was still increasing, and the Dark Continent was becoming of great importance to the British government—a fact that would not have been lost on Victor Buckley, who had been moved to the African department at the Foreign Office. In 1877, in order to deal with the heavy workload now being generated in the department, a subdivision was created for the consular work and Buckley was placed in charge of it.[14]

While Bond and the directors of the African Steam Ship Company had been grappling with their problems, the breakup of its traditional agency structure had provided an opportunity for an enterprising young man by the name of Alfred Jones, who would one day become Britain's most influential figure in the African trade. Jones had started his working life in 1859 at the age of fourteen by joining one of the African Steam Ship Company's vessels as a cabin boy on a return voyage to West Africa. He soon became a junior clerk at the offices of William and Hamilton Laird (at that time the company's agents in Liverpool) before moving on to the Lairds' successors, Fletcher, Parr, and Company, in what was to be the beginning of a long association with Frederick Bond and agents Elder, Dempster. By the time the African Steam Ship Company had decided to dispense with the services of Fletcher, Parr, Jones was climbing the ladder of success.

Under Bond's management the African Steam Ship Company was still the jewel in the crown of African trade, and Jones, who had wisely set up his own business in 1878, was keeping an eye on its shares. He began buying them whenever they came on the market (as indeed he was already doing with shares in the British and African Steam Navigation Company and Elder, Dempster), engineering himself into a position whereby his experience and forceful personality, matched to a substantial share ownership, would eventually reward him with control and, with Bond, an assured entrée to the Foreign Office.

The year 1878 was also a watershed for the British government (now under Disraeli's premiership again) and for the Foreign Office, where a major scandal was about to erupt. Robert Cecil, now the Marquis of Salisbury, had long since recovered from his acute depression arising from the South's defeat in the Civil War. He was now approaching the prime of his political career, but before the coveted premiership came his way he was to fulfill the post of foreign secretary, replacing Lord Derby. Disraeli (now Lord Beaconsfield) was fortunate in his choice; a pending international crisis had reached its climax, and Britain teetered on the brink of war with Russia.

The momentous events leading up to that crisis threatened to redraw the territorial map of the world (the British government fearing Russia would gain control of major trade routes), and a compromise was reached with agreement to convene for the Congress of Berlin on June 13. Disraeli knew that the success of the conference at home in Britain would satisfy the prevailing mood of jingoism. It might also reinforce the contempt he felt for pedantic bureaucracy and for which he had coined the unflattering term "Tenterdenism." However, the Congress of Berlin would not conclude without a monumental scandal emanating from the Foreign Office—one that Victor Buckley may well have observed with interest, if not an uncomfortable reminder of the past.

On February 11 of that year, Buckley had acted as secretary to the Duke of Abercorn's special mission to invest the king of Italy with the Order of the Garter, but in the months following his return, he would find the office overburdened with work and obliged to employ the services of a temporary copyist even in an area of high confidentialty. That copyist was Charles Marvin, who would create a scandal that would shake the Foreign Office and, in doing so, provide an important insight into the ethos of that department of government.

Marvin was a writer and journalist whose modest earnings from freelancing for the press necessitated additional income from another source. He was an intelligent young man with an in-depth knowledge of Russia, where he had lived before returning to England, suffering from ophthalmia, in 1875. Working with his engineer father, and as St. Petersburg correspondent for the *Globe* newspaper, Marvin had traveled throughout the czar's dominions and was fluent in Russian, French, and German. Nevertheless, he was met with rejection slips when he tried to write articles on the country for British periodicals. When he learned that he could earn thirty shillings a week as a writer, or copyist, in the Civil Service, he "gladly acted upon the advice, and wrote to the Commissioners, offering my pen to the Crown." The Civil Service would bitterly regret accepting the offer.[15]

Marvin's intellect exceeded the demands of the monotonous job. His travels had given him a well-tempered view of world affairs, but he maintained a journalistic cynicism. When he was rebuked for working too hard during the time he was assigned to the Customs House, he realized that civil servants paced themselves so that their day was not unduly arduous; from then on he referred to them as "Barnacles."

Marvin considered himself a gentleman, but he was not of that sector of society to which the word was more closely applied by birthright—the Victor Buckleys of the world. He was destined to remain in the cold hinterland between the struggling, working middle class and the prosperous, if not intellectual, breed of gentlemen who peopled the Foreign Office. It was an uncomfortable existence. His experience of life, gained in a variety of posts ranging from working in a city warehouse to teaching languages in Russia, equipped him intellectually but was sniggered at by the junior Civil Service clerks, the "fourpennies" who had access to his curriculum vitae. Marvin did in fact possess one unusual talent; he had developed a system for memorizing written words. By 1877, having fulfilled various mundane roles from the issuing of dog licenses to making entries in countless ledgers, Marvin had sufficient income from his freelance journalism with the *Globe* and the *Morning Advertiser* to consider setting up his own school of linguistics, a plan he abandoned when a letter arrived unexpectedly from the Civil Service Commission offering him a temporary position in the Foreign Office.

The Foreign Office Club, as he dubbed it, provided ample fodder for his cynical observations—the Passport Office, he noted, was the only department having intercourse with the vulgar herd, the "damned British public." Through open doors could be seen "Poodle or Fitzpoodle poring over the *Pall Mall Gazette* and wondering why on earth the public worries itself about such matters which concern the Foreign Office alone." In one room a gigantic window and balcony had "a capital view of the quadrangle and the Barnacles at the India office opposite, hard at work at their papers—I do not mean official documents, but newspapers."[16]

Marvin also concluded that if the Foreign Office concern were farmed out to a city contractor, the whole business of the place might be done with one-third of the staff, at one-sixth of the cost. But the ethos, the tradition, and the privilege of the Foreign Office were unshakable, and Marvin knew it. He tried not to provoke the arrogant permanent clerks—one of them kept a brougham and drove down to the Foreign Office every day from Cadogan Place—who did not hesitate to remind him of his lowly status. While Marvin was paid a meager ten pence an hour, less able men with substantial private incomes received as much as eight hundred pounds a year. "A Garter Mission," like the one attended by Buckley with the Duke of Abercom, Marvin noted, "costs the Queen, or rather the country, between £5,000 and £10,000. Of this sum, a by no means inconsiderable share finds its way into the pockets of the Barnacles at the Foreign Office."[17]

Marvin considered himself a cut above the other supernumerary writers. "I should have had little to remind me that I was only a Tenpenny," he wrote, "but whatever fancies I might gather round my position to hide from my vanity that I was acting as a drudge in the Barnacle Service, I had to cast them off on Monday afternoon when, with the common herd, I had to scramble for my pay at Cannon Row, and to sign for my 30 shillings in the presence of a crowd of shabby-genteel and residium writers. To hear my name called out in connection with such a crew was humiliation. It irritated my self respect."[18]

Remuneration, however, was not quite everything. Marvin found some consolation in the excellent library at the Foreign Office, which kept him supplied with books. Nevertheless, his resentment would eventually reach the boiling point. On asking his superior why he had been chosen for the vacant seat in the Treaty department, he was told that the clerk had wanted no ordinary writer—a mere penman and nothing else—but someone who knew languages and was a gentleman. Marvin compared his £90 a year with the £150 that the messenger who waited on him received and was indignant that "'someone who knew languages and was a gentleman' should be valued at half the pay of a flunkey."[19] That conversation finally destroyed any vestige of loyalty Marvin might have felt for the Foreign Office. He had no wish to be considered a Foreign Office spy, but, in his own words, "I was the only Writer at the F.O. The only writer was a Journalist. This anomaly was a source of exquisite pleasure to me for a while. It was such a good joke that I had not the heart to destroy it." Marvin was also trapped in his dual role. "The Press did not know that I belonged to the F.O. and the F.O. did not know that I belonged to the Press."[20]

Marvin's chance to exact revenge on the Foreign Office came with the Congress of Berlin and was sparked by uncomfortable memories of one of the key figures in the proceedings, Count Peter Schouvaloff, whom he recalled being responsible for political prisoners in St. Petersburg being flogged and held without trial. This, Marvin thought ironically, was the person to whom Lord Salisbury had referred, in his circular of April 1, as "My dear—my dear!—Count Schouvaloff."

By May, Marvin had sufficient freelance work to warrant leaving the Foreign Office, where, to his amusement, his own articles about the Russo-Turkish War were frequently read out loud and, in the library, entered in the Political Register. "It never occurred to Lord Tenterden," he reflected, "to inquire whether I could not assist the Office with my recognised knowledge of Russia."[21]

On the afternoon of Wednesday, May 29, Hervin, one of the clerks in the Treaty department, was summoned to the office of the superintendent to take dictation from Lord Salisbury's private secretary. On one of Hervin's return visits to his desk to collect more paper, Marvin caught the words "la frontière de la Russie en Asie" coming from the office and guessed correctly that, in line with recent rumors, some important compromise had been reached for the projected Congress of Berlin. The following day, Marvin was asked to make copies of a document headed "Memorandum No. 2 for the Use of the Cabinet only," a continuation of work already under way. He employed his "Stokes Memorising Technique" as he wrote, and later had the opportunity to read over Memorandum No. 1 with the superintendent, who wanted to check its correctness. After first having to remove a copy of the *Morning Post* (a paper for which he wrote) from the chair he was invited to sit on, he proceeded to "Stokes" the document. He was later able to "go over it a second time to strengthen the hold of the document upon the memory pegs" before the copies were taken to Lord Salisbury's room for Ambassador Schouvaloff and the foreign secretary to sign.

Marvin thought the terms of the agreement a disgrace, with nothing but concessions to Russia, and overheard the clerks expressing their own astonishment. It had been arranged that a statement would be made in the House that night and that the agreement would be published in *The Times* within a couple of days. Without hesitation Marvin decided to preempt *The Times*. He had not been bound to secrecy, he reasoned, and the public was entitled to read about the Anglo-Russian Agreement immediately. He went straight to the offices of the *Globe* in the Strand. The following afternoon, a furor erupted in the Treaty department when the terms of the agreement, supposed to be still a secret from Austria, appeared in the *Globe*, which had gone to print the previous night. The *Globe* had it before the Queen.

Suspicion eventually fell on Marvin. A delay of one week occurred, however, until an order was received from Salisbury (who tactfully waited until the close of the Berlin Congress) ordering Marvin's arrest for stealing public documents. While detectives searched his rooms, Marvin coolly sat down and penned his resignation from the Foreign Office.

After a night in a bug-ridden cell, he appeared at Bow Street Court, represented by a defense lawyer hired by the *Globe*. He was initially branded "the Foreign Office thief" amid suggestions that Salisbury had considered him to be a spy working for Schouvaloff. The magistrate's decision, however, was unequivocal. He acquitted Marvin, exonerating him of any blame in regard to the initial disclosure of the summary, but condemning divulgence of the full text of the agreement. His verdict, which came even before Marvin's lawyer could rise to his feet, was that there was clearly no case against the defendant. Characteristically, Marvin was aggrieved that only the government's version of events had been aired. Disraeli himself had not favored prosecuting Marvin, and Tenterden, ever the discreet aristocrat, had regarded the matter as "the dirtiest linen ever washed in public by any family."[22]

On the day of Marvin's trial, Disraeli and Salisbury returned to London with their "peace with honour" triumph. Salisbury's later premiership would see the passage of the Official Secrets Act, but in the meantime, Marvin was to achieve further fame. In 1880 he capitalized on his infamy by publishing *Our Public Offices: Embodying an Account of the Disclosure of the Anglo-Russian Agreement.* He followed it with *The Region of Eternal Fire: An Account of a Journey to the Petroleum Region of the Caspian in 1883*, which provided insight into the oil fields of czarist Russia. His in-depth understanding of policies affecting India prompted him to write *The Russians at the Gates of Herat*, one of the first "instant books." Written and published in one week in 1885, it sold 65,000 copies. He became a prolific writer, publishing twelve books and pamphlets on Central Asia, and used his expertise in Russian petroleum products to promote Russian-Anglo oil interests and to call for British involvement in building pipelines and railroads and supplying tanker vessels. Years after his untimely death in 1890 at the age of thirty-six, his voice would be remembered, for by the beginning of the twentieth century Britain was prominent among importers of Russian petroleum products.[23]

Marvin's cynical observations and exposé of the Foreign Office would echo in future satirical texts of the irreverent *Vanity Fair* magazine, but on the issue of a remedy for such a scandal as he had created, the Foreign Office would have the last word. Shortly afterward, in spite of his disapproval of the exposure, Tenterden conducted an inquiry into the affair and concluded, "I hope after this we may have properly appointed clerks for such work and not have to depend on this cheap and untrustworthy class of people."[24]

CHAPTER 20

Arthur Conan Doyle's Revelations

Charles Marvin's Foreign Office scandal would later provide material for one of Britain's most successful authors. The pen of Arthur Conan Doyle would ensure that the intrigues of the Foreign Office and the machinations of the African Steam Ship Company would resonate well into the future. But while historians have long recognized that Marvin's case inspired Doyle, it is highly likely that Victor Buckley and Frederick Bond also found their way into his works. In August 1881 Conan Doyle, fascinated by the criminal psychology practiced by one of his tutors, Dr. Joseph Bell, graduated as a bachelor of medicine and master of surgery from Edinburgh University. His fertile imagination was destined to extend beyond the confines of the medical profession, though. He had other passions, and other subjects tantalized and fascinated him—the sea, Africa, America, and writing.

While at university Conan Doyle had written a short story set in South Africa, "The Mystery of Sasassa Valley," that was published in 1879 by *Chambers Journal.* He sold another story, "The American's Tale," to *London Society*, and these successes spurred him on to begin a romance based on the mystery of the *Marie Celeste*, the ship found abandoned off the coast of West Africa.

Earlier that year an opportunity had presented itself for Conan Doyle, though still a student, to sail as ship's surgeon on the *Hope*, a 400-ton whaler that fished off Greenland.

The rugged experience provided him with ideas for future stories (he would base many of his characters on real people, slightly changing their names or scarcely concealing their identity), and the *Hope*'s captain was assured a place in a later fictional work. When he graduated from university the following year, the call of the sea was still a powerful force and the young surgeon realized an ambition to visit Africa. Later he recalled that following his application, he received a telegram from the British and African Steam Navigation Company offering him a post as medical officer at a salary of twelve pounds per month, but the ship on which Doyle set sail on October 22, 1881, was in fact the 4,000-ton *Mayumba*, a vessel owned by the African Steam Ship Company and bound for the Gold Coast of Africa via Madeira and Tenerife.

It was an eventful voyage. The *Mayumba* carried her usual cargo of general goods and Royal Mail bags along with twenty or thirty passengers, a mixed party that included "some pleasant ladies bound for the Coast, and some unpleasant Negro traders whose manners and bearing were objectionable, but who were patrons of the line and must therefore be tolerated."[1] On the outward journey the *Mayumba* nearly collided with a lighthouse when she put into Madeira and was then caught in a storm as she crossed the Bay of Biscay. Some of the passengers succumbed to malaria and its complication, blackwater fever, and Conan Doyle himself caught typhoid fever in Lagos, Nigeria. On the return journey (when the cargo consisted of palm oil, palm nuts, ivory, and other products) a fire threatened the ship, and she limped unceremoniously back into Liverpool on January 14, 1882. The voyage had satisfied Conan Doyle's hunger for adventure at sea. Thenceforth he would concentrate on his career, maintain his interest in all matters African and American, and shape his hero Dr. Joseph Bell into the incisive and erudite Sherlock Holmes.

The African Steam Ship Company itself was now performing well, and Alfred Jones had indeed been well placed to gain control. Bond was a member of the Royal Colonial Institute, and he and Jones became regular visitors to the Foreign Office, keeping their fingers on the pulse of the African trade and arguing their case when political persuasion might preserve their profits. In 1882, however, the Foreign Office was to mourn the loss of the two men who had been at the center of the *Alabama* affair.

Victor Buckley fell ill in early summer with a fatal rheumatic fever. The family consensus was that exhaustion caused by stress and overwork was the reason he succumbed to the infection.[2] His condition deteriorated into hyperpyrexia, and he died on June 10 at his home in Stanhope Gardens at the age of forty-four. His death notice in *The Times* described him simply as the son of the late General Buckley. The man whose name had once hung on the lips of senior statesmen and who stood precariously at the core of Anglo-American negotiations passed away in virtual anonymity. He was buried close to his parents in the quiet country churchyard of Nunton in Wiltshire.

Tenterden too was in poor health. After the death of his first wife he had married the widow of a barrister whose family came from Devon, and it was at Nelson Cottage, Lynmouth, that he died of a cerebral hemorrhage on September 22. He had suffered physically and emotionally from the Charles Marvin affair, which had rocked the Foreign Office and embarrassed him personally, but there had been other lapses of security under his stewardship, and their cumulative effect had taken its toll.[3] News of the sudden death of the permanent under-secretary of state for foreign affairs was received with shock in London. Tenterden, aged forty-seven, was buried at Brendon, North Devon.

Frederick Bond, in contrast, was doing well. With his increasing prosperity came a move to a more spacious house in London's fashionable Dorset Square. Since 1873 he had been a member of the Oxford and Cambridge University Club, and in 1885 he made an interesting donation to his former college library at Cambridge. He had acquired from F. Westlin, a man who had resided at Shonga on the Upper Nile in 1882, a copy of the Koran written by Africans and procured from Kano, a town in the country of the Hausa people.[4]

The Niger Delta was in fact becoming a hotly contested area for the shipping companies vying for the African trade. The African Steam Ship Company joined forces with the British and African Steam Navigation Company in 1883 to provide discounted voyages in order to eliminate a new competitor, the Anglo-African Steam Ship Company. The strategy worked; the company filed for bankruptcy the following year, encouraging Jones and Bond to maintain their policy and deter competitors. Elder, Dempster became the manager of the British and African and, in 1891, of the African Steam Ship Company. These were astute moves on the chessboard of Jones' ambitions, yet two other competitors, the Royal Niger Company and the African Association, continued to pose a credible threat that had to be addressed.

The Royal Niger Company was intent on acquiring the Niger Delta and amalgamating the small independent traders whose preserve it had been. It was a situation that prompted Jones to lobby friends in the House of Commons and Bond to protest to the Foreign Office. A lengthy dispute followed, with Bond suggesting that the Lagos government should take over the Oil Rivers part of the coast and meeting with the government's reluctance to invest further large sums in the colonies. In the event, Jones won his battle and the proposed new charter that would have so benefited his competitors was dropped.

In 1891 Elder, Dempster formed a syndicate with the Belgian Woermann Line, a new route opening as a direct consequence of the Berlin Congress in 1884–85, which had directed the interests of the world's major powers away from Africa, allowing King Leopold II of Belgium to establish the Congo

Free State. Bulloch's former nemesis, U.S. diplomat Henry Shelton Sanford, emerged as a key player in Leopold's ruthless ambitions to milk the Congo of its natural resources—particularly ivory and rubber, for which world manufacturing was developing an insatiable appetite. The years that followed would bring misery to the people of the Congo.

In the meantime, Bond became the president of the Société Maritime du Congo, a shareholder and director of the Bank of British West Africa, and a director of the Société Français des Asphaltes, which set up an office in London as the French Asphalt Company at Lawrence Pountney Hill. A close family literary friend, editor of the *Court and Society Review*, Alsager Richard Vian (who could claim to have been propositioned by fellow editor Oscar Wilde) became its secretary.[5]

Bond was the perfect business associate for Alfred Jones, his Machiavellian personality preferring to keep a low profile while Jones' larger-than-life character sought total dominance of the African trade. Between them they contributed significantly to the shaping of that trade and to many political considerations, although Macgregor Laird, the abolitionist founder of the African Steam Ship Company, might have flinched at the ethos of a management that tolerated the "unpleasant Negro traders" Conan Doyle had encountered.

By 1892 Arthur Conan Doyle was one of the country's most popular writers, and in June of that year he joined the Reform Club in London, of which Bond had already been a member for some six years. The intriguing question arises as to whether Conan Doyle became acquainted with Bond at the club. Africa was an abiding interest for him still, as was America, which had fascinated him since his childhood. The two men would certainly have found much to discuss. Most important, perhaps, Conan Doyle had been in the employ of the African Steam Ship Company when he sailed on the *Mayumba* eleven years earlier, and within two years of leaving the ship he had begun working on the manuscript of *The Firm of Girdlestone*, a novel that contains some blatant resemblances to the African Steam Ship Company, and indeed to Frederick Bond.

In *The Firm of Girdlestone*, Thomas Dimsdale, a young medical graduate of Edinburgh University, falls in love with Kate Harston, whose father has died, leaving her to the guardianship of John Girdlestone of the African merchants Girdlestone and Company. Financial problems convince John Girdlestone that his only son, Ezra, should marry Kate in order that they can secure her large inheritance, and the two men resort to ever more desperate measures to prevent her from marrying her true love. The novel opens with a description of the firm's offices:

> The approach to the offices of the firm of Girdlestone and Co. was not a very dignified one, nor would the uninitiated who traversed it form any conception of the commercial prosperity of the firm in question. Close to the corner of a broad and busy street, within a couple of hundred yards of Fenchurch Street Station, a narrow doorway opens into a long, white-washed passage. On one side of this is a brass plate with the inscription "Girdlestone and Co., African Merchants" . . . the wayfarer finds himself in a small, square yard surrounded by doors, upon one of which the name of the firm reappears in large white letters. . . . [H]e will make his way into a long, low apartment which is the counting-house of the African traders.[6]

In its early days the African Steam Ship Company had its offices in Mincing Lane, only a few hundred yards from Fenchurch Street Station. The business then moved to Leadenhall Street, and finally to 21 Great St. Helen's, a court of ancient as well as eighteenth- and nineteenth-century buildings leading to St. Helen's Church. The court was located off the busy thoroughfare of Bishopsgate, a five-minute walk to Fenchurch Street station. The offices occupied by the company were all in the heart of London, the area in which Bond and generations of his family had been born and had engaged in gun making and mercantile trade. It was also the commercial hub of the British Empire—home to the Royal Exchange, Lloyd's, East India House, and Jardine Matheson, as well as commodity traders and importers of goods from all corners of the world. At its heart was finance—the Bank of England and bankers such as the Rothschilds and Emile Erlanger, who after the Civil War had taken up residence in Piccadilly at the former home of Lord Byron. While the City's financiers oiled the wheels of trade and industry, Lloyd's provided maritime insurance to shipping businesses such as the African Steam Ship Company.

Within the sanctum of Mr. John Girdlestone there was, above the fireplace,

> a large water-colour painting of the barque *Belinda* as she appeared when on a reef to the north of Cape Palmas. . . . It was generally rumoured that the merchants had lost heavily over this disaster, and there were some who quoted it as an instance of Girdlestone's habitual strength of mind that he should decorate his wall with so melancholy a souvenir. This view of the matter did not appear to commend itself to a flippant member of Lloyd's agency, who contrived to intimate . . . that the vessel may not have been so much under-insured, nor the loss to the firm as enormous as was commonly reported."[7]

Some shipping companies in the nineteenth century engaged in the practice of underinsuring sound vessels and overinsuring older ones less able to withstand the elements; this is a theme in Conan Doyle's book. It does appear, whether by misfortune or otherwise, that the vessels owned by the African Steam Ship Company were not always in good condition, as evidenced by reports of official inquiries into their losses at sea.[8]

The unscrupulous practice of running "coffin ships," as they were known—overloaded old vessels spruced up with new paint or even reregistered, and almost certain to sink sooner or later—cost many lives. It resulted in the introduction of the Plimsoll line, a white line painted on the hull of a ship to measure its draft and indicate the legal limit to which it could be loaded. Among the most notorious shipowners accused of running coffin ships was the wealthy Liverpool-based merchant Edward Bates. In Doyle's book, an angry sea captain reminds John Girdlestone that he had painted out the Plimsoll line and repainted it at a higher level so that a ship could be deliberately overloaded.

Conan Doyle's allusions to the African Steam Ship Company are thinly veiled. John and Ezra Girdlestone are portrayed as heartless and cunning, their lives revolving around their dealings in the City—the price of cotton and the cargoes of palm nuts, barrels of palm oil, gum, ebony, skins, cochineal, and ivory forthcoming when a ship is reported from Madeira. The senior partner boasts of his prestigious house in Eccleston Square and, in a cynical spirit of philanthropy, makes a charitable contribution to the Aboriginal Evolution Society while refusing help to the penniless widow of a seaman who has just died. The reference to the Aboriginal Evolution Society is surely more than coincidental, since a newspaper report of July 26, 1891, listed Frederick Bond present at "a meeting of The Aborigines' Protection Society, held at the Westminster Palace Hotel, to meet Sir Alfred Jones."[9]

The business has a cash-flow problem, which John Girdlestone manages by making insurance claims on his coffin ships. In echoes of the fraud committed by the secretary of the African Steam Ship Company when he invested in jewels, Conan Doyle's characters devise an ill-fated speculation in diamonds.

One the most striking passages in *The Firm of Girdlestone* is the description of John Girdlestone, who in some respects bears an uncanny physical resemblance to Frederick Bond. He is "undeniably a remarkable-looking man. For good or for evil no weak character lay beneath that hard angular face, with the strongly marked features and deep-set eyes. He was clean shaven, save for an iron-grey fringe of ragged whisker under each ear, which blended with the grizzled hair above. So self-contained, hard-set, and immutable was his expression that it was impossible to read anything from it except sternness and resolution, qualities which are likely to be associated with the highest natures as with the most dangerous."[10]

Ezra Girdlestone also has features common to Bond and his brother Edward. Ezra is "a broad shouldered, bull-necked young man" with "something classical in the regular, olive-tinted features and black, crisp, curling hair, fitting tightly to the well-rounded head. . . . It was rather the profile of one of those Roman emperors, splendid in its animal strength, but lacking those subtle softnesses of eye and mouth which speak of an inner life."[11]

Conan Doyle was pleased with his finished manuscript and disappointed when prospective publishers failed to share his enthusiasm; he observed wryly that it came circling back with the precision of a homing pigeon. While the author continued to build on his reputation as a first-class teller of short stories, he was intent on seeing his name on the cover of a book. He made various alterations to the manuscript and ultimately reworked it so that at last, in 1889, he sold the serial rights to the Globe Syndicate for £240, the largest sum he had earned so far. The book was published the following year by Chatto and Windus in London.[12] Later, however, he expressed regret: "I don't suppose any man has ever sacrificed so much money to preserve his ideal of art, as I have done, witness my suppression of Girdlestone."[13]

Among the many myths and legends surrounding the life of Arthur Conan Doyle is one that many Holmes devotees find plausible. Conan Doyle, so the story goes, was having lunch with some friends in one of his clubs when he mentioned his belief that almost every prominent person in society had at least one dark secret in their past which, if revealed, might ruin them. To prove the point, that afternoon he and his friends sent a telegram to several such men in London with the wording, "All is discovered. Leave immediately." The following morning they called at the home of each recipient, only to be informed that the person had been suddenly called away on urgent business.

If, in the sanctuary of the gentlemen's club, Conan Doyle and Frederick Bond had discussed the secrets of the past, the former London Armoury Company manager may well have revealed a story worthy of any Sherlock Holmes mystery—and Conan Doyle was not a man to flinch from tales that involved the aristocracy. A few months after he joined the Reform Club, Conan Doyle wrote "The Adventure of The Naval Treaty," a Sherlock Holmes story. The central character, a young Foreign Office clerk by the name of Percy Phelps, begins a letter requesting help from his old school friend Dr. Watson, explaining: "Through my uncle's influence I obtained a good appointment at the Foreign Office, and . . . I was in a situation of trust and honour until a horrible misfortune came suddenly to blast my career."[14]

Watson recalls the schoolboy Phelps: "He was, I remember, extremely well connected, and even when we were all little boys together we knew that his mother's brother was Lord Holdhurst, the great conservative politician."

Percy Phelps is, at the time of writing to Watson, suffering from "brain fever" brought on by his trauma. Sherlock Holmes and Watson respond to his plea for help by visiting him in Woking, Surrey, where they find the young man attended by his capable fiancée, Annie Harrison, "a girl of strong character" with a "touch of asperity in her voice" as she demands of Holmes whether he will solve the mystery. With the young lady is Phelps' future brother-in-law, Joseph Harrison. The Harrisons do not share Phelps' aristocratic background, their father being in industry in the north.

Phelps recounts the story of how, alone in the office one evening with fellow clerk Charles Gorot, he was copying a naval treaty that addressed concerns over the French fleet gaining ascendancy over that of Italy in the Mediterranean. Phelps left the room for a cup of coffee, and when he returned found that the naval treaty was missing. Gorot was cleared of all possible involvement, and Phelps was accused of stealing the treaty, an allegation that caused him to succumb to brain fever and retreat to his home in Woking and the care of his protective fiancée.

During the course of the investigation, Holmes and Watson visit Phelps' uncle, Lord Holdhurst, "the cabinet minister and future premier of England." "My unfortunate nephew!" Holdhurst exclaims of Phelps. "You can understand that our kinship makes it impossible for me to screen him in any way. I fear the incident must have a very prejudicial effect upon his career."

Sherlock Holmes solves the mystery by identifying Joseph Harrison as the culprit. Harrison has lost money dabbling in stocks and is "ready to do anything on earth to better his fortunes." The naval treaty, he has assumed, is a document of great value.

Conan Doyle undoubtedly based "The Naval Treaty" on the Charles Marvin affair, which had occurred some fifteen years earlier. The fictional Lord Holdhurst is the barely concealed Robert Balfour, whom Conan Doyle had met and who, as Lord Salisbury's nephew, was to be a future prime minister. His cabinet appointment by Salisbury (the former Robert Cecil) and his subsequent practice of promoting members of his own family to high office are the basis of the popular phrase "Bob's your uncle!"

Yet there are other familiar chords in "The Naval Treaty" that suggest Conan Doyle used more than one Foreign Office betrayal in crafting his story. The aristocratic Foreign Office clerk fits Victor Buckley, and there is no character equivalent to Charles Marvin in the plot. Buckley certainly had very influential members of the aristocracy in his immediate family providing patronage, and while no records appear to exist of an internal inquiry into the alleged leak facilitating the escape of the *Alabama*, undoubtedly the matter was so serious as to be worthy of an investigation, albeit at the highest level and with the utmost discretion.

Percy Phelps retreats to his family home in Ripley, Surrey; Balfour had a house at Woking, about fourteen miles away, and the Mangles side of Mary Stirling's family lived at Guildford (where she was a frequent visitor), less than seven miles distant. Her father named a town Guildford in Western Australia and died at the Mangles home, Woodbridge, in 1865.

Conan Doyle's predilection for using variations of real names is relevant here as well. Percy is not far removed from Pery, the prominent family name shared by Buckley's father and grandfather; and Charles Gorot is not so dissimilar from Charles Abbott. Percy Phelps is portrayed as a sensitive character who has relapsed into a near mental breakdown as a result of the theft, while in the Charles Marvin affair, the permanent clerks were quickly eliminated from suspicion.

The naval theme for the story also sits comfortably with the events of 1862, and even Annie Harrison shows shades of Mary Stirling as she brings a hint of maturity and a calming influence into her fiancée's life. In the revelation that the father of Annie and her brother is an ironmaster in the north of England there appears to lurk the ghost of Mary's cousin Thomas Mayne Stirling, who managed the Manchester cotton mill. The Foreign Office code of trust and honor remained sacrosanct at the time Conan Doyle penned his story. Little had changed in the criteria for appointing clerks, and a gulf existed between these aristocratic officials and those less equipped by generational experience—or what has been called "the Foreign Office mind."[15]

Whether or not Bond had confided some, or all, of his own dark past dealings to Conan Doyle remains a mystery, although the writer was certainly interested in the events, noting "the burning question of the *Alabama* Claims" in one of his letters to the press.[16] Coincidentally, Bond's house in London at 15 Dorset Square was just a short walk from the fictional Sherlock Holmes' residence in Baker Street.

One of Buckley's own influential uncles, his mother's brother Edward Pleydell Bouverie, had come to terms with the disappointing reality that the role he so coveted in his political life, that of Speaker of the House, had been denied him, events having come to a head in 1872, the year of the *Alabama* claims. In July of that year the Speaker's chair became vacant, and many in the House thought that Pleydell Bouverie would almost automatically succeed to it. Face-saving rumors suggested he declined the speakership, but in truth, the offer had not been forthcoming. Such blackballing, for whatever reason, was a political twist of inevitable interest to the satirical press that feasted on nuggets of speculation, and *Vanity Fair* published a caricature of Pleydell Bouverie with the caption: "He did not decline the Speakership." The accompanying text observes: "Mr. Bouverie is of that older and steadier school of Liberal politicians who know what politics mean and who are not be led away from that meaning by a caprice for any cause or question."[17]

The same sharp-witted journal would note: "Foreign Office answers are always obscure, commonly misleading and frequently insincere." Of Lord Tenterden *Vanity Fair* had written charitably, "At twenty [he] was introduced into the Foreign Office. Here he distinguished himself from among an idle generation by disclosing good industry . . . a thoroughly steady and reliable official, not eaten up by the trifling fashions of the day . . . an admirable and exalted Freemason."[18]

Vanity Fair likewise lambasted John Laird in 1873 after the Geneva arbitration, commenting on his famous speech in self-defense: "Not for the building of the *Alabama*, nor for her escape, but for the cheers with which British legislators received those words has England now been hunted down to humiliation and the payment of three millions and a half of treasure . . . and the responsibility of the cheers does not lie with Mr. Laird. For all that his name will be coupled, not with statesmanship or policy but with the national disgrace as long as memory remains of it."[19] Harsh words for the man who would die a year later at his home in Hamilton Square, his funeral procession at Birkenhead Priory watched by thousands in meditative silence.

One by one the protagonists in the *Alabama* story passed away, taking with them their private memories of a great drama. Gladstone died in the spring of 1898. Lord Russell (whom *Vanity Fair* had quoted as charging that Gladstone had "tarnished the national honour, injured the national interests and cowered the national character") had died twenty years earlier. Charles Francis Adams, whose keen brain had once engaged in almost daily battle with the Foreign Office, spent his last months in failing mind before his death in America in 1886.

Archibald Hamilton died in 1880 at his home in Kent, a property that had once been owned by the Hankey family, bankers to the ill-fated gun maker Robert Adams. The gun maker himself had emerged from bankruptcy but had indifferent success in business, and died just a few years later in September 1870 following surgery after a firearms accident. Henrietta "Enrica" Hamilton died in Kensington, London, in June 1909.[20]

As the new century dawned, Bond was still active as chairman of the African Steam Ship Company, in which Alfred Jones, now Sir Alfred, maintained a controlling interest. By this time Jones was also in effective control of the country's trade with West Africa, a position he had achieved with considerable help from Bond. Together, the men had outmaneuvered their rivals, shrewdly managed their affairs, and even, ironically, developed a profitable business growing and importing cotton. One of the enduring successes of the business was the importation of fruit, which ships carried from the Canary Islands on their homebound voyage. Jones is credited with introducing bananas to Britain and securing their popularity, against the reluctance of retailers, by bringing costermongers from London to load their barrows from the ships in Liverpool. By allowing the street vendors to sell the bananas for whatever they could get on the streets and keep their takings, he overcame people's suspicion of an unknown fruit and established the banana as a favorite.

On January 7, 1901, the man responsible for building the *Alabama* died at his home in Liverpool. James D. Bulloch, who had become a much-respected resident of the city since being granted British citizenship in 1869, was buried alongside his wife and son in Toxteth Cemetery. The Daughters of the Confederacy later added an inscription on the headstone reminding visitors to his grave that he was an American by birth and an Englishman by choice.[21] Later that month, the country mourned the death of Queen Victoria.

Frederick William Bond died on November 21, 1901, leaving behind an estate worth more than £51,000. He was buried in Highgate Cemetery, which Benjamin Moran had once described as "the most beautiful of the London burial places," in the presence of many of the important people with whom he had been associated: Sir Alfred Jones, Charles Franklin Torrey of the Atlantic Transport Company, Alex Elder, John Dempster, Alsager Vian, William J. Pirrie (of Harland and Wolff, who would build the *Titanic*), Alex and Robert Sinclair, and representatives of Trinity House, the French Asphalt Company, the Bank of British West Africa, and other prominent shipping and commercial organizations. Bond's obituary noted that he had been an active member of the Royal Colonial Institute, had held the position of chairman of the African Steam Ship Company for a quarter of a century, and was "a warm supporter of the Gunmakers' Company."[22]

After Bond's death his name disappeared beneath the layers of history. His life spanned Britain's exploration of the Dark Continent, the American Civil War, and the vast expansion of trade with Africa; yet others held a greater claim to fame. He vanished into the past as surely as one of the African tribes who claimed the ability to make themselves invisible. At the premises of the Gunmakers' Company in London, of which he had several times been elected master, even his picture disappeared from the ornately inscribed page in the official photograph album. Not until the dawn of the twenty-first century would his life again come under scrutiny and his past be revealed.

In the latter years of his life Bond would have known that an observant clerk, Edmund Dene Morel, whom the African Steam Ship Company sent to Belgium every few weeks to supervise the loading and unloading of ships at Antwerp, had been given pause for thought. Morel had observed that while the ships returning from Africa brought valuable cargoes of rubber and ivory, the passengers on those return voyages were army officers, and the holds also held arms and ammunition. He correctly surmised that there was no legitimate trading, and these goods were the product of slave labor.[23] King Leopold's colony became an international scandal when Morel embarked upon an exposé of the brutality behind the economic miracle of the Belgian Congo. He eventually took his crusade to America, and to the president of the United States, who was by then Bulloch's nephew, Theodore Roosevelt. But in a story full of coincidences and unexpected connections, another was yet to occur.

In the 1920s Arthur Conan Doyle bought as a second home a house at Bignell Wood in Hampshire, a secluded retreat where he could indulge his interest in spiritualism and hold regular séances. Conan Doyle died in 1930 at his principal residence in Crowborough, Sussex, and he and his wife were buried within the grounds there. When his heirs decided to sell the property in 1955, the bodies were removed to another burial site. Such was Conan Doyle's fame that transportation of the coffins had to take place late at night, with an innocuous laundry van being used as a subterfuge; the vehicle proceeded to the graveyard of a church in Hampshire, close to the Doyles' beloved Bignell Wood, which had agreed to allow the burial. Conan Doyle's embrace of spiritualism had not endeared him to the Church of England, and his final resting place was a corner of the churchyard at a discreet distance from the building itself. That burial placed him at the very heart of one of the nineteenth century's most intriguing stories, for Bignell Wood is in the parish of Minstead, the birthplace of Victor Buckley, who was baptized in the church. Admirers of Conan Doyle still make pilgrimages to Minstead Church, little knowing that a complex mystery destined to fascinate historians for many years began in this very place with a birth into one of the country's aristocratic families.

Time passed, but the quest for the truth behind the *Alabama* story continued unabated. The people, the politics, the ships, and the war all belonged to the past, yet a relentless desire to know the facts was handed down to future generations. The search for the truth is as much about understanding the mindset, the prejudices, and the passions of the people involved as about following the chronology of the extraordinary events. To this end, numerous researchers and historians have taken on the challenge, but no one has offered an explanation more appropriate than that given by Brooks Adams, the son who accompanied Charles Francis Adams to Geneva at the time of the *Alabama* Claims.

In 1911, as a respected historian, he presented his paper "The Seizure of the Laird Rams" to the Massachusetts Historical Society and revealed that although he had been a schoolboy during the years of the American Civil War when his father served as minister to Great Britain, he had long since harbored contempt for the British government of that time and what he viewed as "a system of fraudulent neutrality."[24] He believed his father had stood "between an exasperated people in America and an insolent, contemptuous, unscrupulous and vindictive aristocracy in England" who desired to sever the bonds of the Union to strengthen themselves, and hence undertook to build a navy for the South. After Waterloo, he reasoned, England became the heart of modern civilization, the center of the world's economic system, and as such wielded an unquestioned supremacy.

On the subject of the *Alabama*'s departure—which, Adams reminded his audience, had been acknowledged as a scandal by Lord Russell himself—he referred to his father's diary entry of December 22, 1865, in which he recorded that Moran had shown him a copy of the short note from V. Buckley. And Adams then made his unwitting mistake, claiming that the note was addressed to "Mr. [Caleb] Huse."

In Brooks Adams' view, the aristocracy's hold on power had met its nemesis on the night of February 23, 1864, when a debate on the seizure of the Laird rams was held in the House of Commons. The sitting became highly charged and acrimonious, and threatened to become a vote on a motion to censure that might possibly bring down the government. That debate, Adams contended, and the political division that followed, marked the rise of new social forces in Britain and the advent of a new ruling class. The type of English aristocrat represented by Lord Palmerston had been discarded. During the debate, Thomas Baring, a prominent Conservative, censured Lord Russell for not having prevented the departure of the *Alabama*; but in the event, the ministers who represented the aristocracy had to appeal to the radical MPs such as Bright, Cobden, and Forster, for support. That turning point, as Adams saw it, changed Britain's ruling structure.

The modern-day historian and biographer of Gladstone Roy Jenkins chose the *Alabama* claims settlement as a turning point in Anglo-American relations, suggesting it "not only was the greatest nineteenth century triumph of rational internationalism over short-sighted jingoism, but also marked the break point between the previous hundred years of Anglo-American strain and the subsequent century and more of two world wars fought in alliance . . . and several decades in which at least some people in Washington and London believed strongly in a special relationship between the two countries."[25]

If indeed the *Alabama*'s departure, and the part young Victor Buckley allegedly played in it, gave rise to such an international accord, then Brooks Adams' explanations are worthy of consideration, for bitter though he was toward Britain for its support for the Confederacy, he struck at the heart of the matter when he referred to the prevailing attitudes of the time. History reveals that the Age of Empire was, at that time, morphing into the Age of Capital, an era that found a new word, "entrepreneur," to describe the ability of men like Archibald Hamilton and Frederick William Bond to exploit opportunities, create vast wealth, and determine the course of history.

The confidence with which Palmerston and the aristocracy protected Britain's, and their own, interests was indeed fueled by the mood of their youth. Adams spoke of the era of the arrogance of Waterloo, and in that he touched on the truth.

NOTES

Chapter 1. Family and Foreign Office

1. Sir Edward Hertslett, *Recollections of the Old Foreign Office* (London: John Murray, 1901), 108.
2. Lady Catherine Pleydell Bouverie was the daughter of William, 3rd Earl of Radnor, by his first wife, Katherine Pelham Clinton, only daughter of Henry, Earl of Lincoln (Burke's Peerage).
3. W. A. Lindsey, *The Royal Household* (London: K. Paul, Trench, Trübner, and Company, 1898).
4. The memorial in Minstead Parish Church, Hampshire, notes that Ensign George Richard Buckley died of battle fatigue August 15, 1815.
5. An equerry (a senior military officer) attended the monarch on formal occasions as a member of the royal household.
6. Journal of Queen Victoria 1838, RA VIC/MAIN/QVJ/23 February.
7. The cup was inscribed: "The Gift of Her Majesty Queen Victoria to Victor Buckley Her Godson May 1838."
8. South Audley Street: East Side, *Survey of London, vol. 40: The Grosvenor Estate in Mayfair, pt. 2, The Buildings,* (1980) pp. 291–303, http://www.british-history .ac.uk (accessed February 2013).
9. In the Salisbury by-election of November 1853 Buckley won 255 votes to 88 in an electorate of 580.
10. Hon. John Colborne and Frederick Brine, *The Last of the Brave* (The Strand: Ackerman and Company, 1857). A memorial appears in the Royal Military Chapel, Wellington Barracks; Buckley's death is also recorded in the Royal Garrison Church, Portsmouth, in a list of men killed in the Crimean War. Tim Backhouse *Memorials and Monuments in Portsmouth*, http://www.memorials .inportsmouth.co.uk/churches/royal_garrison/etonians.htm.
11. Journal of Queen Victoria RA VIC/MAIN/QVJ9 September.
12. Charles Marvin, *Our Public Offices* (London: Swann Sonnenschein and Allen, 1880), 200.
13. Louise Atherton, *Never Complain, Never Explain: Records of the Foreign Office and State Paper Office 1500–c. 1960* (PRO, 1994).
14. Ibid.

15. Canon Walter King, "Victor Buckley, 1838–1882" (unpublished thesis, 2007) (Canon King is the great-grandson of Victor Buckley).
16. Ray Jones, *The Nineteenth-Century Foreign Office: An Administrative History*, LSE Research Monographs 9 (London: London School of Economics, 1971), 61.
17. Atherton, *Never Complain, Never Explain.*
18. *The FCO Policy, People and Places, 1782–1997* (London: Foreign and Commonwealth Office Publications, April 1991), 2.
19. Marvin, *Our Public Offices*, 209.
20. Ibid., 211.
21. Jasper Ridley, *Lord Palmerston* (London: Constable, 1970), 414.
22. Gordon Waterfield, *Layard of Ninevah* (New York: Frederick A. Praeger, 1963), 263.

Chapter 2. Guns, Ships, and Victorian Values

1. *London Gazette*, August 29, 1834; *Spectator*, August 30, 1834.
2. The Worshipful Company of Gunmakers took their charter in 1637, and a member of the Barnett family became the first president of the Gunmakers Guild.
3. D. F. Harding, *Small Arms of the East India Company 1600–1856*, vol. 1 (London: Foresight Books, 1999); Barry "Buck" Conner, *Success in the North American Fur Trade* (Macon, Ga.: Blanket Series Books, 2005); Carl Parcher Russell, *Guns on the Early Frontiers: A History of Firearms from Colonial Times to the Years of the Western Fur Trade* (New York: Dover, 2005), 113–14.
4. W. H. J. Chamberlain and A. W. F. Taylerson, *Prospectus of the London Armoury Company 1856: Adams' Revolvers* (London: Barrie and Jenkins, 1976), 43–44.
5. Ibid.
6. A. W. F. Taylerson, Ronald A. N. Andrews, and James Frith, *The Revolver 1818–1865* (London: Herbert Jenkins, 1966), 130. Adams' banker was Thomas Alers Hankey of Hankey and Company, 7 Fenchurch Street, in the City.
7. Ibid. Adams was paying royalties to Hankey, who may have been acting as a nominee for the bank.
8. Chamberlain and Taylerson, *Prospectus of the London Armoury Company 1856*, 70.
9. Ibid., 75.
10. After his mother's death in 1861 Archibald Hamilton erected a memorial window to her memory, designed by Dante Gabriel Rossetti, in the church at Old West Kirk. Ninian Hill, *The Story of the Old West Kirk at Greenock 1591–1898* (Greenock: James McKelvie and Sons, 1898), https://www.inverclyde.gov.uk/education-and-learning/libraries/local-and-family-history/local-history-books-online/ninian-hill-old-west-kirk-1898. For the family of Menzies Sinclair, see *Views and Reminiscences of Old Greenock 1891*, pt. 1 (Greenock: James McKelvie and Sons, 1891), https://www.inverclyde.gov.uk/

community-life-and-leisure/local-history-and-heritage/views-reminscences-old-greenock+1891.

11. Caleb Huse, *The Supplies for the Confederate Army: How They Were Obtained in Europe and How They Were Paid For* (Boston: T. R. Marvin and Son, 1904), 19–20.
12. Benjamin La Fevre, *Campaign of '84. Biographies of S. Grover Cleveland and Thomas A. Hendricks* (New York: Baird and Dillon 1884), 111.
13. Bulloch's middle name was spelled Dunwody until his naturalization as a British citizen in 1869.
14. Ethel Trenholm Seabrook Nepveux, *George Alfred Trenholm and the Company That Went to War, 1861–1865* (Charleston, S.C.: privately printed, 1973).
15. Andrew Roberts, *Salisbury: Victorian Titan* (London: Weidenfeld and Nicolson, 1999), 48.
16. Keith Hill, "On Track to Westminster," *Backtrack* 17, no. 9 (September 2003): 523–26.
17. Wynne Jones, "America's Secret War in Welsh Waters," in *Cymru a'r Môr / Maritime Wales*, vol. 1 (Gwynedd Archive Service). Edward Bates bought Gyrn Castle, Llanasa, Clwyd, in 1853. He later became member of Parliament for Plymouth and was created a baronet (hereditary title) in 1880.
18. Pamela Statham-Drew, *James Stirling: Admiral and Founding Governor of Western* (Perth: University of Western Australia Press, 2003), 454.
19. Ibid., 407.
20. Ibid., 525.
21. A Drawing Room was a court reception that marked the "coming out" into society of young ladies, and their presentation to Queen Victoria.
22. *Punch*, March 30, 1861.
23. The act further prohibited the enlistment (without royal licence) of any natural-born British subject "as a soldier in any military operation in the service of any foreign state, or as a sailor or marine on board any ship of war or other ship fitted out or equipped or intended to be used for any warlike purpose." The barristers concurred that although there was the contention of intent to cruise against a friendly state, the mere building of a ship within Her Majesty's dominions by any person was no offense, *whatever may be the intent of the parties* because the offense was not the *building* but the *equipping*.

Chapter 3. The Honorable Members for the United States

1. Henry Adams, *The Education of Henry Adams* (Boston: Houghton Mifflin, 1930), 114–15.
2. Frank J. Merli, *Great Britain and the Confederate Navy* (Bloomington: Indiana University Press, 1970), 38.
3. Francis Russell, *Adams: An American Dynasty* (New York: American Heritage Publishing, 1976), 262–63.

4. Merli, *Great Britain and the Confederate Navy*, 31.
5. George Macaulay Trevelyan, *The Life of John Bright* (London: Constable and Company, 1913), 299.
6. Andrew Roberts, *Salisbury: Victorian Titan* (London: Weidenfeld and Nicolson, 1999), 48.
7. Brooks Adams, "The Seizure of the Laird Rams," *Proceedings of the Massachusetts Historical Society* 45 (October 1911–June 1912): 243–333, 250.
8. John Bright's address to trade unionists in St. James's Hall, London, March 26, 1863.
9. Russell, *Adams*, 263.
10. Frank Hardie, *The Political Influence of Queen Victoria, 1861–1901* (Oxford: Oxford University Press, 1935), 188.
11. "The Life of Queen Victoria," *Graphic*, January 26, 1901.
12. Evelyn Ashley, *Henry John Temple: The Life of Viscount Palmerston, 1846–1865*, 2 vols. (London: Richard Bentley and Sons, 1876), 2:209–10.
13. Edward Boykin, *Sea Devil of the Confederacy* (New York: Funk and Wagnalls, 1959), 83.
14. Horace White, *Fossetts: A Record of Two Centuries of Engineering* (Bromborough: Fawcett Preston and Company, 1958), 45.
15. *The Times*, April 10, 1861; David Hollett, *The* Alabama *Affair* (Wilmslow: Sigma Leisure, 1993), 9.
16. When John Laird Sr. entered Parliament, the business name was changed from John Laird and Sons to Laird Brothers.
17. David Hollett, *The Conquest of the Niger by Land and Sea from the Early Explorers and Pioneer Steamships to Elder Dempster and Company* (Gwent: P. M. Heaton, 1995).
18. P. N. Davies, *The Trade Makers: Elder Dempster in West Africa, 1852–1972.* (London: George Allen and Unwin, 1973), 42.
19. John Raymond Harris, *Liverpool and Merseyside: Essays in the Social and Economic History of the Port and Its Hinterland* (London: Routledge, 1968), 235.
20. James D. Bulloch, *The Secret Service of the Confederate States in Europe* [hereinafter *Secret Service*], 2 vols. (New York: Thomas Yoseloff, 1959), 1:61–62.
21. Russell, *Adams*, 263.
22. Joseph A. Fry, *Henry S. Sanford: Diplomacy and Business in Nineteenth-Century America* (Reno: University of Nevada Press, 1982), 16–19.
23. Ibid., 44.
24. Bulloch to Mallory, August 13, 1861, in *Official Records of the Union and Confederate Navies in the War of the Rebellion* [hereinafter ORN] (Wilmington: Broadfoot Publishing for the National Historical Society, 1987), 2 series, 31 vols., series II, vol. 2, 84.
25. FCO letter to author, June 7, 2000: The old Foreign Office buildings in Downing Street and Fludyer Street (running parallel) were in use until October

1, 1861, although the move to temporary accommodation in Pembroke House and Malmesbury at Whitehall Gardens began on August 27, 1861, the most likely time for the group of clerks to be photographed as a memento.

26. Sanford to Seward, July 4, 1861, in Fry, *Henry S. Sanford*, 41.

Chapter 4. Money Will Accomplish Anything in England

1. Ashley, *Life of Palmerston*, 2:211.
2. Ibid., 208.
3. Ridley, *Lord Palmerston*, 53.
4. Gordon W. Batchelor, *The Beresfords of Bedgebury Park* (Goudhurst: William J. C. Musgrave, 1996), 115.
5. James Spence, *The American Union: Its Effect on National Character and Policy* (London: Richard Bentley, 1861), 304–5; James Spence, *On the Recognition of the Southern Confederation* (London: Bentley, 1862).
6. J. Ewing Ritchie, *Life and Times of the Right Hon. W. E. Gladstone* (London: James Sangster, n.d.), 4, 126.
7. *Liverpool Evening Star*, October 1861.
8. *Manchester Examiner*, October 1861.
9. W. Stanley Hoole, ed., *Confederate Foreign Agent: The European Diary of Major Edward C. Anderson* [hereinafter Anderson diary] (Tuscaloosa, Ala.: Confederate Publishing Company, 1976), August 2, 1861.
10. Ibid., Saturday August 3, 1861, n. 36. Hoole states this to be Hamilton of the London Armoury Company.
11. Adams to Russell, August 15, 1861, ORN I, 6:176–77.
12. Anderson diary, September 15, 1861.
13. Charles Francis Adams to Charles Francis Adams Jr., March 24, 1865, in *A Cycle of Adams' Letters, 1861–1865*, ed. Worthington Chauncey Ford, vol. 2 (Boston: Houghton Mifflin, 1920), 259.
14. Robert Bruce Murray, *Legal Cases of the Civil War* (Mechanicsburg, Pa.: Stackpole Books, 2003), 43; James D. Bulloch, *The Secret Service of the Confederate States in Europe* [hereinafter *Secret Service*], 2 vols. (New York: Thomas Yoseloff, 1959), 1:110.
15. Anderson diary, September 26, 1861.
16. Ibid.
17. William Acton, *Prostitution, Considered in Its Moral, Social, and Sanitary Aspects* (London: John Churchill and Sons, 1870), 19; Kellow Chesney, *The Victorian Underworld* (London: Penguin Books, 1989), 366.
18. Daniel Joseph Kirwan, *Palace and Hovel; Phases of London Life. Being Personal Observations of an American in London by Day and Night; with Vivid Illustrations of the Manners, Social Customs and Modes of Living of the Rich and the Reckless, the Destitute and the Depraved* (Hartford, Conn.: Belknap and Bliss, 1870), 229, 483, 476.

19. Derek Hudson, *Man of Two Worlds: The Life and Diaries of Arthur J. Munby, 1828–1920* (London: John Murray, 1972).
20. Kirwan, *Palace and Hovel*, 231, 472.
21. Anderson diary, October 1, 1861, 67–68; Kirwan, *Palace and Hovel*, 588.
22. Trevelyan, *Life of John Bright*, 310.
23. Ridley, *Lord Palmerston*, 552.

Chapter 5. Our Friend in the Foreign Office

1. Benjamin Moran, *The Journal of Benjamin Moran*, 2 vols., ed. Sarah Agnes Wallace and Frances Elma Gillespie (Chicago: University of Chicago Press, 1948), 1:xii–x.
2. Henry Wilding to Seward, August 17, 1861, ORN I, 6:171.
3. Dudley to Seward, December 6, 1861, ORN I, 6:510.
4. Adams to Seward, September 6, 1861, ORN I, 6:265.
5. Mallory to North, September 27, 1861, ORN II, 1:96.
6. Adams to Seward, September 14, 1861, ORN I, 6:330–31.
7. Anderson diary, September 23, 1861.
8. H. Waddington (Under-Secretary of the State, Home Department) to the Commissioners of Customs, October 3, 1861, copy transmitted to the Collector at Greenock, Glasgow City Archives CE60/2/134; Collector of Customs, Greenock, to Commissioners of Customs, October 4, 1861, Glasgow City Archives CE60/2/134.
9. Anderson diary, October 6, 1861.
10. Telegram, Secretary of Customs London to the Collector at Greenock, October 5, 1861, Glasgow City Archives CE60/2/134.
11. Anderson diary, October 6, 1861.
12. Anderson diary, October 10, 1861.
13. Ibid.
14. Edward Brennan to J. Pollaky, October 10, 1861, ORN I, 6:370.
15. "Historic Andrew Low House," http://www.visit-historic-savannah.com/andrew-low-house.html.
16. Morse to Seward, October 16, 1861, ORN I, 12:330.
17. Anderson diary, October 2, 1861.
18. Bulloch, *Secret Service*, 1:115.
19. Ibid., 1:119.
20. Ibid., 1:127.
21. Morse to Seward, October 16, 1861, ORN I, 12:330.
22. Seth Grosvenor Porter was married to Annette, sister of Bulloch's second wife, Harriott (Hattie).
23. Merli, *Great Britain and the Confederate Navy*, 79.

24. Ibid., 85; and *The Times*, January 11, 1862.
25. Merli, *Great Britain and the Confederate Navy*, 61–62.

Chapter 6. Choice Foreign Office Fiction

1. Bulloch, *Secret Service*, 1:156.
2. Prioleau to North, February 5, 1862, ORN II, 2:142.
3. Lt. David D. Porter to Hon. Gideon Wells, August 13, 1861, ORN I, 1:65.
4. Chester G. Hearn, *Gray Raiders of the Sea* (Baton Rouge: Louisiana State University Press, 1992), 48.
5. Pegram to the Duke of Somerset, January 27, 1862, ORN II, 2:750–51.
6. Craven to Hon. Gideon Welles, February 3, 1862, ORN I, 1:299.
7. Moran diary, February 27, 1862.
8. Anderson diary, October 4 and 5, 1862.
9. Henry Hotze, ed., Count Joseph Arthur de Gobineau, *The Moral and Intellectual Diversity of the Races* (Philadelphia: J. B. Lippincott, 1856), 91; Charles P. Cullop, *Confederate Propaganda in Europe, 1861–1865* (Miami: University of Miami Press, 1969), 19.
10. Cullop, *Confederate Propaganda in Europe*, 19.
11. Moran diary, September 1, 1858.
12. Cullop, *Confederate Propaganda in Europe*, 19–20.
13. A guinea was one pound and one shilling in "old money." There were twenty shillings to a pound. When Britain converted to decimal currency in 1971, the guinea (and the shilling, of course) was discontinued.
14. Patricia McNealy, *Knights of the Quill: Confederate Correspondents and Their Civil War Reporting* (West Lafayette, Ind.: Purdue University Press, 2006), 226.
15. Hotze to Hunter, February 28, 1865, ORN III, 3:354.
16. Regina Rapier, *Saga of Felix Senac* (Atlanta, Ga.: privately printed, 1972), 80.
17. Ibid., 130; John George Witt, *Life in the Law* (London: T. Werner Laurie, 1906), 147.
18. Rapier, *Saga of Felix Senac*, 54.
19. Ibid., 132.
20. Ibid., 137.
21. Hotze to Hunter, February 23, 1862, ORN II, 3:346.
22. Ibid.
23. Ibid., 353.
24. Rapier, *Saga of Felix Senac,* 133.
25. Ibid.
26. James Dugan, *The Great Iron Ship* (London: Hamish Hamilton, 1953), 117–18.
27. Hotze to Benjamin, August 4, 1862, ORN II, 3:506.

Chapter 7. The *Enrica* Is Launched and the *Florida* Is Freed

1. Hotze to Hunter, April 25, 1862, ORN II, 3:399.
2. Ridley, *Lord Palmerston*, 555.
3. Ibid., 555–57.
4. Raphael Semmes, *Memoirs of Service Afloat during the War between the States* (London and Baltimore: Kelly, Piet, and Company, 1869), 402.
5. Bulloch, *Secret Service*, 1:227–30.
6. William Stanley Hoole, *Four Years on the* Alabama*: The Career of Captain John Low on the CSS* Fingal, Florida, Alabama, Tuscaloosa, *and* Ajax (Athens: University of Georgia Press, 2012), 39–40. Harriet and Harriott were originally known as the "spoken form" of Henrietta.
7. Bulloch, *Secret Service*, 1:228.
8. Spy Report, July 4, 1862, W. S. Hoole Special Collections Library, University of Alabama.
9. Peter Hamilton, *The Hamilton Heritage*, http://www.islandconnections.eu/1000003/1000005/0/29005/interview.html (accessed November 2012); Agustin Guimerá *Ravina, La Casa Hamilton: Una empressa británnica en Canarias 1837–1987 (Santa Cruz de Tenerife, 1989), 163.*
10. Rob Roy MacGregor (1671–1734); Mary Hamilton (1753–1777); Gregor Macgregor (1740–1799).
11. George Stewart, *Curiosities of Glasgow Citizenship as Exhibited Chiefly in the Business Career of Its Old Commercial Aristocracy. Short biographical notices of the magistrates and merchants of Greenock in 1783* (Glasgow: James Maclehose, 1881), Glasgow Digital Library, University of Strathclyde, http://gdl.cdlr.strath.ac.uk/stecit/stecit15.htm https://www.strathuk/cdlr/services/glasgowdigitallibrary (accessed September 2013).
12. Henrietta Newton Duncan Hamilton (1828–1909); Alexander Duncan (1783–1839) married Margaret Newton (1789–1864).
13. Isabella Newton Duncan (1823–1895) married John Scott (1815–1885).
14. Frank J. Merli, *The* Alabama, *British Neutrality and the American Civil War*, ed. David M. Fahey (Bloomington: Indiana University Press, 2004), 128.
15. Author's correspondence with Miss Joan Butcher, granddaughter of Mathew Butcher.
16. M. J. Butcher, *A Chapter of Unwritten History*: *The* Alabama's *Escape, Memoir,* December 12, 1880. By kind permission of Miss Joan Butcher.
17. Bulloch, *Secret Service*, 1:231.
18. Ibid., 237.
19. Bulloch *Secret Service*, 1:157n.
20. Frank Lawrence Owsley Jr., *The CSS* Florida*: Her Building and Operations* (Tuscaloosa and London: University of Alabama Press, 1987), 26.
21. Emma Martin Maffitt, *The Life and Services of John Newland Maffitt* (New York and Washington: Neale, 1906), 239.

22. Boykin, *Sea Devil of the Confederacy,* 102.
23. Merli, *Great Britain and the Confederate Navy,* 31.
24. Bulloch to Mallory, April 11, 1862, ORN II, 2:184.
25. Ibid., 183.
26. North to Mallory, March 29, 1862, ORN II, 2:177.
27. J. M. Stribling to Capt. J. H. North, May 29, 1862, ORN II, 2:204.
28. Huse to Gorgas, ORA IV, 1003; Caleb Huse, *Reminiscences* (Boston: T. R. Marvin and Son, 1904), 20.
29. Adams to Russell, June 23, 1862, in *Papers Relating to the Treaty of Washington; Geneva Arbitration* [hereinafter referred to as *Geneva Arbitration*] *(Washington, D.C.: Government Printing Office, 1873),* vol. 3, pt. 7, p. 81, http:digital.library.wisc.edu/1711.dl/FRUS.
30. Ibid.

Chapter 8. Intended for a Ship of War

1. Affidavit of Richard Broderick, Spy Report, July 4, 1862, W. S. Hoole Special Collections Library, University of Alabama.
2. Mallory to Bulloch, May 3, 1862, ORN II, 2:190.
3. Ibid.
4. Warren F. Spencer, *The Confederate Navy in Europe* (Tuscaloosa: University of Alabama Press, 1997), 80
5. Semmes, *Memoirs,* 353–54.
6. Bulloch to North, July 10, 1862, ORN II, 2:214.
7. Adams to Russell, June 23, 1862, *Geneva Arbitration,* 81; Charles C. Beaman, *The National and Private "*Alabama *Claims" and Their "Final and Amicable Settlement"* (Washington, D.C: W. H. Moore, 1871), 70; and *Geneva Arbitration,* pt. 6, 308.
8. Law Officers of the Crown to Earl Russell, June 30, 1862, *Geneva Arbitration,* 310.
9. Ibid.
10. Thomas F. Fremantle and Grenville C. L. Berkeley, Commissioners of Customs, to the Lords of Her Majesty's Treasury, July 1, 1862, *Geneva Arbitration,* 311.
11. Ibid.
12. Dudley to Collector of Customs, July 9, 1862, *Geneva Arbitration,* 312–13.
13. Samuel Price Edwards to Dudley, July 10, 1862, *Geneva Arbitration,* 313.
14. Report of F. J. Hamel, July 11, 1862, *Geneva Arbitration,* 314.
15. Douglas H. Maynard, "Union Attempts to Prevent the Escape of the *Alabama,*" *Mississippi Historical Review* 41 (June 1954–March 1955): 49.
16. Ibid.
17. Sir Austen Henry Layard, *Autobiography and Letters from His Childhood until His Appointment as H.M. Ambassador at Madrid,* ed. Hon. William N. Bruce, with

a Chapter on His Parliamentary Career by the Rt. Hon. Sir Arthur Otway (London: John Murray 1903), 229.

18. Gordon Waterfield, *Layard of Ninevah* (New York: Frederick Praeger, 1968), 294.
19. Ibid., 296.
20. Philip Guedalla, *Palmerston* (London: E. Benn, 1926), 427–28.
21. Opinion of Sir Robert Collier, July 16, 1862, *Geneva Arbitration*, 323.
22. Squarey to Board of Customs, July 23, 1862, Beaman, *The National and Private "*Alabama *Claims,"* 83.
23. George A. Hamilton to Layard, July 22, 1862, *Geneva Arbitration*, 319; Merli, *The* Alabama, *British Neutrality, and the American Civil War*, 78.
24. Beaman, *The National and Private "*Alabama *Claims,"* 85–86.

Chapter 9. Information from a Private and Most Reliable Source

1. Bulloch, *Secret Service*, 1:229.
2. Dudley to Adams, June 21, 1862, *Geneva Arbitration, Case of Great Britain*, pt. 1, 109.
3. John Bassett Moore, *History and Digest of International Arbitrations* (Washington, D.C.: Government Printing Office, 1898), 1:680.
4. Nugent Chaplin, *A Short Account of the Families of Chaplin and Skinner and Connected Families* (Croyden: privately printed, 1902). Extract by kind permission of Alan Ray-Jones.
5. Ibid.
6. Harding also wrote "Historical Account of the Castles of Glamorgan and Monmouth," *Transactions of the Cymmrodorion or Metropolitan Cambria Institution* 2, London (1828).
7. Kirwan, *Palace and Hovel*, 159.
8. E. D. Steele, *Palmerston and Liberalism, 1855–1865* (Cambridge: Cambridge University Press, 1991), 363.
9. Deposition of Edward Roberts, July 22, 1862, *Geneva Arbitration, Case of the United States*, pt. 6, 322.
10. Opinion of Sir Robert Collier, July 23, 1862, *Geneva Arbitration*, pt. 4, 457.
11. Merli, *The* Alabama, *British Neutrality, and the American Civil War*, 71.
12. Adams to Russell, July 24, 1862, *Geneva Arbitration, Case of the United States*, pt. 6, 323.
13. Spencer Walpole, *The Life of Lord John Russell*, 2 vols. (New York: Greenwood Press, 1968), 2:354; Mountague Bernard, *Historical Account of the Neutrality of Great Britain during the American Civil War* (London: Longman, Green, Reader, and Dyer, 1870), 345.
14. Ibid.
15. Dean B. Mahin, *One War at a Time: The International Dimensions of the American Civil War* (Washington, D.C.: Brassey's, 1999), 150.

16. Adams to Seward, August 1, 1862, in *Correspondence concerning Claims against Great Britain: Transmitted to the Senate of the United States, in Answer to the Resolutions of December 4 and 10, 1867, and of May 27, 1868* (Washington, D.C.: Government Printing Office, 1870), 608.
17. Bulloch, *Secret Service*, 1:238.
18. *HC Deb 06 March 1868 vol. 190 cc1150–98* Hansard, http://hansard.millbanksystems.com/commons/1868/mar/06/motion-for-an-address.
19. Walpole, *Life of Lord John Russell*, 2:354; Brooks Adams, "Seizure of the Laird Rams," 260.
20. Thomas Mozley, *Reminiscences*, vol. 2 (London: Longman, Green, 1882), 92.
21. Chaplin, *Short Account of the Families of Chaplin and Skinner*, extract.
22. Mozley, *Reminiscences*, 2:92.
23. Moore, *History and Digest of International Arbitrations*, 1:678.
24. Harding to Archibald Campbell Tait, Dartmouth, December 1, 1862, Lambeth Palace Library: Tait 79 ff.32730.
25. Ibid.
26. Memoir of Mathew Butcher, edited for publication by Dr. Frank Merli and Renata Eley Long (by kind permission of Miss Joan Butcher), in Merli, *The* Alabama, *British Neutrality, and the American Civil War*, 129–40.
27. *HC Deb 27 March 1863 vol. 170 cc33–72 Hansard.*
28. Raphael Semmes, *The Cruise of the* Alabama *and the* Sumter (Carlisle, Mass.: Applewood Books, 2008), 99.
29. Brooks Adams, "Seizure of the Laird Rams," 259.
30. Dudley to Seward, *July 25, 1862, Correspondence concerning Claims against Great Britain, 15*; Coy F. Cross II, *Lincoln's Man in Liverpool* (DeKalb: Northern Illinois University Press, 2007), 62.
31. Report of William Passmore, Saturday, July 26, 1862, Union Spy Reports from the Birkenhead Shipyards, A. William Stanley Hoole Papers, box 2250, folder 94, University of Alabama, www.lib.ua.edu/content/libraries/hoole/digital/cssala/spy.htm (accessed September 1, 2013).
32. *Dictionary of American Naval Fighting Ships* (Washington, D.C.: Department of the Navy), http://www.history.navy.mil/danfs/cfa1/agrippina.htm (accessed February 2014).
33. Edwin de Leon to Judah P. Benjamin, September 30, 1862, ORA IV, 2.
34. Memorandum, Layard to Russell, July 29, 1862; Walpole, *Life of Lord John Russell*, 1:355.
35. Bulloch, *Secret Service*, 1:242–43.
36. Ibid.
37. *Vanity Fair*, April 17, 1869.
38. Brooks Adams, "Seizure of the Laird Rams," 60.

39. E. D. Adams, *Great Britain and the American Civil War* (New York: Longman, Green, 1925), 120; George W. Dalzell, *The Flight from the Flag* (Chapel Hill: University of North Carolina Press, 1940), 135.
40. Norman C. Delaney, "The *Alabama*'s Bold and Determined Man," *Naval History* magazine (August 2011).
41. Trevelyan, *Life of John Bright*, 309.
42. William Otto Henderson, *The Lancashire Cotton Famine, 1861–65* (Manchester: Manchester University Press, 1904), 76.
43. The full text of the letter to the president and his reply is on the plinth of a statue of Abraham Lincoln now standing in Lincoln Square, Manchester.

Chapter 10. Everlasting Infamy

1. Merli: *The* Alabama, *British Neutrality, and the American Civil War*, 60.
2. John Morley, *Life of Gladstone*, 2 vols. (London: Macmillan, 1906), 1:713.
3. Dudley Mann to Benjamin, October 7, 1862, ORN III, 3:551.
4. Hotze to Benjamin, August 4, 1862, ORN II, 3:506.
5. Trevelyan, *Life of John Bright*, 306–7.
6. House of Commons debate: The United States–Foreign Enlistment Act Question, HC Deb 27 March 1863 Vol. 170 cc 33-72; D. P. Crook, *Diplomacy during the American Civil War* (New York: John Wiley and Sons, 1975), 133.
7. Richard I. Lester, *Confederate Finance and Purchasing in Great Britain* (Charlottesville: University Press of Virginia 1975), 27.
8. Huse to Colonel J. Gorgas, June 12, 1863, ORA IV, 2:646.
9. Charles Mackay, *Extraordinary Popular Delusions and the Madness of Crowds* (first published in 1841), examines financial bubbles such as the South Sea Bubble and the Dutch Tulip Mania.
10. Lester, *Confederate Finance and Purchasing in Great Britain*, 155–60.

Chapter 11. Humble Submission to Yankee Bullying

1. Moran diary, March 16, 1863.
2. Bulloch, *Secret Service*, 1:330–33.
3. Beaman, *The National and Private "Alabama" Claims*, 151.
4. Bulloch, *Secret Service*, 1:341.
5. Beaman, *The National and Private "Alabama" Claims*, 152–53.
6. Moran diary, June 25,1863.
7. Ibid., June 9, 1863.
8. Ibid., March 14, 1863.
9. Brooks Adams, "Seizure of the Laird Rams," 290.
10. Ibid.
11. Bulloch to Mallory, February 3, 1862, ORN II, 2:345.

12. Bulloch to Mallory, November 7, 1862, ORN II, 2:292.
13. Beaman, *The National and Private "Alabama" Claims*, 164.
14. David Dixon Porter, *The Naval History of the Civil War* (New York: Dover, 1998), 817.
15. Brooks Adams, "Seizure of the Laird Rams," 297; Merli, *Great Britain and the Confederate Navy*, 201.
16. Brooks Adams, "The Seizure of the Laird Rams," 301. Russell defended his stance before Parliament on February 15, 1864 (*HL Deb 15 February 1864 vol. 173 cc. 544-500, Hansard*).
17. Walpole, *Life of Lord John Russell*, 2:359.
18. Merli, *Great Britain and the Confederate Navy,* 206; Ridley, *Lord Palmerston*, 561.
19. Merli, *Great Britain and the Confederate Navy,* 211.
20. Ibid., 129.
21. Ibid.
22. Ibid.
23. Ibid.
24. Ibid., 128.

Chapter 12. War-Torn Waters

1. Bulloch to Mallory, July 20, 1863, ORN II, 2:469.
2. Pascal Boissel, *Grand-Hôtel, Café de la Paix: Two Centuries of Parisian Life* (Paris: Éditions Italiques 2004), 48–49.
3. Sinclair, Hamilton & Co. to Nelson Clements, May 4, 1863, ORN II, 3:941.
4. Adams to Seward, May 1, 1863, ORA III, 3:213.
5. C. J. McRae to Hon. O. G. Memminger, October 7, 1863, ORA IV, 2:983.
6. Edmund Hammond to Archibald Hamilton, October 10, 1863, ORN II, 3:943.
7. Benjamin to Slidell, January 8, 1864, ORN II, 3:990.
8. Moran diary, November 20, 1863.
9. E. D. Adams, *Great Britain and the American Civil War*, 129; W. H. Dall, "Is Alaska a Paying Investment?" *Harper's* 44 (1871): 252–53. For the political reasoning, see Frederick W. Seward, "The Story of Alaska: The Treaty of Purchase 1867," in *Reminiscences of a War-Time Statesman and Diplomat, 1830–1915* (New York: G. P. Putnam's Sons, 1916), 360–61.
10. Bulloch, *Secret Service*, 2:41.
11. Log of the *Alabama*, May 21, 1864, ORN I, 3:674.
12. Ibid., Friday, June 10, 676.
13. ORN I, 3:677.
14. Cullop, *Confederate Propaganda in Europe*, 122.
15. Sinclair, *Two Years on the* Alabama, 251; *London Daily News*, June 27, 1864.
16. Warren Armstrong, *Cruise of a Corsair* (London: Cassell, 1963), 177–78.

17. Statement of Evan Parry Jones, in Sinclair, *Two Years on the* Alabama, 287–91.
18. *The Collected Letters of George Meredith* (New York: Charles Scribner's Sons, 1912), 1:152–53. The publication by Saunders and Otley was *The Cruise of the* Alabama *and the* Sumter *from the Private Journals and Other Papers of Commander R. Semmes C.S.N. and Other Officers*, 2 vols. (London, 1864).
19. Rapier, *Saga of Felix Senac*, 158.

Chapter 13. The War Is a Thing of the Past

1. William Marvel, *The* Alabama *and the* Kearsarge (Chapel Hill: University of North Carolina Press, 1996), 249.
2. Semmes, *Memoirs of Service Afloat*, 756.
3. Norman C. Delaney, *John McIntosh Kell of the Raider* Alabama (Tuscaloosa: University of Alabama Press, 1973), 165.
4. Sinclair, *Two Years on the* Alabama, 262.
5. Dalzell, *The Flight from the Flag: The Continuing Effect of the Civil War upon the American Carrying Trades* (Chapel Hill: University of North Carolina Press, 1940), 171.
6. Semmes, *Memoirs of Service Afloat*, 461–62.
7. *The Times*, June 21, 1864; Merli, *Great Britain and the Confederate Navy*, 99; Van Doren Stern, *The Confederate Navy: A Pictorial History* (Cambridge, Mass.: Da Capo Press, 1992), 96.
8. Rapier, *Saga of Felix Senac*, 158.
9. Capt. John A. Winslow to Hon. Gideon Welles, July 30, 1864, ORN I, 3:77.
10. Hon Gideon Welles to Capt. John A. Winslow, July 12, 1864, ORN I, 3:75.
11. Edward Boykin, *Sea Devil of the Confederacy*, 291.
12. Bulloch to Lt. William C. Whittle, October 6, 1864, ORN II, 2:731.
13. A. A. Hoehling, *Damn the Torpedoes: Naval Incidents of the Civil War* (Winston Salem, N.C.: John F. Blair, 1989), 182.
14. Dalzell, *The Flight from the Flag.*

Chapter 14. Black Friday

1. Henry Adams, *The Education of Henry Adams*, 196.
2. Frances Leigh Williams, *Matthew Fontaine Maury, Scientist of the Sea* (New Brunswick, N.J.: Rutgers University Press, 1963), 414–15.
3. James Ford Rhodes, *History of the Civil War, 1861–1865* (New York: Macmillan, 1917), 418.
4. *Cycle of Adams Letters*, 2:256.
5. Chamberlain and Taylerson, *Adams' Revolvers*, 109.
6. *London Gazette*, September 14, 1866.
7. Records of London Small Arms Co. Ltd., 1866–1920, the Royal Bank of Scotland GB 1502 GM/2047.

8. *London Gazette*, July 9, 1867.
9. For Manchesterism, see Eric Hobsbawm, *The Age of Capital, 1848–1875* (Preston, Lancashire: Abacus, 2004), 129.
10. The medals are still awarded at VMI.
11. Roberts, *Salisbury*, 48.
12. Moran diary, May 1, 1865.
13. Ibid., May 6, 1865.
14. Walpole, *Life of Lord John Russell*, 370.
15. Ibid., 357.

Chapter 15. "Little Hudson"

1. Charles Francis Adams, Diary, July 1, 1865, no. 27, ms. N-1776, Massachusetts Historical Society.
2. Moran diary, July 22, 1865.
3. Alfred Jackson Hanna, *Flight into Oblivion* (Baton Rouge: Louisiana State University Press, 1999), 225.
4. Merab-Mical Favorite, "What the Civil War Meant to Manatee County 150 Years Ago," *Bradenton Times*, April 10, 2011.
5. Eli N. Evans, *Judah P. Benjamin: The Jewish Confederate* (New York: Free Press, 1988), 329.
6. Moran diary, September 7, 1865.
7. Richard Burton had become well known for his expedition with fellow explorer John Speke into the African interior in search of the source of the Nile. Illness curtailed their quest, and a bitter quarrel followed. In 1864 Speke died of a gunshot wound in unexplained circumstances, judged to be an accident or suicide. Burton joined the Foreign Office and was appointed consul at Fernando Po, an island off the coast of West Africa.
8. R. J. M. Blackett, *Divided Hearts: Britain and the American Civil War* (Baton Rouge: Louisiana State University Press, 2001), 42.
9. Moran diary, November 7 and 10, 1864.
10. J. F. Jameson, "The London Expenditures of the Confederate Secret Service," *American Historical Review* 35, no. 4 (July 1930): 811–24.
11. Rapier, *Saga of Felix Senac*, 189.
12. A list of the major Erlanger Loan bondholders appears in Richard I. Lester, *Confederate Finance and Purchasing in Great Britain* (Charlottesville: University of Virginia Press, 1975), app. 3.
13. Moran diary, October 21, 1865.
14. *New York Times*, November 13, 1865.
15. Sidney Root Memorandum MSS 293f., Kenan Research Center at the Atlanta History Center, Atlanta, Ga.

16. Ibid.; Sharon G. Whitney, "Sidney Dwight Root, 1824–1894: From New England Yankee to Southern Secessionist and Philanthropist," *Georgia Genealogical Quarterly* 47 (winter 2011): 293–319.
17. Sidney Root, *Exotic Leaves Gathered by a Wanderer* (London: William Freeman, 1865).
18. Moran diary, October 23, 1865.
19. Ibid.
20. Stuart J. Reid, *Lord John Russell* (London: Dent, 1895), 326.
21. Charles Francis Adams to John Russell, October 21, 1865, *The Official Correspondence on the Claims of the United States in Respect to the* Alabama (Ulan Press, 2012), 172.
22. Ibid.
23. *Edinburgh Gazette*, December 26, 1865.
24. Elizabeth Harcourt Mitchell, *The Crosses of Monmouthshire* (Newport: privately printed for Caerleon and Monmouthshire Antiquarian Association, 1893).
25. *The Times*, December 25, 1865.

Chapter 16. Britain Is Condemned out of Her Own Mouth

1. Moran diary, December 15, 1865.
2. Ibid., December 20, 1865.
3. Ibid.
4. Charles Francis Adams, Diary, December 22, 1865, no. 27, ms. N-1776, Adams Family Papers, Massachusetts Historical Society.
5. Martin B. Duberman, *Charles Francis Adams, 1807–1886* (Stanford: Stanford University Press, 1968), 323.
6. Among these were the Hon. Evelyn Ashley, son of the Earl of Shaftesbury and private secretary to Palmerston; the Hon. W. Ashley, the earl's brother and an officer under the Lord Chamberlain; John Laird Sr., MP; J. S. Gilliat, director of the Bank of England, and other members of his family; the MP William Gregory, Lord Campbell; the Marquis of Bath; the Earl of Fitzhardinge, a privy councillor; J. Cunard of the famous shipping line (Captain Butcher's previous employer); the Marquis of Lothian; and Lord Gifford.
7. *New York Times*, December 9, 1865.
8. Charles Stirling to Walter Stirling, in Statham-Drew, *James Stirling*, 538.
9. Moran diary, March 24, 1866.
10. Ibid., May 7, 1866.
11. Ibid., July 9, 1866.
12. Mann to Benjamin, July 5, 1862, ORN II, 3:454.
13. Moran diary, November 24, 1866.
14. Duberman, *Charles Francis Adams*, 267.
15. King, "Victor Buckley," 6.

16. John Pendleton Kennedy, *At Home and Abroad: A Series of Essays with a Journal in Europe, 1867–8* (New York: G. P. Putnam and Sons 1872), 351.
17. National Archives, 31-Victoria C 211/37/1-47.
18. Bill Wright, *Happy Have We Met: A History of the Joshua Nunn Lodge Number 2154, 1886–2004* (privately printed for the Joshua Nunn Lodge, 2005). Joshua Nunn founded the Eclectic Lodge number 1201, a Temperance Lodge, in 1867 and served as master for two years.

Chapter 17. Prospects for a Solution

1. Ray Jones, *The Nineteenth-Century Foreign Office,* 67.
2. Adrian Cook, *The* Alabama *Claims: American Politics and Anglo-American Relations, 1865–1872* (Ithaca, N.Y.: Cornell University Press, 1975), 39.
3. J. Sexton, "The Funded Loan and the *Alabama* Claims," *Diplomatic History* 27 (2003): 449–78.
4. Charles Francis Adams, Diary, December 24, 1867, Adams Family Papers Microfilm Edition, P-54, reel 79, Massachusetts Historical Society.
5. Adrian Cook, *American Politics and Anglo-American Relations, 1865–1872* (Ithaca, N.Y.: Cornell University Press, 1975), 41.
6. Moran diary, February 28, 1867.
7. Walpole, *Life of Lord John Russell,* 2:372–73.
8. Frank Warren Hackett, *Reminiscences of the Geneva Tribunal of Arbitration, 1872: The* Alabama *Claims* (Boston: Houghton Mifflin, 1911), 40 and n. 64.
9. Duberman, *Charles Francis Adams,* 330.
10. Moran diary, December 8, 1868.
11. Ibid.
12. *Glamorgan Gazette,* December 4, 1868.
13. Cook, *American Politics and Anglo-American Relations,* 75.
14. *The Times,* May 27, 1869.
15. Thomas Paterson, J. Garry Clifford, and Shane J. Maddock, *American Foreign Relations: A History to 1920.* (Boston: Houghton Mifflin, 2005), 1:179.
16. Ray Jones, *The Nineteenth Century Foreign Office,* 67.
17. Tenterden and Moran's friend and confidant, Vice Consul Joshua Nunn, were both members in London of the Freemasons' prestigious Grand Lodge of England.
18. Moran diary, May 14, 1870.
19. J. Sexton, *Debtor Diplomacy: Finance and American Foreign Relations in the Civil War Era, 1837–1873* (Oxford: Oxford University Press, 2005), 215; Hackett, *Reminiscences of the Geneva Tribunal,* 60.
20. Log book of the *Deerhound,* R.Y.S. Sir Geo. Stucley Bart., October 21, 1869, to February 6, 1870, Bonhams, New Bond Street, London, June 24, 2008.

Chapter 18. The Massive Grievance

1. Andrew Lang, *Life, Letters and Diaries of Sir Stafford Northcote, First Earl of Iddesleigh* (Edinburgh and London, 1890), 2:12; Hackett, *Reminiscences of the Geneva Tribunal of Arbitration*, 64n.
2. Morley, *Life of Gladstone*, 2:9.
3. Hackett, *Reminiscences of the Geneva Tribunal*, 66.
4. Sir Stafford Northcote to Lord Granville, May 5, 1871, in Hackett, *Reminiscences of the Geneva Tribunal*, 66n.
5. Albert Gallatin Mackey, *Mackey's National Freemason, October 1871 to September 1872* (reprint, Kessinger Publishing's Rare Mystical Reprints, May 2003), 48.
6. Ibid., 50.
7. *Masonic Mirror* 24, n.s. (January–June 1871). Earl de Grey and Ripon later confirmed his views in an address (*Freemason*, May 27, 1922, 633–34).
8. *Geneva Arbitration*, pt. 1, *Statement of the Matter Referred to the Arbitrators as It Is Understood by the Government of Her Britannic Majesty*, 207, http://images.library.wisc.edu/FRUS/EFacs/1872p2v1/reference/frus.frus1872p2v1.i0016.pdf.
9. Hackett, *Reminiscences of the Geneva Tribunal*, 46.
10. "*International Arbitration*: Explanation of the Picture" ("The following is the substance of the artist's explanatory remarks regarding the picture as given by Mr. Carpenter on its departure from New York"). Source unknown. Copy article from the private collection of A. George Scherer III, great-great-grandson of Francis B. Carpenter.
11. Letter from Frederick W. Seward to John Russell Young and others [journalists meeting at Astor House, New York], November 25, 1891. From the private collection of A. George Scherer III.
12. Hackett, *Reminiscences of the Geneva Tribunal*, 105.
13. Tenterden's notes at the Geneva Arbitration, February 4, 1873; Morley, *Life of Gladstone*, 2:20.
14. *Geneva Arbitration, Counter Case of the United States*, 437.
15. Beaman, *The National and Private "*Alabama *Claims" and Their "Final and Amicable Settlement,"* 91.
16. Ibid., quoted from "The Cruise of the *Alabama*," compiled from Semmes' journal, 100.
17. *Geneva Arbitration, Case of the United States*, pt. 1, 150.
18. Ibid., 152.
19. Brooks Adams, "Seizure of the Laird Rams," 259–60.
20. Frank J. Merli, "On the Baleful Influence of Error," draft paper published as "E. D. Adams, Roundell Palmer and the Escape of the *Alabama*, in *The* Alabama, *British Neutrality and the American Civil War*, ed. David Fahey (Bloomington: Indiana University Press, 2004), 36.
21. *Geneva Arbitration, Counter Case of the United States*, pt. 4: Wherein Great Britain Failed to Perform Its Duties as a Neutral, 100.

22. Hackett, *Reminiscences of the Geneva Tribunal*, 275.
23. Ibid., Henry William Gegg Markheim to Frank Warren Hackett, January 19, 1873, p. 362.
24. Ibid., 340.

Chapter 19. The Foreign Office Thief

1. Duberman, *Charles Francis Adams*, 385.
2. Bulloch's middle name was Dunwody, but he appears to have used Dunwoody after his naturalization.
3. Bulloch, *Secret Service*, 1:260.
4. Ibid., 229.
5. Bulloch to Mallory, August 4, 1862, ORN II, 2:233.
6. *Liverpool Telegraph*, September 20, 1864.
7. John George Witt, *Life in the Law* (London: T. Werner Laurie, 1906), 154–55.
8. Ibid., 159.
9. Rapier, *Saga of Felix Senac*, 204.
10. The crayon portrait is believed to be the image that appears in Moran's published journals. Author's correspondence with Karie Diethorn, Chief Curator, Independence National Park, Philadelphia, 2014.
11. King, "Victor Buckley."
12. Ibid., 6.
13. P. N. Davies, *Sir Alfred Jones: Shipping Entrepreneur par Excellence* (Europa Publications, 1978), 26–27.
14. Ray Jones, *Nineteenth-Century Foreign Office*, 90.
15. Marvin, *Our Public Offices* (London: Samuel Tinsley, 1879), 2.
16. Ibid., 205.
17. Ibid., 221.
18. Ibid., 242.
19. Ibid., 247.
20. Ibid., 251–52.
21. Ibid., 261–62.
22. Ibid., 105n.; Disraeli to Tenterden, July 2, 1878, PRO FO 363/5, Tenterden Papers.
23. Alexander Yefimov, "Russian Oil in the Eyes of a Briton," in *Oil of Russia*, LUKOIL International Magazine, no. 3 (2005), http://www.oilru.com/or/24/414.
24. David Vincent, *The Culture of Secrecy: Britain 1832–1998* (Oxford: Oxford University Press, 1998), 81n; Tenterden to Salisbury, June 15, 1878, PRO FO/363/3 Tenterden Papers.

Chapter 20. Arthur Conan Doyle's Revelations

1. Sir Arthur Conan Doyle and David Stuart Davies, *Memories and Adventures: An Autobiography* (London: Wordsworth Literary Lives, 2007), 40.
2. Walter King, "Victor Buckley."
3. Keith Neilson and Thomas G. Otte, *The Permanent Under-Secretary for Foreign Affairs, 1854–1946* (London: Routledge, 2009), 41.
4. St. John's College, Cambridge University Library, African Qur'an, Arabic. A card enclosed reads "Alkoran: written by African natives and procured from Kano in the Houssa Country by F. Westin while resident at Shonga on the Upper Nile in 1882. Presented by Fredk. W. Bond, Esqre 20 Jan/85."
5. A collection of letters from Oscar Wilde to Vian was sold at auction in Britain in 2010 by Bamfords, Auctioneers, Derby.
6. Arthur Conan Doyle, *The Firm of Girdlestone* (Bibliobazaar, 2006), 13.
7. Ibid., 16.
8. Reports on inquiries subsequent to losses at sea can be found in Shipping Intelligence and articles in the archives of the *London Times.*
9. *London Morning Post,* July 26, 1891. The article mistakes the initials, giving "E. W. Bond, Chairman of the African Steamship Company."
10. Doyle, *Girdlestone,* 17.
11. Ibid., 14.
12. Andrew Lycett, *The Man Who Created Sherlock Holmes: The Life and Times of Sir Arthur Conan Doyle* (New York: Free Press, 2007), 162.
13. Arthur Conan Doyle, *Arthur Conan Doyle: A Life in Letters,* ed. Jon Lellenberg, Daniel Stashower, and Charles Foley (New York: Harper Perennial, 2008), 512.
14. Arthur Conan Doyle, "The Adventure of the Naval Treaty," pts. 1 and 2, *Strand,* October and November 1893.
15. T. G. Otte, *The Foreign Office Mind: The Making of British Foreign Policy, 1865–1914* (Cambridge: Cambridge University Press, 2011), 3.
16. *The Times,* January 7, 1896.
17. *Vanity Fair,* July 17, 1872.
18. Ibid., August 17, 1878.
19. Ibid., May 1873.
20. *London Gazette,* August 6, 1909.
21. James Dunwody Bulloch applied for British citizenship on January 16, 1869. His application was granted on January 21, and he later adopted the spelling Dunwoody.
22. *The Times,* November 30, 1901; *Journal of Commerce,* November 29, 1901.
23. Adam Hochschild, *King Leopold's Ghost: A Story of Greed, Terror and Heroism in Colonial Africa* (Pan Books, 2006), 180.
24. Brooks Adams, "Seizure of the Laird Rams," 260.
25. Roy Jenkins, *Gladstone* (Papermac, 1996), 356.

BIBLIOGRAPHY

Books

Acton, William. *Prostitution, Considered in Its Moral, Social, and Sanitary Aspects.* London: John Churchill and Sons, 1870.

Adams, Charles Francis, and Henry Adams. *A Cycle of Adams Letters, 1861–1865.* Edited by Worthington Chauncey Ford. 2 volumes. Boston: Houghton Mifflin, 1920.

Adams, E. D. *Great Britain and the American Civil War.* New York: Longman, Green, 1925.

Adams, Henry. *The Education of Henry Adams: An Autobiography.* Boston: Houghton Mifflin, 1930.

Adelman, Paul. *Victorian Radicalism: The Middle-Class Experience, 1830–1914.* London and New York: Longman Higher Education, 1984.

Anderson, Col. Edward. *Confederate Foreign Agent: The European Diary of Major Edward C. Anderson.* Edited by W. Stanley Hoole. Atlanta: Confederate Publishing Company, 1976.

Armstrong, Warren. *Cruise of a Corsair.* London: Cassell and Company, 1863.

Ascherson, Neal. *The King Incorporated: Leopold the Second in the Age of Trusts.* London: George Allen and Unwin, 1963.

Ashley, Hon. Evelyn, MP. *The Life of Henry John Temple Viscount Palmerston, 1846–1865.* 2 volumes. London: Richard Bentley and Son, 1876.

Atherton, Louise. *Never Complain, Never Explain: Records of the Foreign Office and State Paper Office, 1500–c.1960.* London: Public Records Office Publications, 1994.

Ball, Douglas B. *Financial Failure and Confederate Defeat.* Champaign-Urbana: University of Illinois Press, 1991.

Batchelor, Gordon W. *The Beresfords of Bedgebury Park.* Goudhurst: William J. C. Musgrave, 1996.

Beaman, Charles Cotesworth. *The National and Private* "Alabama *Claims" and Their "Final and Amicable Settlement."* Washington, D.C.: W. H. Moore, 1871.

Bell, Herbert C. F. *Lord Palmerston.* London: Longman, Green, 1936.

Benson, A. C., and Viscount Esher, eds. *Letters of Queen Victoria, 1837–1861.* 3 volumes, 1854–1861. London: John Murray, 1908.

Bernard, Mountague. *A Historical Account of the Neutrality of Great Britain during the American Civil War.* London: Longman, Green, Reader, and Dyer, 1870.

Blackett, R. M. J. *Divided Hearts: Britain and the American Civil War.* Baton Rouge: Louisiana State University Press, 2001.

Blackmore, Howard L. *A Dictionary of London Gunmakers, 1350–1850.* Oxford: Phaidon, 1986.

Blake, Robert. *Disraeli.* New York: St. Martin's Press, 1967.

Boaz, Thomas. *Guns for Cotton: England Arms the Confederacy.* Shippensburg, Pa.: Burd Street Press, 1996.

Bolitho, Hector. *Victoria: The Widow and Her Son.* New York: D. Appleton–Century, 1934.

Bourne, Kenneth, and D. Cameron Watt, eds. *British Documents on Foreign Affairs: Reports and Papers from the Foreign Office.* Confidential print, series C, part 1: *North America 1837–1914,* volume 6. University Publications of America, 1986.

Bowden, Mark. *Pitt Rivers: The Life and Archaeological Work of Lieutenant-General Augustus Henry Lane Fox Pitt Rivers, DCL, FRS, FSA.* Cambridge: Cambridge University Press, 1991.

Boykin, Edward. *Sea Devil of the Confederacy.* New York: Funk and Wagnalls, 1959.

Braynard, Frank O. *S.S.* Savannah*: The Elegant Steam Ship.* New York: Dover, 1988.

Brown, Ivor. *Conan Doyle: A Biography of the Creator of Sherlock Holmes.* London: Hamish Hamilton, 1972.

Bulloch, James D. *The Secret Service of the Confederate States of America; or How the Confederate Cruisers Were Equipped.* 2 volumes. New York and London: Thomas Yoseloff, 1959.

Burnett, Lonnie A. *Henry Hotze: Confederate Propagandist. Selected Writings on Revolution, Recognition and Race.* Tuscaloosa: University of Alabama Press, 2008.

Case, Lynn M., and Warren F. Spencer. *The United States and France: Civil War Diplomacy.* Philadelphia: University of Pennsylvania Press, 1970.

Case of Great Britain as Laid before the Tribunal of Arbitration Convened at Geneva under the Provisions of the Treaty between the United States of America and Her Majesty the Queen of Great Britain, Concluded at Washington, May 8, 1871. Washington, D.C.: Government Printing Office, 1872.

Case of the United States, to Be Laid before the Tribunal of Arbitration, to Be Convened at Geneva under the Provisions of the Treaty between the United States of America and Her Majesty the Queen of Great Britain, Concluded at Washington, May 8, 1871. Senate Document 31, 42nd Congress, 2nd session, 1871. Washington, D.C.: Government Printing Office, 1872.

Chamberlain, W. H. J., and A. W. F. Taylerson. *Adams' Revolvers.* London: Barrie and Jenkins, 1976.

Chaplin, Nugent. *A Short Account of the Families of Chaplin and Skinner and Connected Families.* Croyden: privately printed, 1902.

Chesney, Kellow. *The Victorian Underworld.* London: Maurice Temple Smith, 1970. Reprint, London: Penguin Books, 1989.

Colborne, Hon. John, and Frederick Brine. *The Last of the Brave.* The Strand: Ackerman and Company, 1857.

Conner, Barry Buck. *Success in the North American Fur Trade.* Macon, Ga.: Blanket Series Books, 2005.

Cook, Adrian. *The* Alabama *Claims and Anglo-American Relations, 1865–1872.* Ithaca, N.Y.: Cornell University Press, 1975.

———. *American Politics and Anglo-American Relations, 1865–1872.* Ithaca, N.Y.: Cornell University Press, 1975.

Cowden, J. E., and John Duffy. *The Elder Dempster Fleet History.* Coltishall: Mallett and Bell, 1986.

Creevey, Thomas. *Thomas Creevey's Papers, 1793–1838.* Edited by John Gore. London: Penguin Books, 1984.

Cross, Coy F. *Lincoln's Man in Liverpool.* DeKalb: Northern Illinois University Press, 2007.

Cullop, Charles P. *Confederate Propaganda in Europe, 1861–1865.* Miami, Fla.: University of Miami Press, 1969.

Currie, C. R. J., gen. ed. *The Victoria History of the Counties of England.* Oxford: Oxford University Press, 1999.

Dalton, Kathleen. *Theodore Roosevelt: A Strenuous Life.* New York: First Vintage Books, 2004.

Dalzell, George W. *The Flight from the Flag.* Chapel Hill: University of North Carolina Press, 1940.

Davies, P. N. *Sir Alfred Jones: Shipping Entrepreneur par Excellence.* London: Europa Publications, 1978.

———. *The Trade Makers: Elder Dempster in West Africa, 1852–1972.* London: George Allen and Unwin, 1973.

Davis, Jefferson. *Private Letters, 1823–1889.* Edited by Hudson Strode. New York: Harcourt, Brace and World, 1966.

———. *The Rise and Fall of the Confederate Government.* Urbana, Ill.: Sagamore Press, 1958.

Delaney, Norman C. *John McIntosh Kell of the Raider* Alabama. Tuscaloosa: University of Alabama Press, 1973.

Dictionary of American Naval Fighting Ships. Washington, D.C.: Department of the Navy; http://www.history.navy.mil/danfs/cfa1/agrippina.htm.

Dove, P. E. *The Revolver.* Edinburgh: Adam and Charles Black, 1858.

Doyle, Arthur Conan. *The Firm of Girdlestone.* London: Chatto and Windus, 1899. Reprint, Bibliobazaar, 2006.

———. *Letters to the Press. The Unknown Conan Doyle.* Edited by John Michael Gibson and Richard Lancelyn Green. London: Martin Secker and Warburg, 1986.

———. *A Life in Letters.* Edited by Jon Lellenberg, Daniel Stashower, and Daniel Foley. London: Harper Press 2007.

———. *Memories and Adventures*. Oxford: Oxford University Press, 1989.

Duberman, Martin. *Charles Francis Adams, 1807–1866*. Boston: Houghton Mifflin 1960. Reprint, Stanford: Stanford University Press, 1968.

Dugan, James. *The Great Iron Ship*. London: Hamish Hamilton, 1953.

Dullum, John. *Unremitting Vigilance: Naval Intelligence and the Union Blockade during the American Civil War*. Biblioscholar, 2012.

Edwards, William B. *Civil War Guns*. Mechanicsburg, Pa.: Stackpole Books, 1962.

Evans, Eli N. *Judah P. Benjamin: The Jewish Confederate*. New York: Free Press, 1988.

Fitzmaurice, Lord Edward. *The Life of Granville George Leveson Gower, Second Earl Granville, K.G., 1815–91*. London and New York: Longman, Green, 1905.

Foner, Philip S. *British Labor and the American Civil War*. New York: Holmes and Meier, 1981.

Foreign and Commonwealth Office. *The FCO: Policy, People and Places, 1782–1997*. Fifth edition, revised. Historians LRD no. 2. London: Foreign and Commonwealth Office General Services, August 1997.

Fry, Joseph A. *Henry S. Sanford: Diplomacy and Business in Nineteenth-Century America*. Reno: University of Nevada Press, 1982.

Fry, Richard. *Bankers in West Africa: The Story of the Bank of British West Africa*. London: Hutchinson, 1976.

Gobineau, Count Joseph Arthur de. *The Moral and Intellectual Diversity of the Races*. Edited by Henry Hotze. Philadelphia: J. B. Lippincott, 1856.

Guedalla, Philip. *Palmerston*. London: E. Benn, 1926.

Hackett, Frank Warren. *Reminiscences of the Geneva Tribunal*. Boston and New York: Houghton Mifflin; Cambridge: Riverside Press, 1911.

Hanna, Alfred Jackson. *Flight into Oblivion*. Baton Rouge: Louisiana State University Press, 1999.

Hardie, Frank. *The Political Influence of Queen Victoria, 1861–1901*. Oxford: Oxford University Press, 1935.

Harding, D. F. *Small Arms of the East India Company, 1600–1856*. London: Foresight Books, 1997.

Harris, John Raymond. *Liverpool and Merseyside: Essays in the Economic and Social History of the Port and Its Hinterland*. London: Frank Cass, 1969.

Hearn, Chester G. *Gray Raiders of the Sea*. Camden, Me.: International Marine Publishing, 1992.

Henderson, William Otto. *The Lancashire Cotton Famine, 1861–65*. Manchester: Manchester University Press, 1904.

Henrick, Burton J. *Statesmen of the Lost Cause*. New York: Literary Guild of America, 1939.

Hertslett, Sir E. *Recollections of the Old Foreign Office*. London: John Murray, 1901.

Hobsbawm, Eric. *The Age of Capital, 1848–1975*. London: Weidenfeld and Nicolson, 1975. Reprint, Abacus, 1997.

Hochschild, Adam. *King Leopold's Ghost: A Story of Greed, Terror and Heroism in Colonial Africa*. New York: Pan Books, 2006.

Hoehling, A. A. *Damn the Torpedoes: Naval Incidents of the Civil War*. Winston-Salem, N.C.: John F. Blair, 1989.

Hollett, David. *The* Alabama *Affair*. Wilmslow: Sigma Press, 1993.

———. *The Conquest of the Niger by Land and Sea*. Abergavenny: P. M. Heaton, 1995.

———. *Men of Iron: The Story of Cammell Laird Shipbuilders, 1828–1991*. Birkenhead: Countyvise, 1991.

Hoole, William Stanley. *Four Years in the Confederate Navy*. Athens: University of Georgia Press, 1964.

Hope, Bryan D. *A Curious Place: The Industrial History of Amlwch (1550–1950)*. Wrexham: Bridge Books, 1994.

Hope, Eva. *Our Queen: The Life and Times of Victoria, Queen of Great Britain and Ireland, Empress of India, etc.* "By the author of Grace Darling." London: Walter Scott, 1897.

Horn, Stanley F. *Gallant Rebel: The Fabulous Cruise of the CSS* Shenandoah. New Brunswick, N.J.: Rutgers University Press, 1947.

Hudson, Derek. *Man of Two Worlds: The Life and Diaries of Arthur J. Munby, 1828–1910*. London: John Murray, 1972.

Hudson, Frederic. *Journalism in the United States, from 1690 to 1872*. New York: Ardent Media, 1968.

Hughes, Robert. *The Fatal Shore: The Epic of Australia's Founding*. New York: Alfred A. Knopf, 1987.

Huse, Caleb. *Reminiscences*. Boston: T. R. Marvin and Son, 1904.

———. *The Supplies for the Confederate Army. How They Were Obtained in Europe and How Paid For*. Boston: T. R. Marvin and Son, 1904.

Jones, Howard. *Blue and Gray Diplomacy: A History of Union and Confederate Foreign Relations*. Chapel Hill: University of North Carolina Press, 2010.

———. *Union in Peril: The Crisis over British Intervention in the Civil War*. Chapel Hill: University of North Carolina Press, 1992.

Jones, Ray. *The Nineteenth-Century Foreign Office: An Administrative History*. LSE Research Monographs 9. London: Weidenfeld and Nicholson, 1971.

Kennedy, John Pendleton. *At Home and Abroad: A Series of Essays with a Journal in Europe, 1867–8*. New York: G. P. Putnam and Sons, 1872.

Kirwan, Daniel Joseph. *Palace and Hovel: Phases of London Life*. Hartford, Conn.: Belknap and Bliss, 1870.

La Fevre, Gen. Benjamin. *Campaign of '84: Biographies of Cleveland and Henricks*. Chicago: Baird and Dillon, 1884.

Lang, Andrew. *Life, Letters and Diaries of Sir Stafford Northcote, First Earl of Iddesleigh*. Volume 2. Edinburgh and London: William Blackwood and Sons, 1890.

Law, Henry William, and Irene Law. *The Book of the Beresford Hopes*. London: Heath Cranton, 1925.

Layard, Sir A. Henry. *Autobiography and Letters from His Childhood until His Appointment as H.M. Ambassador at Madrid.* Edited by Hon. William N. Bruce, with a chapter on his parliamentary career by the Rt. Hon. Sir Arthur Otway. London: John Murray, 1903.

Lee, Sir Sidney. *King Edward VII.* London: Macmillan, 1925.

Lester, Richard I. *Confederate Finance and Purchasing in Great Britain.* Charlottesville: University Press of Virginia, 1975.

Lindsey, W. A. *The Royal Household.* London: K. Paul, Trench, Trübner, and Company, 1898.

Lockwood, Alison. *Passionate Pilgrims: American Traveller in Great Britain, 1800–1914.* Teaneck, N.J.: Fairleigh Dickinson University Press, 1982.

Lorne, Marquis of. *The Queen's Prime Ministers: A Series of Political Biographies.* New York: Harper and Brothers, 1895.

Luraghi, Raimondo. *A History of the Confederate Navy.* London: Chatham Publishing, 1996.

Lycett, Andrew. *The Man Who Created Sherlock Holmes: The Life and Times of Sir Arthur Conan Doyle.* New York: Free Press, 2007.

Mackay, Charles. *Extraordinary Popular Delusions and the Madness of Crowds.* New York: Crown, 1980.

Mackey, Albert Gallatin. *Mackey's National Freemason, October 1871 to September 1872.* Kessinger Publishing's Rare Mystical Reprints, Whitefish, Mt., May 2003.

Maffit, Emma Martin. *The Life and Services of John Newland Maffitt.* New York: Neale, 1906.

Mahin, Dean B. *One War at a Time: The International Dimensions of the American Civil War.* Washington, D.C.: Brassey's, 1999.

Marvin, Charles. *Our Public Offices.* London: Samuel Tinsley, 1879; and Swan Sonnenschein and Allen, 1880.

Matthews, Roy T., and Peter Mellini. *In "Vanity Fair."* London: Scolar Press, 1982.

Maxwell, Rt. Hon. Sir Herbert, ed. *The Creevey Papers, 1793–1838.* London: John Murray, 1934.

Mayhew, Henry. *London Labour and the London Poor.* London: Griffon Bohn and Company, 1861.

———. *London's Underworld.* Edited by Peter Quennell. London: Spring Books, 1983.

McNealy, Patricia, Debra Reddin van Tuyll, and Henry H. Schulte, eds. *Knights of the Quill: Confederate Correspondents and Their Civil War Reporting.* West Lafayette, Ind.: Purdue University Press, 2006.

McPherson, James M. *Battle Cry of Freedom.* Oxford: Oxford University Press, 1988.

Meredith, George. *The Collected Letters of George Meredith.* 2 volumes. New York: Charles Scribner's Sons, 1912.

Merli, Frank J. *The* Alabama, *British Neutrality, and the American Civil War.* Edited by David M. Fahey. Bloomington: Indiana University Press, 2004.

———. *Great Britain and the Confederate Navy, 1864–1865*. Bloomington: Indiana University Press, 1970.

Milton, David Hepburn. *Lincoln's Spymaster: Thomas Haines Dudley and the Liverpool Network*. Mechanicsburg, Pa.: Stackpole Books, 2003.

Mitchell, Elizabeth Harcourt. *The Crosses of Monmouthshire*. Newport: privately printed for Caerleon and Monmouthshire Antiquarian Association, 1893.

Montgomery, James. *A Practical Detail of the Cotton Manufacture of the United States of America; and the State of the Cotton Manufacture of That Country Contrasted and Compared with that of Great Britain; with Comparative Estimates of the Cost of Manufacturing in Both Countries*. Glasgow: J. Niven, 1840.

Moore, John Bassett. *History and Digest of International Arbitrations*. 6 volumes, volume 1. Washington, D.C.: Government Printing Office, 1898.

Moran, Benjamin. *The Journal of Benjamin Moran, 1857–1865*. 2 volumes. Edited by Sarah A. Wallace and Frances E. Gillespie. Chicago: University of Chicago Press, 1948.

Morgan, James Morris. *Recollections of a Rebel Reefer*. Boston: Houghton Mifflin, 1917.

Morley, John. *The Life of William Ewart Gladstone*. 2 volumes. London: Macmillan, 1905.

Mozley, Thomas. *Reminiscences*. London: Longman, Green, 1882.

Murray, Robert Bruce. *Legal Cases of the Civil War*. Mechanicsburg, Pa.: Stackpole Books, 2003.

Neilson, Keith, and Thomas G. Otte. *The Permanent Under-Secretary for Foreign Affairs, 1854–1946*. Abingdon: Routledge, 2009.

Nepveux, Ethel Trenholm Seabrook. *George Alfred Trenholm and the Company That Went to War*. Charleston, S.C.: privately printed, 1973.

Official Records of the Union and Confederate Navies in the War of the Rebellion [ORN]. Washington, D.C.: Government Printing Office, 1921.

O'Neil, John. *A Lancashire Weaver's Journal, 1856–1864, 1872–1875*. Edited by Mary Brigg. Record Society of Lancashire and Cheshire, volume 122, 1982.

Otte, T. G. *The Foreign Office Mind*. Cambridge: Cambridge University Press, 2011.

Owsley, Frank Lawrence. *King Cotton Diplomacy*. Second edition, revised. Chicago: University of Chicago Press, 1959.

Owsley, Frank Lawrence, Jr. *The CSS* Florida. Tuscaloosa: University of Alabama Press, 1987.

Paterson, Thomas G., Shane J. Maddock, Deborah Kisatsky, J. Garry Clifford, and Kenneth J. Hagan. *American Foreign Relations: A History to 1920*. Andover: Cengage Learning, 2009.

Pearsall, Ronald. *Conan Doyle: A Biographical Solution*. Worthing: Littlehampton Book Services, 1977.

Porter, David Dixon. *The Naval History of the Civil War*. New York: Dover, 1998.

Rapier, Regina. *Saga of Felix Senac: Being the Legend and Biography of a Confederate Agent in Europe.* Atlanta, Ga.: privately printed, 1972.

Ravina, Agustin Guimerá. *La Casa Hamilton: Una empressa británica en Canarias, 1837–1987.* Santa Cruz de Tenerife: no publisher, 1989.

Reid, Stuart J. *Lord John Russell.* London: Dent, 1895.

Rhodes, James Ford. *History of the Civil War, 1861–1865.* New York: Macmillan, 1917.

Ridley, Jasper. *Lord Palmerston.* London: Constable, 1970.

Ritchie, J. Ewing. *Life and Times of the Right Hon. W. E. Gladstone.* London: James Sangster and Company, no date.

Roberts, Andrew. *Salisbury: Victorian Titan.* London: Weidenfeld and Nicolson, 1999.

Robinson, Charles M., III. *Shark of the Confederacy: The Story of the CSS* Alabama. Annapolis, Md.: Naval Institute Press, 1995.

Root, Sidney. *Exotic Leaves Gathered by a Wanderer.* London: William Freeman, 1865.

Russell, Carl Parcher. *Guns on the Early Frontiers: A History of Firearms from Colonial Times through the Years of the Western Fur Trade.* Lincoln: University of Nebraska Press, 1980. Reprint, Mineola, N.Y.: Dover, 2005.

Russell, Francis. *Adams: An American Dynasty.* New York: American Heritage, 1976.

Sankey, W. H. O. *Lectures on Mental Disease.* London: H. K. Lewis, 1884.

Semmes, Raphael. *The Cruise of the* Alabama *and the* Sumter. *From the Private Journals and Papers of Commander R. Semmes C.S.N., and Other Officers.* London: Saunders and Otley, 1864.

———. *Memoirs of Service Afloat during the War between the States.* Baltimore: Kelly, Piet, 1869.

Seward, F. W. *Reminiscences of a War-Time Statesman and Diplomat 1830–1915.* New York and London: G. P. Putnam's Sons, 1916.

Sexton, Jay. *Debtor Diplomacy: Finance and American Foreign Relations in the Civil War Era, 1837–1873.* Oxford Historical Monographs, 2005.

Sinclair, Arthur. *Two Years on the* Alabama. New York: Konecky and Konecky, 1998.

Smith, George Barnett. *The Life of the Right Honourable William Ewart Gladstone.* 6 volumes bound as 3. London: Cassell, no date.

Spence, E. Lee. *Treasures of the Confederate Coast: The "Real Rhett Butler" and Other Revelations.* Miami, Fla.: Narwhal Press, 1995.

Spence, James. *The American Union: Its Effect on National Character and Policy.* London: Richard Bentley, 1861.

———. *On the Recognition of the Southern Confederation.* London: Richard Bentley, 1862.

Spencer, Warren F. *The Confederate Navy in Europe.* Tuscaloosa: University of Alabama Press, 1983.

Statham-Drew, Pamela. *James Stirling: Admiral and Founding Governor of Western Australia.* Perth: University of Western Australia Press, 2003.

Steele, E. D. *Palmerston and Liberalism, 1855–1865.* Cambridge: Cambridge University Press, 1991.

Stewart, George. *Curiosities of Glasgow Citizenship as Exhibited Chiefly in the Commercial Career of the Old Commercial Aristocracy.* Glasgow: James Maclehose, 1881.

Summersell, Charles G., ed. *The Journal of George Townley Fullam.* Tuscaloosa: University of Alabama Press, 1973.

Taylerson, A. W. F., Ronald A. N. Andrews, and James Frith. *The Revolver, 1818–1865.* London: Herbert Jenkins, 1966.

Taylor, Jocelyn Pierson. Assisted by Robert G. Koolakian. *Grosvenor Porter Lowrey: A Biographical Sketch of the Founder of the Edison Electric Light Companies.* Dearborn, Mich.: Edison Institute, 1978.

Taylor, John M. *Confederate Raider: Raphael Semmes of the* Alabama. London: Brassey's, 1994.

Timmins, Geoffrey. *Four Centuries of Lancashire Cotton.* Preston: Lancashire County Books, 1996.

Toplis, Ian. *The Foreign Office: An Architectural History.* London: Mansell, 1987.

Trevelyan, G. M. *The Life of John Bright.* London: Constable, 1914.

Ure, Andrew. *The Philosophy of Manufactures.* London: 1835.

U.S. Department of State. *Papers relating to the Foreign Relations of the United States. Transmitted to Congress with the Annual Message of the President, December 2, 1872.* Washington, D.C.: Government Printing Office, 1872. University of Wisconsin Digital Collections, http://digital.library.wisc.edu/1711.dl/FRUS.FRUS1872p2v1.

———. *Papers relating to the Treaty of Washington; Geneva Arbitration: Containing the Argument of Her Britannic Majesty's Government; and Supplementary Statements of Arguments Made by the Respective Agents or Counsel.* Washington, D.C.: Government Printing Office, 1872–74.

Van Doren Stern, Philip. *The Confederate Navy: A Pictorial History.* Cambridge, Mass.: Da Capo Press, 1992.

———. *When the Guns Roared.* New York: Doubleday, 1965.

Vincent, David. *The Culture of Secrecy: Britain, 1832–1998.* Oxford: Oxford University Press, 1998.

Walpole, Spencer. *Life of Lord John Russell.* 2 volumes. Reprint, New York: Greenwood Press, 1968.

The War of the Rebellion: Official Records of the Union and Confederate Armies [ORA]. Series I, volume 1. Washington, D.C.: Government Printing Office, 1880.

Warren, Kenneth. *Steel, Ships and Men: Cammell Laird and Company, 1824–1993.* Liverpool: Liverpool University Press, 1998.

Waterfield, Gordon. *Layard of Ninevah.* New York: Frederick A. Praeger, 1963.

Weinreb, Ben, Christopher Hibbert, Julia Keay, and John Keay. *The London Encyclopaedia.* London: Macmillan, 2008.

Weintraub, Stanley. *Disraeli: A Biography*. New York: Truman Talley Books/E. P. Dutton, 1987.

———. *Victoria: An Intimate Biography*. New York: Truman Talley Books/Plume, 1992.

White, Horace. *Fossets: A Record of Two Centuries of Engineering*. Bromborough, 1958.

Williams, Frances Leigh. *Matthew Fontaine Maury, Scientist of the Sea*. New Brunswick, N.J.: Rutgers University Press, 1963.

Williams, K. J. *Ghost Ships of the Mersey: A Brief History of Confederate Cruisers with Mersey Connections*. Birkenhead: Countyvise, 1983.

Wise, Stephen R. *Lifeline of the Confederacy: Blockade Running during the Civil War*. Columbia: University of South Carolina Press, 1988.

Witt, John George. *Life in the Law*. London: T. Werner Laurie, 1906.

Woldman, Albert A. *Lincoln and the Russians*. New York: Greenwood Press, 1952.

Wright, Bill. *Happy Have We Met. A History of the Joshua Nunn Lodge* No. 2154, 1886–2004. Privately printed for the Joshua Nunn Lodge, Halstead, Essex, 2005.

Papers, Magazines, and Manuscripts

Adams, Brooks. "The Seizure of the Laird Rams." *Proceedings of the Massachusetts Historical Society* 45 (October 1911–June 1912): 243–333.

Adams, Charles Francis. Diary of Charles Francis Adams. Microfilm copy consulted by kind permission of Massachusetts Historical Society and Cambridge University Library. MS microfilm 2089–2090.

Butcher, M. J. (Commanding SS *Moray*). "A Chapter of Unwritten History." July 29, 1862. Typescript supplied by Miss Joan Butcher [granddaughter of Capt. M. J. Butcher].

Careless, Virginia Ann Stockford. "The Ethnological Society of London 1843–1871." Master's thesis, University of British Columbia, 1974, https://circle.ubc.ca/bitstream/id/62733/UBC_1974_A8%20C37.pdf.

Collis, Sheila. "Peter Hamilton: The Hamilton Heritage." *Island Connections*, http://www.islandconnections.eu/1000003/1000005/0/29005/interview.html.

Cowden, J. E. "Compagnie Belge Maritime du Congo, S.A." *Sea Breezes* 70 (1996).

Crockfords' Clerical Directory: A Directory of the Clergy of the Church of England, the Church in Wales, the Scottish Episcopal Church, the Church of Ireland. London, 1887.

Dall, W. H. "Is Alaska a Paying Investment?" *Harpers New Monthly* 44 (1872): 252–58.

Delaney, Norman C. "The *Alabama*'s 'Bold and Determined Man.'" *Naval History* 25, no. 4 (August 2011): 18–25.

Doyle, Arthur Conan. "The Missing Naval Treaty." Parts 1 and 2. *Strand*, nos. 34 and 35 (October and November 1893).

Favorite, Merab-Mical. "What the Civil War Meant to Manatee County 150 Years Ago." *Bradenton Times*, April 10, 2011, http://www.thebradentontimes.com/index.php?cid=3846173&src=news&refno=3787&category=ArtandCulture&curlid=9975#.VEO.

Freemasons Magazine and Masonic Mirror. N.s., 24 (January–June 1871). London: published for the Freemasons Magazine Company, 1871.

The Graphic. *The Life of Her Majesty the Queen.* January 26, 1901.

Hansard House of Commons Debates. The "Alabama" Claims Motion for an Address. HC Deb 06 March 1868, vol. 190 cc1150-98.

Hill, Keith. "On Track to Westminster." *Backtrack* 17, no. 9 (September 2003): 523–26.

Jameson, J. F. "The London Expenditures of the Confederate Secret Service." *American Historical Review* 35, no. 4 (July 1930): 814–15, http://www.jstor.org/stable/1837575.

Jarvis, R. C. "The *Alabama* and the Law." *Transactions of the Historic Society of Lancashire and Cheshire* 3 (1959): 189–98.

Jones, Ivor Wynne. "America's Secret War in Welsh Waters." Cymru a'r Môr/Maritime Wales. Gwynedd Archive Service, 1976.

Journal of Queen Victoria, 1838. Royal Archives, RAVIC/MAIN/QVJ/23 February 1838.

King, Canon Walter. "Victor Buckley, 1838–1882." Unpublished paper, 2007 [Canon King is the great-grandson of Victor Buckley].

Maynard, Douglas H. "Union Efforts to Prevent the Escape of the *Alabama*." *Mississippi Valley Historical Review* 41 (June 1954): 41–60.

Moran, Benjamin. Benjamin Moran Papers, 1851–1875. Library of Congress, Washington, D.C., http://lccn.loc.gov/mm81033407, 42 volumes, 13 containers.

Root, Sidney Dwight. "Memorandum of My Life." 1893. Kenan Research Center, Atlanta History Center, Atlanta, Ga.

Sanford, Henry Shelton. Henry Shelton Sanford Papers. Sanford Historical Society, Sanford, Fla.

Sexton, Jay. "The Funded Loan and the *Alabama* Claims." *Diplomatic History* 27 (2003): 449–78.

Taylerson, A. W. F. "The London Armoury Company." *Journal of the Arms and Armoury Society*, 1956.

Yefimov, Alexander. "Russian Oil in the Eyes of a Briton." *Oil of Russia. LUKOIL International Magazine*, 3 (2005), http://www.oilru.com/or/24/414/.

INDEX

ABOUT THE AUTHOR

Renata Eley Long is a freelance writer and historian who has lived and worked on both sides of the Atlantic. Her childhood in Cornwall and Bristol fostered an early interest in maritime history that developed into a passion for research and unearthing the untold stories of the past.

The Naval Institute Press is the book-publishing arm of the U.S. Naval Institute, a private, nonprofit, membership society for sea service professionals and others who share an interest in naval and maritime affairs. Established in 1873 at the U.S. Naval Academy in Annapolis, Maryland, where its offices remain today, the Naval Institute has members worldwide.

Members of the Naval Institute support the education programs of the society and receive the influential monthly magazine *Proceedings* or the colorful bimonthly magazine *Naval History* and discounts on fine nautical prints and on ship and aircraft photos. They also have access to the transcripts of the Institute's Oral History Program and get discounted admission to any of the Institute-sponsored seminars offered around the country.

The Naval Institute's book-publishing program, begun in 1898 with basic guides to naval practices, has broadened its scope to include books of more general interest. Now the Naval Institute Press publishes about seventy titles each year, ranging from how-to books on boating and navigation to battle histories, biographies, ship and aircraft guides, and novels. Institute members receive significant discounts on the Press's more than eight hundred books in print.

Full-time students are eligible for special half-price membership rates. Life memberships are also available.

For a free catalog describing Naval Institute Press books currently available, and for further information about joining the U.S. Naval Institute, please write to:

Member Services
U.S. Naval Institute
291 Wood Road
Annapolis, MD 21402-5034
Telephone: (800) 233-8764
Fax: (410) 571-1703
Web address: www.usni.org